GOODNESS PERSONIFIED

SOCIAL PROBLEMS AND SOCIAL ISSUES

An Aldine de Gruyter Series of Texts and Monographs

SERIES EDITOR

Joel Best

Southern Illinois University at Carbondale

Joel Best (*editor*), **Images of Issues: Typifying Contemporary Social Problems**

Joel Best (*editor*), **Troubling Children: Studies of Children and Social Problems**

James A. Holstein, **Court-Ordered Insanity: Interpretive Practice and Involuntary Commitment**

James A. Holstein and Gale Miller (*editors*), **Reconsidering Social Constructionism: Debates in Social Problems Theory**

Gale Miller and James A. Holstein (*editors*), **Constructionist Controversies: Issues in Social Problems Theory**

Philip Jenkins, **Intimate Enemies: Moral Panics in Contemporary Great Britain**

Philip Jenkins, **Using Murder: The Social Construction of Serial Homicide**

Valerie Jenness, **Making It Work: The Prostitutes' Rights Movement in Perspective**

Stuart A. Kirk and Herb Kutchins, **The Selling of *DSM*: The Rhetoric of Science in Psychiatry**

Bruce Luske, **Mirrors of Madness: Patrolling the Psychic Border**

Leslie Margolin, **Goodness Personified: The Emergence of Gifted Children**

William B. Sanders, **Gangbangs and Drivebys: Grounded Culture and Juvenile Gang Violence**

Wilbur J. Scott, **The Politics of Readjustment: Vietnam Veterans since the War**

Wilbur J. Scott and Sandra Carson Stanley (*editors*) **Gays and Lesbians in the Military: Issues, Concerns, and Contrasts**

Malcolm Spector and John I. Kitsuse, **Constructing Social Problems**

GOODNESS PERSONIFIED

The Emergence of Gifted Children

LESLIE MARGOLIN

ALDINE DE GRUYTER
New York

About the Author

Leslie Margolin is Assistant Professor, Department of Counselor Education, University of Iowa. His research on children and adolescents has been widely published in professional journals. Dr. Margolin received his M.S.W. from Hunter College and his Ph.D. from the University of Nebraska.

ALDINE DE GRUYTER
A division of Walter de Gruyter, Inc.
200 Saw Mill River Road
Hawthorne, New York   10532

This publication is printed on acid-free paper ⊗

Library of Congress Cataloging-in-Publication Data

Margolin, Leslie, 1945–
    Goodness personified : the emergence of gifted children / Leslie Margolin.
        p.   cm. — (Social problems and social issues)
    Includes bibliographical references and index.
    ISBN 0-202-30526-0 (cloth : acid-free paper). — ISBN
0-202-30527-9 (paper : acid-free paper)
    1. Gifted children—Education—Social aspects—United States.
2. Gifted children—United States—Social Conditions.   I. Title.
II. Series.
LC3993.9.M35   1994
371.95'00973—dc20   93-47411
                                                       CIP

Manufactured in the United States of America

10   9   8   7   6   5   4   3   2   1

For Mary, Josie, Jamie, and Andrew

The guide-post which first put me on the *right* track was this question—what is the true etymological significance of the various symbols for the idea "good" which have been coined in the various languages? I then found that they all led back to *the same evolution of the same idea*—that everywhere "aristocrat," "noble" (in the social sense), is the root idea, out of which have necessarily developed "good" in the sense of "with aristocratic soul," "noble," in the sense of "with a soul of high calibre," "with a privileged soul"—a development which invariably runs parallel with that other evolution by which "vulgar," "plebeian," "low," are made to change finally into "bad."

Friedrich Nietzsche
Genealogy of Morals

Contents

Preface

In this book I attempt to tell several different stories: the story of a social movement; of a particular educational practice; of hidden racism and classism; of upper middle-class ideals and obsessions; of language and rhetoric; of the relation of virtue to power. I also represent an effort to appropriate and blend two rather different styles of writing and analysis: American ethnomethodology and the aesthetics of Nietzsche and Foucault.

I chose gifted child education as the target of this blending quite by accident. About three years ago, when I was having some difficulty finding a job in sociology, the College of Education at The University of Iowa offered me a home. When I arrived, I was intrigued by educators' confidence in the existence of certain special populations of children. In particular, I was fascinated by how often and how easily they talked about gifted children. I wondered how and why they were able to do that.

Several people helped me in this inquiry. First, I wish to thank Merry Morash, the editor of *Social Problems*, for putting together a wonderful team of reviewers for the article, also titled "Goodness Personified" (*Social Problems* 40:510–532, 1993), that led to the book. Reviews by Richard A. Hilbert, Melvin Pollner, Dorothy Pawluch, and Steven J. Taylor were incredibly helpful. Two chapters of the book were presented at The University of Iowa's Project on the Rhetoric of Inquiry, resulting in lots of encouragement and interesting suggestions. Rick Fumerton was quite helpful in his review of Chapter 7. Joel Best provided a great deal of support and many valuable suggestions for the entire book. Melvin Pollner also reviewed the entire book, providing detailed criticism and analysis. I particularly wish to thank James C. Kimberly and Carl J. Couch for their inspiring teaching and friendship.

The staff of the Connie Belin National Center for Gifted Education were very generous in allowing me to use their research library and to incorporate their materials. Special thanks to Virginia Travis and Reta Litton for their excellent typing and clerical assistance.

To my wife, Mary, and my children, Josie, Jamie, and Andrew, I owe the greatest debt. To them, with love, I dedicate this book.

Introduction

The book's title, *Goodness Personified*, is taken from the way gifted child experts portray these children. According to them, the gifted are not characterized by having some specific ability, but by having all abilities. They are portrayed as a distinct class of human beings superior to non-gifted children in every way. This book's central questions are: By what means have we been persuaded that such children exist? Who benefits by this belief? And how is this belief sustained although it clashes with the commonsense reality in which there are no consistently virtuous children but merely ordinary children with their share of virtues and vices, strengths and weaknesses?

Despite widespread questioning in the academic literature of the various methods used to conceptualize, describe, and identify human intelligence, giftedness and gifted education have somehow managed to escape comparable critical analysis. Perhaps because sociologists focus on "deviance," "social problems," and other troubling phenomena, they have considered giftedness outside their field of interest.[1] As a result, gifted education has been studied mostly by insiders with a stake in seeing gifted education continue: gifted child educators themselves. Although gifted education currently serves over 5% of all school-age children and represents an enormous and complex source of social influence, it has rarely been examined by social scientists who are not members of the gifted child movement.

Seven academic journals specialize in studies of gifted children.[2] Yet, there are no studies on the social construction of giftedness. Researchers who study gifted children attempt to determine their characteristics, but neglect the approach utilized in deviance and social problems research (Best 1987, 1989; Blumer 1971; Gusfield 1981; Spector and Kitsuse 1977) of studying the ways conceptions of such characteristics are developed. Thus, researchers have addressed the etiology of giftedness but not the etiology of the meaning of giftedness. They ask how the gifted can be recognized, how many gifted there are, how giftedness is supported and produced, but so far no one has asked how giftedness became a possibility. The emergence of giftedness as a recognized, enforceable social category has never been explored.

We "know" that gifted children exist, or more exactly, we know we can talk about gifted children. However, we do not inquire into how we developed this knowledge and capacity; rather, we accept the appearance and existence of gifted children without inquiring into the processes that created our perceptions. As members of society, we take the existence of gifted children for granted because we routinely hear these words used in standard, stable, typical ways. We are everywhere confronted by gifted children, gifted child educators, classes, theories, and stories. As sociologists, however, we must challenge these understandings. We must ask how gifted children can possibly exist as a social category. We must ask how people could possibly come to believe in the existence of gifted children.

Since Foucault (1977a, 1980) argued that power in contemporary society is becoming increasingly "positive"—that is, less a matter of coercion than of inducing and seducing—an examination of how a positive concept such as giftedness is established may offer a key to understanding modern social control (see Stanley Cohen 1985; Gross 1970; Rodger 1988). However, this examination is precarious because, unlike repressive forms of control where power operates self-consciously, where there is a clear distinction between the deviant and the agent, positive power operates invisibly and effortlessly. Among gifted child educators, for example, there is little awareness of who the objects and agents of control are, or that social control is operating at all. The prevailing voices speak only in terminologies of liberation, self-actualization, and creative freedom. In the words of gifted child scholars, "Children who produce and create well beyond our expectations invigorate us and show us the possibilities of human potential. . . . In our own experience we have never met teachers more excited about teaching than when they work with gifted children" (Colangelo and Davis 1991, p. 4).

Because giftedness represents the nonproblematic and virtuous, it is taken for granted. Like Schutz's (1945, p. 370) conception of "home," virtue represents the familiar, the reassuring, the unquestioned and unquestionable, "a set of traditions, habits, institutions, timetables for activities of all kinds" that can be used to master the problems of daily life. Attributions of virtue thus represent a sanctuary from uncertainty, a place where critical analysis appears out of place, illegitimate. And, in Foucault's scheme, virtue's capacity to reassure is precisely what makes it essential to sociological interpretation: virtue conceals power.

It may also be difficult to associate the gifted and their activities with social control given the belief that positive labeling promotes self-esteem and achievement—the "Pygmalion effect" (Cooper and Good 1983; Rosenthal and Jacobson 1968). Nonetheless, the fact that positive labels are selectively assigned implies that some groups are given fewer advantages than others. In this regard, it is noteworthy that, although African-American children make up 16% of the nation's school enrollment, only 8% of the students in programs for the gifted are of African-American descent (*New York Times* 1988). By implication, the selective distribution of positive labels in our schools parallels and supports the class differences and racial discrimination found in society as a whole (Bowles and Gintis 1976; Lawler 1978; Mensh and Mensh 1991).

Another, and perhaps more subtle, way in which positive labeling results in social control is that use of the positive implicitly constructs its negation. Good and evil are mutually defined; each is meaningful only in relation to the other. Thus, discourse on the gifted only occurs alongside an implied (or explicit) discourse on the nongifted. And one can easily argue that any distinction between levels of worth is not only a matter of degree, that is, a comparison in terms of better or worse; it is absolute or categorical (Douglas 1970, p. 5). Establishing the gifted as a social type also establishes the nongifted as a social type. However, unlike other "dividing practices" (Foucault 1965, 1973, 1977a) whereby abnormals are defined and segregated from normals (e.g., the insane from the sane, the sick from the healthy, the criminal from the law-abiding), here the social hierarchy is formed by attention to the positive idealization. This is consistent with Foucault's (1977a, pp. 304, 183) characterization of the modern "disciplines" as primarily engaged in "making" people, as procedures used to assign qualities and characteristics to human individuals. In Foucault's (1977a, p. 170) words, theirs "is the specific technique of power that regards individuals as both the objects and instruments of its exercise."

Because the categories used to identify people are taken for granted, they lead us to "see" the expected types as natural, as the only possible reality. They minimize and obscure differences among people belonging to the same categories and similarities to those not so categorized (Bogdan and Taylor, 1982, p. 13). Moreover, because the categories used to identify "good" people are the least likely to be recognized in terms of the decisions and constitutive work that produced them, they are least likely to be challenged. Positive labels not only prevent awareness of alternative ways of seeing people, but also deflect and resist scrutiny as historical, cultural accomplishments.

A SUDDEN CONVERGENCE

Scholars' writings on the gifted may be a particularly good example of "people making," as there was no public discourse on gifted children till social scientists first named and described them during the second and third decades of the twentieth century.[3] At the beginning of the twentieth century, stories of "child prodigies" appeared with increasing regularity in magazines and newspapers, but these children were seen as curiosities, more as accidents of nature or individualistic anomalies than as representatives of a stable class of people.[4] It was not until psychologists such as Lewis M. Terman, Henry H. Goddard, and Leta S. Hollingworth began reporting "findings" on gifted children that this social category received widespread acceptance. By making giftedness appear predictable, orderly, and explainable, psychologists assimilated the gifted into natural law and made it possible to include them in everyday discourse.

Psychologists' interest in assessing differences in children's intellectual capacities can be traced to the sudden swelling of the school population at the turn of the century.[5] Between 1890 and 1915, the public elementary school enrollment in the United States increased by 47% (Chapman 1988, p. 42). The new students included children previously in the labor force before compulsory education and child labor laws were passed and the vast number of children who had recently migrated from rural areas of the United States and eastern Europe. The sudden influx of these populations meant that the school systems not only had to provide for large numbers of new students, but also that they had to deal with students from diverse cultural backgrounds, many of whom spoke different languages (Oakes 1985, pp. 19–21). On top of everything else, a large proportion of these new students were beyond normal school entry age. These "overage" students presented an enormous challenge to teachers, because they did not fit into the first grade, yet because of their academic deficiency, they could not be placed anywhere else. As a result, the first grade in most urban elementary schools was enormously overpopulated, while the more advanced grades were proportionally underused. To illustrate the scope of this bottleneck, in 1904 the superintendent of New York City schools noted that 39% of the students were above the expected age for their grades (Ayres 1909). Three years later, the Russell Sage Foundation surveyed 30 cities to determine the percentage of overage children in their school systems and found percentages ranging from 19% to 51% (Ayres 1914). Given such numbers and the strain on the educational systems, educators began to discuss methods for distinguishing overage children who could catch up from those who could not. They reasoned that if children's learning potential or intelligence could be estimated, teachers' attention could be channeled to those students more likely to advance. Thus, pressure to allocate limited educational resources created interest in methods for distinguishing and separating students with low, average, and above average, native capacities (Chapman 1988).

We should also note a shift in the valuation of children at the turn of the century: "from 'object of utility' to object of sentiment and from producer asset to consumer good" (Zelizer 1981, p. 1036). The clearest documentation of this change comes from the data on children's labor force participation. A conservative estimate placed 1,750,178 children or slightly over 18% of those between 10 and 15 years old in the labor force in 1900. By 1930, however, that number had shrunk to 667,118 children. This change was even more pronounced among 10- to 13-year-olds, 186,358 of whom were in the labor force in 1900, whereas only 30,000, or one-sixth that number, were in the labor force in 1930 (Sanderson 1974; Zelizer 1986). Thus, although children were a significant economic resource to their families in nineteenth-century America, "contributing income in normal times, and supporting their families in especially difficult times" (Goldin 1981, p. 284), in twentieth-century America the basis for parent-child relations appeared as something more emotional and sentimental (Dizard and Gadlin 1990). In keeping with these new imperatives, we will see how emotional, sentimental images energized and infused discourse on gifted children.

Still, it would be a mistake to believe that these were the only ways children were seen. From the perspective of education and industry, children had not suddenly become economically useless or emotionally priceless. Although humanitarian groups led by Felix Adler, Florence Kelley, and Jane Addams lobbied for effective child labor legislation by appealing to people's affectional and sentimental regard for exploited children (Sanderson 1974), close inspection of these efforts reveals a pragmatic appeal: What sort of citizens and workers are we providing for tomorrow, reformers asked, if we do not protect and educate our children today? In this regard, educators and social critics such as John Dewey (1916) and Charles Eliot (1909) argued that a modern democratic society not only requires a healthy, informed electorate but also a workforce sufficiently sophisticated to master the complications of new technologies. Thus, the impulse to pull children from sweatshops and place them in schools was not based solely on sentiment and Christian piety but also was rooted in the new perception of children as long-term social and economic capital. As capital, they had to generate profit. And to accomplish this, they should be trained and used according to their capabilities. They had to be ranked, judged, categorized more precisely than ever before.

These practical considerations ignited experts' interest in how to sort children according to their intellectual capacities. However, the eugenics movement provided this discourse's form and direction. By 1914, the year of the first National Conference on Race Betterment, the eugenics movement had become a major influence over educators, medical professionals, and charitable organizations (Hofstadter 1959). From Galton's (1869, 1883, 1889) first inquiries into human heredity, there was a growing fascination in the United States with identifying, protecting, and preserving genetically superior cultural and racial groups. As the first chapter shows, the eugenicist identification of superiority or "fitness" with membership in the upper classes and white race was shared by gifted child experts and was critical to their understanding of giftedness (Hofstadter 1959, pp. 161–167).

Another intellectual current that influenced the emergence of gifted child discourse was social Darwinism. Although Darwin is usually credited with the expression "survival of the fittest," Herbert Spencer first used it in 1852 to explain people's intellectual evolution. Spencer, and other social Darwinists such as William Graham Sumner, reasoned that if the most intelligent and skillful people have the best chances of surviving, then the population should increase in intelligence with each successive generation (Hofstadter 1959, p. 39). The significance of this mode of reasoning was that it provided a way of seeing intelligent people as something other than accidents of nature. From this perspective, intelligent people were not only the inevitable outcome of the adaptation to the environment, but also they now had a moral dimension. They could be seen as the achievement or favorable end product of the struggle to survive, whereas the stupid, weak, and malformed could be seen as the negative residue. Thus, social Darwinism provided the soon-to-emerge "gifted children's" movement with a theoretical framework for expecting profound differences in children's mental capacity, for interpreting these differences as genetically determined, and for responding to them with differential solicitude, with brighter children seen as a natural aristocracy, deserving better treatment because nature—not God or tradition or birth—had endowed them with special qualities.

Finally, we should note the invention of the intelligence test by Binet in 1908 and the astonishing speed with which it moved from its creation in France to mass use in the United States. Consider this chronology: In 1909, only one year after Binet introduced the test, it was translated into English by Henry Goddard who immediately began administering it to the "feebleminded" (Mensh and Mensh 1991, pp. 25–26). In 1912, the U.S. Public Health Service commissioned Goddard to administer the test to new arrivals at Ellis Island. Four years later, Lewis Terman published an adaptation of the Binet test for general school usage. In 1917, 1.75 million American soldiers were given the IQ test. And in 1919 alone, over half a million copies of the "National Intelligence Test" were sold to psychologists and educators (Kevles 1985, p. 82). Apparently, large segments of these professional groups grasped IQ technology as if it were the social and educational equivalent of Newtonian physics and Galilean mechanics. For them, the IQ test was the "Christopher Columbus's egg"[6] of intelligence, the innovation that would finally allow them to master prodigious children, to possess them completely and definitely.

What marks the origins of giftedness, then, is a sudden convergence, the extreme rapidity of a progress that could hardly have been anticipated; a mode of discourse that seemed to spring from everything and nothing. This book tells how this discourse took root and survived.

HOW THE BOOK IS ORGANIZED

Conceptualizing gifted child experts' findings as accounts (Garfinkel 1967; Hilbert 1990; Zimmerman and Wieder 1970), that is, as an effort to shape people's belief in giftedness, I deliberately avoid the question of whether there "really" are gifted children or whether the methods used to describe them are empirically valid. Rather, I am interested in the ways experts see, describe, and explain gifted children. The purpose of this methodological stance is to specify the language and imagery used to make the concept *gifted children* appear representative of something real, obdurate, and objective. Put somewhat differently, this book explores the methods used to display gifted children as objects of nature rather than of human imagination, as something discovered rather than something created. This book, then, is not about the "emergence" of a new vocabulary or a new class of people. Nor is it primarily a description of claims made in conjunction with the gifted child label. Instead, this book examines the methods by which and through which claims about an intended object—the gifted—were (and are) taken as true (Zimmerman and Pollner 1970).

Given giftedness's intimate association with scholarly activity, much of this book focuses on a group of players—-scholars, researchers, social scientists—who have received little attention in the sociological and social movement literatures. Most discussions of the cultural formulation of social problems focus on the press and other popular media; however, social issues are also advocated within the framework of scientific writing.[7] Although scholars are usually portrayed as the disinterested interpreters of social change, here they are portrayed as a dynamic force in their own right. I examine how scholars' investigations defined, legitimated, and inspired gifted child activities and campaigns. I pay particular attention to the writings of Leta Hollingworth and Lewis Terman, because they are widely recognized as the "mother" and "father" of the gifted child movement (Davis and Rimm 1989, p. 6). Although Henry Goddard is more famous for his writings on "feeblemindedness" than "giftedness," he is highlighted here to emphasize the linkage between these discourses.

However, the book makes clear that scholars are not the only players engaged in "making" gifted children. As shown in Chapter 1, scholars require a receptive audience, and, as noted in the other chapters, gifted children appear to require educators, therapists, counselors, programs, government intervention, parental support, and more. Given the variety of voices engaged in attributing qualities to gifted children, I consider the spectrum of images and expectations that have dominated this discourse and the likelihood that these definitions legitimize the power and serve the interests of some, rather than other, cultural groups. Following Foucault (1977b, p. 203), I presume that historical origins are more derisive and ironic than lofty, that self-interest comes before knowledge, and that knowledge is an instrument of self-interest.

My methodology: I make no distinction between establishing the truth of a social category and the ascription of particular qualities to members of that category. Although there is a difference between the argument that witches can fly and the argument that witches exist, it is also true that when we start talking about whether witches can or cannot fly, we are simultaneously affirming, constructing, defining the category *witches*. Our belief in social categories depends on instances, detail, events, activities. Abstractions have no life of their own. Certainly we can refer to "witches" in general; however, we start believing in them when they are seen; when stories are told about them; when they are described. Consider Heritage's (1984, pp. 84–86) discussion of sense making: Every social object is constituted as a unity from a succession of images generated over time; every social category, regardless of how general or finite, is permeated with temporal specifications: "Social objects such as 'a cheerful person' or 'a woman walking down to the shops' are the products of complicated judgements in which an 'underlying pattern' is built up from a temporally qualified succession of appearances" (p. 86). Although social categories are not themselves perceptions, they are the framework of relations in which all perceptions tally: "If a sick man sees the devil, he sees at the same time his smell, his flames and smoke, because the significant unity 'devil' is precisely that acrid, fire-and-brimstone essence. There is a symbolism in the thing which links each sensible quality to the rest" (Merleau-Ponty 1964, p. 319).

In keeping with this point of view, Chapter 1 examines how scholars "assembled" gifted children piece by piece, how they provided detailed documentation of the gifted's characteristics, and managed to spread that vision to a community of believers. Because this social category did not receive widespread public acceptance until psychologists such as Lewis Terman, Henry Goddard, and Leta Hollingworth reported on gifted children, the book begins by examining the ways these writers represented gifted children.[8]

Chapter 2 deals with continuities and discontinuities in later gifted child writings. In particular, we note that, although early gifted child scholars emphasized the superiority of the white upper classes and the inferiority of dark-skinned and working-class peoples, contemporary scholars stridently disavow racist, classist postures. I argue, however, that these disavowals mask what may be a fundamental continuity in this discourse. Despite the current discussion of "cultural relativism," "pluralism," and "inclusion," within gifted child education, the themes of racism and classism are still evident.

In setting forth the characteristics of giftedness and of the educational systems most befitting gifted children, scholars were not only engaged in "people making," that is, they were not only engaged in attributing characteristics to a new category of people, but also they were engaged in recruiting advocates. They were continually motivating people to do something about and for gifted children. This theme constitutes the main topic of Chapters 3 and 4. As shown in Chapter 3, gifted child scholars galvanized a social movement by portraying the sufferings of gifted children denied appropriate recognition, support, and educational programming. This line of rhetoric dramatized the "plight" of the gifted as child victims, as a population acutely vulnerable to various forms of harm and deprivation.

A second, more utilitarian line of rhetoric aimed at portraying the gifted as a national resource, is described in Chapter 4. In this chapter, we examine how the failure to nurture gifted children was displayed as equivalent to squandering and stifling America's future leadership. Through longitudinal studies of gifted children's accomplishments and retrospective analyses of the eminent, gifted child scholars continuously emphasized gifted children's productive capacities. We shall see that the cautionary message underlying these reports has always been that gifted children's productive capacities can easily be wasted if not properly nurtured.

Chapter 5 examines classroom practices associated with gifted education. In this chapter, I argue that gifted education is the flip side of the "pedagogy of the oppressed"; that it is a strategy to single out the children of the affluent for training in leadership and dominance. Contrary to the stereotypes usually associated with gifted education, this pedagogy is not characterized by academic rigor, but is organized around the personal and social traits associated with the gifted themselves.

Despite all appearances to the contrary, this social movement does not

survive as a result of naivete or the absence of self-reflection. The opposite is true. Chapter 6 argues that giftedness occurs as an "incorrigible"
truth to members of this culture specifically because they are self-critical,
because members acknowledge their own uncertainty and error. We will
see that by reiteratively identifying what is spurious about gifted education, scholars highlight and affirm a "core meaning" of giftedness that
cannot be questioned (Hilbert 1992, pp. 93–95).

Chapter 7 shows that the various procedures used to support and
confirm giftedness in one target population, support and confirm the
nongiftedness of the excluded. For the gifted to be elevated, other children have to be downgraded. I argue that the effects of gifted education
are global, systemic, affecting the way all children are seen.

Using Foucault as a resource, in Chapter 8 I explore attributions of
giftedness occurring within a social agency devoted to assessing and
treating gifted children. Through examination of the recorded dialogue
between gifted child professionals and their clients, I show that giftedness is not merely an accomplishment of the way people talk about those
defined as gifted. It is also a function of the institutional rituals that
guarantee that agency personnel and clients conform to sanctioned
modes of talk. Specifically, the "faceless gaze," Foucault's term for continuous unseen surveillance, ensures that, once children are defined by
the agency as gifted, nothing occurs that can dislodge, nullify, or under-
mine this identification.

The concluding chapter considers how and why virtue is appropriated
by gifted education. Nietzsche's (1901/1909, 1887/1910) doctrines guide
us here: First, that there are no moral or immoral activities but only
moral interpretations; second, that command of these interpretations—
the right to say who or what is virtuous—belongs to the powerful and is
not only the method by which the powerful legitimize their superior
privilege and status but also the chief reward accruing to that status.
Power and virtue belong to one another as parts of a single process. In
this sense, it is by invoking the imperatives of Christianity and democracy that gifted education achieves the right to judge who has the loftier
soul, who is more noble, who has higher value with regard to human
progress, utility, and prosperity in general. And, as we will see through-
out the book, command of the language of virtue also makes it possible
to identify the bad, the low, the plebeian and vulgar (Nietzsche 1887/1910,
pp. 22–23).

Finally, some precaution is in order. I make no claim that this is a
scientific book. Since my analysis examines the means by which gifted
child scholars lay claim to impartiality and universality, it would be
unwise to claim an equivalent impartiality and universality for myself. A
book aiming to account for scientific objectification should not be li-

censed to enact an objectification of its own. To avoid misreadings, then, readers should bear in mind that this book is not a personification of gifted child scholarship—although, paradoxically, it is impossible to engage in accessible argument without the appearance of objectification. Rather, this is an effort to dramatically confront the epistemological problem of how we have come to believe and value the reality of gifted children.

1

From Facial Beauty to Pubic Hair: Assembling Gifted Children

> She is an attractive, merry, wholesome girl, who does all mental work with
> an ease, accuracy and expertness, which entitles her to be called a *"gifted
> child."*
>
> From "The Mentality of a Gifted Child" by Genevieve Coy (1918)

If a conceptualization of a group's identity is to be adopted by a particular audience, it must be grounded in the "native tongue" of that audience's culture (Scott 1970). Thus, to communicate successfully the
message that a social type exists, that message must be couched in
language and documented by examples that express and support the
culture's prevailing attitudes, beliefs, and values. The new social type
must be defended in terms of people's "thinking as usual" (Schutz 1944,
p. 501). Since experts on gifted children and the consumers of their
reports are from the upper middle class, portrayals of gifted behavior
and thinking can be expected to make sense to them—that is, appear
valid and legitimate—to the extent that they reflect upper middle-class
experience. To illustrate, the following dialogue was originally offered
by Hollingworth (1926, p. 257) as an example of how exact a gifted
child's thinking can be. What should be noted, however, is that the
"exact" thinking that is displayed is not general or abstract. It is "exact"
only in terms of the vocabulary, values, and institutions representative
of upper middle-class culture[1] (Mills 1940).

Q: What do you think is the most interesting vocation? What would you
 like to be when you grow up?
A: Well, the answer to those two questions is not the same.
Q: Then tell us first what you think is the most interesting vocation.
A: Science, especially astronomy.
Q: And what vocation would you like to follow when you grow up?

1

A: To be a medical doctor.
Q: But why not be what is most interesting?
A: Because a person cannot make much money being an astronomer. I never heard of anyone at the Lick Observatory earning fifty thousand dollars a year.
Q: But do medical doctors earn fifty thousand dollars a year?
A: It is possible for one to do it. Some of them do.
Q: Do you think being a medical doctor is the most lucrative occupation?
A: No. It would be more lucrative to get into Standard Oil.
Q: Then why not go into Standard Oil?
A: Because it isn't so interesting as being a medical doctor.

The gifted children described by Hollingworth (1926) are portrayed as interested in upper-middle class occupations and their career choices are explained, defended, and qualified in terms of upper-middle class vocabularies motive (Mills 1940).

There is also a gender difference in presentation of the gifted child that is consistent with higher class values and norms. Gifted girls "make sense" of their occupational choices in language grounded in upper middle-class conceptions of feminine behavior (Hollingworth 1926, pp. 141–142, 253).

Girl, IQ 159: Will teach school. "I think I am better fitted for that work." Also music. "I like to hear the notes blend together in beautiful harmonies."
Girl, IQ 133: Will be "a piano soloist." Expects "to graduate from university at 21 years, then marry and go on with piano work."
Girl, IQ 148: "I want to be an authoress, actress, artist, and musician."

Gifted boys, on the other hand, explain their career choices with language that "makes sense" in terms of upper middle-class conceptions of masculinity.

Boy, IQ 162: Will take up the oil business, "because there is a lot of money in it, and because I like the work, and I have a lot of relatives in that business."
Boy, IQ 143: Will study zoology, "because father is a zoologist, and animals are so interesting."
Boy, IQ 187: "I want to work at whatever has the most mathematics in it, when I grow up."

Not only is giftedness portrayed as a mirror to upper middle-class values, the gifted are portrayed as actual members of the upper middle class. For example, in the first volume of *Genetic Studies of Genius*, an examination of 1,528 gifted children, Terman (1925, p. 63) reported that among the 560 fathers of gifted children questioned, only one was a laborer. This was at a time when 15% of the population was in this job category. Similarly, only two fathers were listed as farmers. By contrast, there were 33 lawyers, 38 engineers (with college degrees), 30 teachers, 32 physicians and dentists, and 103 executives, managers, and manufacturers. On average, parents of gifted children had covered twice as many school grades as other adults in the population. They lived in neighborhoods rated as "superior" and homes rated as "very superior." Each gifted child's home contained an average of 328 books.

For Schutz (1944, p. 500), a person's assessment of what is real within any sphere is guided primarily by self-interest: "He groups the world around himself (as the center) as a field of domination. . . . He singles out those of its elements which may serve as means or ends for his 'use and enjoyment,' for furthering his purposes, and for overcoming obstacles." From this perspective, gifted child experts and consumers not only more readily comprehend gifted children's thinking as more intelligent, as truly "gifted," when that thinking is expressed in their cultural vernacular, they are more likely to support this designation because it conforms with their practical interests. After all, their children and values are labeled as gifted. This portrayal rings true for readers of this literature, then, because the linkage of superior intellectual capacity to their own social class elevates their status and provides a rationale for their superior privilege and wealth.

This is my key hypothesis: Behind gifted child knowledge there is a definite purpose: the preservation of a social order, a class, a race, a community, a culture (Nietzsche 1901/1909, p. 215). Behind gifted child knowledge lies something completely different from itself: desires, fears, interests, the will to appropriate (Foucault 1977b, pp. 202–203). In which case, the judgment *gifted* did not originate because giftedness was seen; rather, giftedness was seen because of a disposition and capacity to judge. It was "the good themselves, that is, the aristocratic, the powerful, the high-stationed, the high-minded, who have felt that they themselves were good, and that their actions were good, that is to say of the first order, in contradistinction to all the low, the low-minded, the vulgar, and the plebeian" (Nietzsche 1887/1910, pp. 19–20).

THE ROLE OF HEREDITY

A particularly soothing, self-serving and, hence, convincing, dimension of gifted child discourse during the early part of this century was the effort to portray upper middle-class status as a sequela or reward arising from giftedness. This is exhibited in Hollingworth's explanation of why most fathers of the gifted are highly educated, successful, and wellplaced in professions or business. Although Hollingworth (1926, pp. 57–58) acknowledges that "a few of the very gifted are born into homes where the father is an unskilled or semi-skilled manual laborer, and reared without 'advantages,'" she claims "these cases teach us that the gifted are not absolutely confined to any one set of environmental conditions." They do not become gifted because they are given specific environmental stimuli or superior learning opportunities. Rather, gifted people earn and select superior environments. "If superior environment were the cause of high scores on [IQ] tests, no child living from birth in squalor could score high" (Hollingworth 1926, p. 58).

How, then, do gifted children come to live in "superior" environments? The answer was that their parents were gifted or, at least, came very close to this standard. Because giftedness is seen as resulting from heredity, not the social "advantages" that appear to accompany giftedness, the significant correlation between giftedness and wealth is explained by the fact that "modern men, both voluntarily and involuntarily, allow more money to the more gifted. . . . Modern civilization bestows medals, appointments, professional, political, and military titles upon its best performers. It is clear that people always, even when their theories are aggressively democratic, create aristocracy within their group" (Hollingworth 1926, pp. 2–3). In the words of Terman (1922, p. 660), "The common opinion that the child from a cultured home does better in tests by reason of his superior home advantages is an entirely gratuitous assumption. . . . The children of successful and cultured parents test higher than children from wretched and ignorant homes for the simple reason that their heredity is better."

So great was researchers' belief in the correspondence between social class and giftedness that Catherine Cox (1926), working under Terman's guidance, used "family standing" as a means of estimating the intelligence of children who did not take IQ tests. According to her methodology, a "family standing" at the "lower business and skilled labor level" was treated as equivalent to IQ 100, "semiprofessional and higher business" equalled IQ 110, and "professional" equalled IQ 120. Thus the fact that John Bunyon's father was only a "brazier or tinker" accounted for Bunyon not being considered gifted as a child. Cox added, however, that some credit should be given to the finding that Bunyon's father was not a run-of-the-mill tinker but "a tinker of recognized position in the village"; moreover, "the mother was not of the squalid poor, but of people who were 'decent and worthy in their ways.' This was sufficient for Bunyon to get an IQ rating of between 90 and 100" (p. 90).

Although social class is portrayed as correlated to giftedness, race has a cause-and-effect relation to giftedness: Whites are portrayed as superior, and dark-skinned people as inferior, intellectual stock. Hollingworth (1926, p. 69) notes several surveys testing the intelligence of black children but contends "these surveys unexceptionally show a low average of intellect among children having negro blood. Comparatively few of these children are found within the range which includes the best one per cent of white children." Terman (1916, pp. 91–92) is even more direct: "Their [dark-skinned people's] dullness seems to be racial, or at least inherent in the family stocks from which they come. The fact that one meets this type with such extraordinary frequency among Indians, Mexicans, and Negroes suggests quite forcibly that the whole question of racial differences in mental tests will have to be taken up anew and by experimental methods. The writer predicts that when this is done there will be discovered enormously significant racial differences in general intelligence, differences which cannot be wiped out by any scheme of mental culture."

To reinforce the claim that giftedness is inborn (and, by implication, that upper middle-class status results from hereditary advantage rather than socioeconomic opportunity), Hollingworth, Terman, and other psychologists from this period focused their analyses on individual-level data and variables. For example, descriptions of gifted children's early childhood address developmental questions such as their age when they first stood, walked, spoke their first words, spoke complete sentences, learned the alphabet, began to read, and so forth. Thus, the first volume of Terman's *Genetic Studies of Genius* (1925), subtitled *Mental and Physical Traits of a Thousand Gifted Children*, contains chapters on "racial and social origin," "intellectually superior relatives," "vital statistics," "anthropometric measurements," "health and physical history," "medical examinations," "reading interests," "tests of character and personality traits," but little information on social interaction and context. How these children were cared for, got along with other family members, were taught to speak, introduced to reading, and so on is almost wholly ignored. Other family members are displayed solely to demonstrate the heritability of giftedness. Thus, when siblings are discussed, it is to show that they, like their gifted brothers and sisters, have unusually high IQs. With regard to parents of gifted children, their genetic giftedness is displayed through detailed accounts of their occupational accomplishments, because "we know that occupational status, especially if it is high, is a fairly good indication of intellectual endowment" (Hollingworth 1926, p. 181).

The gifted are portrayed as scions of an aristocracy to which members are born, not raised. Consider, for example, Terman's (1925, pp. 91–92) efforts to trace gifted children's ancestry to members of the Hall of Fame and *Who's Who*. Even Goddard's (1928, pp. 135–141) text on gifted children in the school setting provides documentation of giftedness' heritability. He reported one- or two-line comments made by a "home visitor" addressing gifted family members' lineage (e.g., "maternal great-grandfather descendant of William Penn," "paternal aunt an M.D. and lecturer," "mother niece of Gen. Robert E. Lee," "maternal family of elite of Prague," and so on).

Early gifted child texts contain lengthy descriptions of the educational and professional achievements of gifted children's ancestors but little or no information on how these individuals influenced gifted children's development. For example, although Hollingworth (1926, pp. 234–235) tells us nothing about J.M.'s family interactions, upbringing, or the emotional and intellectual stimulation she received, we are told:

> [Her] father was educated as an electrical engineer, but subsequently went into investment banking. J.M.'s paternal grandfather was an architect who attended Edinburgh University, and was trained in the Manchester School of Science. The paternal great-grandfather was an architect and ship builder, who engaged in laying out factories, and came from a line of builders. . . . J.M.'s maternal grandfather was first a teacher, then a merchant, very wealthy, and mayor of a southern town for eighteen years. The line of his descent was through southern planters. The maternal grandmother was the daughter of a college professor, who in turn was the son of a physician and surgeon coming from a long line of . . .

This attention to ancestors' social status appears to be modeled after Goddard's (1912) *The Kallikak Family*, a study that traces the genealogy of a family of feebleminded people by documenting members' long history of social and occupational failure. Just as Hollingworth and other gifted child experts provide seemingly endless documentation of gifted children's upper middle-class lineage, Goddard documents children's feeblemindedness through detailed accounts of their ancestors' poverty, immodesty, and lack of sexual discrimination. These efforts to connect intellectual capacity to income and social class are fully compatible with, and implicitly supported by, a culture that views financial success as a general indicator of worth. According to Douglas (1970, p. 7), a linkage between poverty and general moral devaluation precedes and underlies upper middle-class language, "where the very means of saying that someone is both poor and virtuous—that is, 'poor but virtuous'—involves the presumption that one must normally . . . expect the poor to be wicked, since this 'but' implies a contradiction in normal expectation." This use of language also suggests the converse, that being well-off is presumed to correlate with every virtue.

OTHER VIRTUES

If upper middle-class status represents general moral elevation, then the gifted, as the repository of these idealizations, can be expected to be superior in every area of human worth. Accordingly, they should be cognitively, as well as morally and spiritually, superior. Goddard's (1928, p. 81) exchange with a gifted education teacher confirms these beliefs. When asked how she disciplined her students, she responded incredulously, "Discipline, what do you mean by discipline?" Goddard attempted to clarify:

Q: Why punishment—what kind of punishment do you use?
A: Oh, we don't use any.
Q: Well, what do you do with the children who are bad?
A: Why, they are never bad.
Q: Oh, I mean when they are disobedient or don't do their work.
A: But there is no such thing in these classes. There is no such thing as not doing their work.

The Protestant "valuation of restless, continuous, systematic work . . . as the highest means to asceticism, and at the same time the surest and most evident proof of rebirth and genuine faith" (Weber 1930, p. 172), is everywhere evident in scholars' descriptions of gifted children.[2] From the earliest days of the gifted children's movement, these children were characterized as tireless, obsessive, driven: At 7 years of age, D. was typing and editing his own newspaper (Hollingworth 1926, p. 244). "By her eighth birthday, Betty had read approximately seven hundred books, many of them twice" (Hollingworth 1926, p. 226). At the age of 5, R.W. was taking four violin lessons per week and practiced three to four hours daily (Stedman 1924, p. 25). At 3, K.D. made all her dolls' clothes (Stedman 1924, p. 52). At 6, H.H. kept his family's accounts and made out the bills (Terman 1919, p. 237). When L.M. was 10 he ran a lending library for the neighborhood children: His "interests take in the whole world;—prohibition, Red Cross, Y.M.C.A., Boy Scouts, Athletics. Gives morality talks to any one he thinks in need of them. Walks miles distributing literature for all the 'drives'" (Terman 1919, p. 213).

According to Davis (1924, p. 132), teachers frequently refer to gifted children's "higher standards," their "truthfulness," their "ability to govern themselves," to "assume responsibility," and to "respect the rights of others." To illustrate, Davis noted that the remark, "Refined people do not chew gum in public," needed to be made only once to a group of gifted pupils for the offensive behavior to cease. By contrast, "in a class composed of normal children, exposed to the same suggestions, no fewer than fifteen pupils in a period of one week were asked to remove gum from their mouths!" (p. 134).

Gifted children are also less likely to cheat, lie, or steal:

> One teacher cites an illustrative case which arose when both a dull and a gifted child were found with pencils that did not belong to them. She handled the situation in an identical manner with the two children, explaining that they had no right to the property of others without the owner's consent. In the case of the gifted child, this single correction was enough. The offense was never repeated and the child took the trouble later to call attention to the fact that he was thereafter using his own pencil. In the case of the dull child, the offense was repeated on the afternoon of the same day. He was spoken to again more forcibly. The following day, the same action was repeated for the third time. It was only after a severe session that the dull child was brought to the point where he no longer took the pencils that belonged to other children. (Davis 1924, pp. 132–133)

In Goddard's (1928, p. 76) text, the gifted are paragons of classroom comportment. Each child appears cooperative, yet self-reliant, independent but not self-centered: "He doesn't ask, 'May I get a pencil?' He goes and gets it, or a piece of paper or a book. If on his way to get the book he sees something that interests him and he stops to look at it, no one shouts at him to take his seat. If something strikes him as being funny, he laughs and no one reproves him unless he laughs unbecomingly loud, in which case very likely another child says, 'William, I shouldn't laugh so loud as that; it isn't polite.' And William accepts the reproof good-naturedly and has learned another lesson."[3]

Because our society regards masculinity as a primary virtue for boys, evidence that gifted boys are more masculine provides further support for the reality of giftedness. In conformity to these expectations, Terman (1925, p. 413) shows that gifted boys are not only more likely to be white, and upper middle class, their "Masculinity Index" is significantly higher. Terman shows that gifted boys are less likely to play with dolls or "play dress up" (p. 401) and are only one-fourth as likely to consider going into domestic and personal service occupations as nongifted boys.

Lulu Stedman (1924, pp. 13–14) was particularly impressed by gifted children's unusual command of English: "By the age of nine or ten years they frame sentences with precision and show a mastery of style which is hardly equalled in the compositions of average high school students." Some are so talented "one is reminded of Goldsmith's description of the village schoolmaster" (Stedman, p. 14):

> And still they gazed and still the wonder grew,
> that one small head could carry all he knew.

According to Stedman (p. 14), the gifted are often heard using such sophisticated expressions as "the policies of government," "changing personalities," "the climax of a story," and "details of a composition." She took special note of the language of a gifted 9-year-old, who, when asked about formulating regulations for controlling stairway traffic, replied, "Why do you need a rule for stairways? You have already made rules for the halls, and a stairway is only a terraced hall." This same girl was also overheard making these comments on a hike: "Don't you think it would be worth while to pause for a moment and admire the beautiful scenery? I don't know whether it is the heat or the effect of the atmosphere which makes the hills appear so lovely, but I must admire the harmonious blending of the shrubbery."

Reflecting what Berger and Luckmann (1967, p. 64) call our "built-in need" to integrate meanings, to see the different dimensions of our experience as elements of some consistent whole, we expect that virtue be displayed in an orderly, coherent fashion. We expect that people who excel in one way will excel in all ways. Thus, descriptions of the feeble-minded as people born to every manner of vice and the gifted as people born to every manner of goodness make sense in terms of our expectation that phenomena hang together, that they "appear . . . in coherent arrangements of well-circumscribed objects having determinate properties" (Schutz and Luckmann 1973, p. 4). By demonstrating the congruence of the various details comprising giftedness, it is transformed from a "mere congery of particulars" into a determinate ensemble (Pollner 1987, p. 34). For this reason, the texts most influential in establishing the facticity of gifted children are those showing cognitive excellence to be correlated with other human virtues. As Hollingworth (1926, p. 202) put it: "If a child is better than average in one performance, he will probably fall on the plus side of average in any other performance undertaken."

DOCUMENTING GIFTEDNESS

To demonstrate this positive correlation among capacities, Hollingworth and Terman document gifted children's superiority in a wide range of areas, including musical talent, artistic and mechanical ability, mental health, character, leadership, ambition, and discipline. In addition, an entire chapter, or about one-tenth of Hollingworth's (1926) text, is devoted to displaying gifted children's superior physical and athletic endowments. Three chapters, or almost one-fifth, of Terman's (1925) text are devoted to describing such qualities. Although both volumes provide an abundance of detail, Terman's is especially distinctive in this

regard. To give one illustration, not only is the pubic hair development
of gifted children compared to that of the nongifted, but also subcatego-
ries are provided for children who have kinky and straight hair. In
keeping with the anticipated pattern of gifted children's early matura-
tion, they are shown to acquire pubic hair earlier than the nongifted
regardless of whether their hair type is kinky or straight (Terman 1925,
p. 207). This heaping up of detail creates a sense of giftedness' inev-
itability, its omniscience and prominence. Through these means, giftedness becomes a "master status" (Hughes 1945), a characteristic that can
always be counted on to set the identified child apart from others.

For Terman (1925), no detail of gifted children's lives was too small
to be identified, categorized, compared, measured, tested. Thus, he
showed how many gifted children were born through normal, induced,
breach, or caesarian delivery, how many gifted were breastfed, how long
breastfeeding continued, what diseases and injuries they experienced,
how often they had headaches and urinary problems, their ratio of
mouth breathing to nose breathing, the exact width and depth of their
hips and chest, and length and circumference of each arm, their grip and
breathing capacity, height standing and sitting.

Consistent with Hollingworth and Terman, Goddard establishes the
separate existence of gifted children by continually contrasting the impressions they inspire with those that might be anticipated in classes for
the nongifted. However, Goddard's imagery is more personal than that
used by Hollingworth and Terman ("It was a thrilling moment when the
principal of the school led us to the room where the special class for
gifted children was held" [p. 7]) and more oriented to the ambience of
giftedness ("The room made me think of a boys' and girls' camp on a
rainy day, except that the sun was shining outside and everything was
bright and pleasant" [p. 7]). Also, instead of ranking and rating gifted
children's attentiveness, obedience, and wholesomeness, he provides
readers with opportunities to discover these qualities for themselves:
"We walk into the room for our visit. Instantly there is a little commotion
as three or four, perhaps five or six, boys rush to get us chairs. This
courtesy done, they get back to work, and in a few seconds you would
not know that we were there. For the rest of the time the children pay no
more attention to us than if we were not there unless we take part in the
work exercises" (p. 77).

Because truth is understood in opposition to myth, Goddard establishes the truth of giftedness by continually emphasizing the mythic
foundations of beliefs opposing giftedness. For instance, he claims that
many consider the gifted to be "conceited little prigs," but he quickly
points out that the gifted are more humble than ordinary children: "The
narrowly conceited person who is snobbish and intolerant is not the

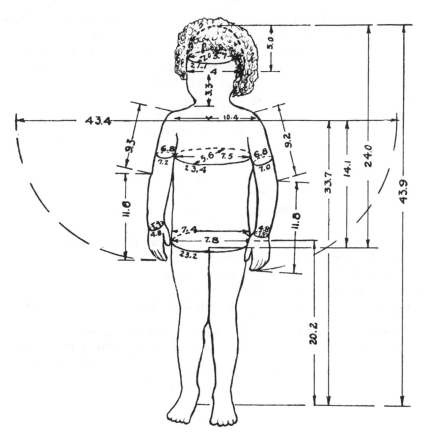

Terman's (1925) depiction of the measurements made on the gifted children in his study.

person of ability" (p. 26). According to Goddard (1928, p. 24), many say that the gifted are flighty: "they cannot stick to anything that requires hard work." However, Goddard warns that such a belief is not only unjust and untrue, but also it "is often expressive of jealousy." He writes: "Let anyone who thinks that gifted children have no perseverance watch one of them working on a program of his own" (p. 25). Many are inclined to imagine the gifted are bookish, says Goddard, "that they are interested in little except reading" (p. 92). But this too is false. "These children quickly become interested in mechanics, manual training, physical culture, music, foreign language, typewriting, nature study, art, anything which is within the reach of their mentality and which is presented to them in the right way" (p. 92).

He says that many consider the separation of gifted children a form of elitism, but then he argues the contrary is true: Excluding gifted children from their own classes deprives them of equal opportunity. "Instead of the special class for gifted children being undemocratic, it is the only truly democratic procedure—the only plan that gives the bright child a chance" (pp. 28–29). Similarly, Goddard says it is often believed that separating the gifted deprives the nongifted of opportunities to interact with positive role models. Again, Goddard (1928, p. 29) shows that the fact of the matter is the opposite: "Experience has proved that when the exceptionally bright child is taken out of the room those that are left are happier and get along better."

The rhetorical form for Hollingworth's discussion of gifted children also consists of the contrast between myth and fact. The recurrent differentiation between folk versions of reality and "scientifically proven assessments" creates the impression that experts' versions of gifted children are sophisticated, nonidealogical, and independent of any cultural stereotype. Above all, it creates the impression that any version of giftedness except that which is offered by Hollingworth and other scientists is capricious, arbitrary, and false (cf. Goode 1969). To illustrate, Hollingworth (p.78) begins her chapter on "Physique and Movement" by noting,

> There is a current belief that very bright children are likely to be puny, weak, and undersized. It is supposed that the brain is active at the expense of the body, and that health is liable to deterioration in consequence. Thus the scholar has come down to us in poetry "sicklied o'er with the pale cast of thought." When the cartoonist wishes to portray the bright child, he draws a species of monstrosity, with large head, spindle legs, and a facial expression of deep melancholy.

The remainder of Hollingworth's chapter is devoted to demolishing this imagery by showing that "objective" tests reveal gifted children as prodigously large, strong, healthy, speedy, well-proportioned, and well-coordinated. She shows, for example, that height bears a positive and linear correlation with intelligence: "The gifted group has a median height of 52.9 inches, as compared with a median of 51.2 inches for the children of average intelligence, and of 49.6 inches for the very stupid" (p. 83). Gifted children are also shown to be heavier than other children. Moreover, "the superstition that very bright children are inclined to be thin and frail receives an especially pointed correction from inspection of the facts with regard to the relationship prevailing between their height and weight" (p. 84). These "facts" reveal that gifted children not only have more weight than ordinary children, they have more weight per unit of height. She documents gifted children's greater size with two photographs displaying rows of gifted children standing next to a significantly smaller child, who, according to the caption, represents "average

These photos were intended as a demonstration of gifted children's superior size; they are also a demonstration of their wealth and status (from Hollingworth 1926).

height per age" (Figure 1.2). Although Hollingworth acknowledges that tests reveal that gifted children do indeed have larger heads than other children, she emphasizes they need larger heads to fit the proportions of their comparatively larger bodies. As regards motor control, Hollingworth (pp. 110–111) states that "we have few precise data." However, "such as we have show the gifted to be stronger and swifter than unselected children, as a group." She then illustrates their motor superiority with a photograph of a baby reclining on his back, apparently holding—she says "balancing"—a ball between his hands and another between his feet. This photograph is displayed as evidence of giftedness because five years later the boy tested at IQ 187.

Photographs are used not only to demonstrate gifted children's size and physical capacities but also, more generally, to underscore their realness as a class of people, to embody their goodness, and to create the appearance of linkage between social class and intellectual endowment. Through the "retrospective illusion" whereby the impressions constituted by our sense perceptions are felt to represent something that has a reality all its own (Merleau-Ponty 1964, p. xiii), pictures of gifted children permit observers to experience this social type as something perceived, as part of a world "out there" rather than an imagined world existing only in people's minds. For example, the photographs in Hollingworth's book display the gifted as a group of extremely well-dressed, smiling, attractive children. This is also true of Goddard's (1928) book on gifted children where photographs show smiling, comely children—the boys almost always dressed in white shirt and tie—standing next to their science projects or reading books, as if demonstrating their giftedness. One of Goddard's photographs shows a group of children doing a variety of activities such as painting, typing, sewing, reading, and some sort of electronics work. The caption under this picture reads: "A high I.Q. class of children from first, second, and third grades. The children are not posing; this is a normal scene" (p. 61).

Perhaps the apotheosis of gifted child imagery is contained in the second volume of Terman's *Genetic Studies of Genius* (Cox 1926), a retrospective analysis of gifted children from earlier times. There, across from the title page, a portrait appears of a prepubescent youth who closely resembles Gainsborough's *Blue Boy* in silken attire and idealized facial beauty (John Milton at the Age of 10 by David Masson). By contrast, the feebleminded displayed in textbooks during the first decades of the century are posed as if in mug shots, in side-by-side profile and full-faced photographs, their arms rigidly at their sides, wearing overalls and other garments conspicuously cheaper than those of the gifted. On the whole, these people appear unsmiling, unkempt, and uncomfortable (e.g., Goodard 1914; Huey 1912; Holmes 1912; Tredgold 1915).

Compare Goddard's portrayal of a classroom scene involving feebleminded children (upper picture) and a scene involving gifted children. The photographs are from Goddard's *School Training of Defective Children* (1914) and his
   School Training of Gifted Children (1928).

Again, Goddard's *The Kallikak Family* serves as the archetype for this
negative imagery, as the photographs in this book not only show the
feebleminded dressed in working-class outfits and posed beside or within shacks, farms, and institutions for defectives, but also their faces were
retouched with heavy dark lines around the eyes, eyebrows, mouth,

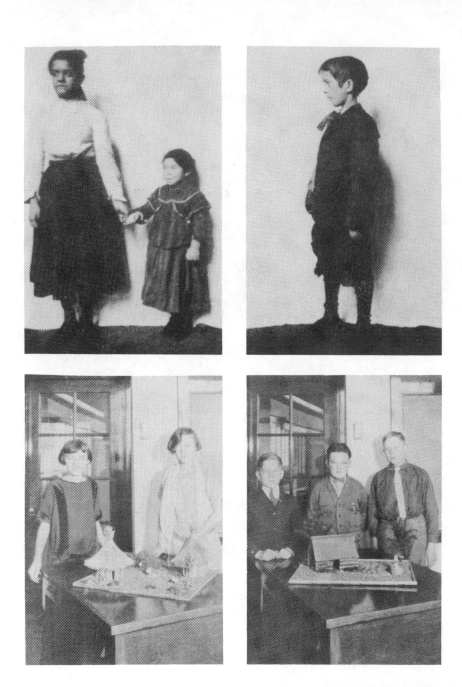

Note the sad expressions of the feebleminded children in Goddard's *School Training of Defective Children*, (1914) their rigid postures, shabby clothing, the
boy's malnutrition, the overall starkness. By contrast, the gifted children in
the lower pictures (from *School Training of Gifted Children*) appear as the
occupants of a bright, optimistic world.

nose, and hair to make them appear ugly and sinister (Gould 1981, p. 171). These photographs support the belief that intelligence (or the lack of it) shines through as a series of physical characteristics, adorning the gifted, stigmatizing the backward. Through such imagery, the difference between the gifted and the feebleminded is no longer solely a matter of something abstract and equivocal such as cognitive ability. This difference is now visual, palpable, and concrete.

In the middle 1930s, Hollingworth attempted to establish the superior beauty of gifted children in a dramatically different way, by proving it scientifically. She had a panel of judges rate the faces, heads, and shoulders of 40 gifted adolescents and compare them to those of a group of ordinary adolescents. The results are reported as clear-cut: "The photographed faces of highly intelligent adolescents are more attractive (more beautiful) to adult judges than are those of adolescents who represent the average population of adolescents" (Hollingworth 1935, p. 279).

Terman (1954, p. 224) summarized his findings from the 1920s with the following adjectives: Gifted children are "appreciably superior" in physique, health, and social adjustment; "markedly superior" in moral attitudes and character traits; and "vastly superior" in academic performance. Goddard's (1928, p. 35) findings are remarkably similar: "These groups of children are physically the best in the system. Mentally they are more alert, they think quicker, they are more observing, they can see relationships more promptly. They have more good habits and fewer detrimental ones. They have a better use of language. . . . They have more curiosity and more energy. They see the end from the beginning more promptly. In short, they 'live' better, using that term with its fullest significance."

For her part, Hollingworth does not find gifted children inferior in any area. Although she finds them no better than others in music, drawing, mechanical aptitude, and some physical activities, they are no worse either. Moreover, Hollingworth shows that some of this apparent equality reveals other dimensions of gifted children's superiority. For example, the fact that gifted children are equal to ordinary children in the standing broad jump is taken as evidence of "their superior neuromuscular energy" (Monahan and Hollingworth 1927, p. 95), because the gifted have to compete in this athletic event with the handicap of weighing 7 pounds more than their nongifted peers. Although Hollingworth found the gifted to be more conforming than other children, she interprets this as an unmitigated virtue, since this behavior pattern is believed to result from their superior intelligence: "They quickly learn that 'it pays' in emotional tranquility, personal security, and sense of duty done, to regard the attitudes of others, and to meet the responsibility fully and promptly regardless of inclinations" (p. 124). Similarly, behav-

ior that might be taken as evidence of gifted children's emotional instability or, at the very least, as an ambiguous indicator of emotional stability, is seen only as evidence of their advanced development. This is
apparent in her story of a gifted 6-year-old boy who was heard weeping
one night after he was put to bed. When his parents asked him the cause
of his weeping, he said, "I was crying to think how awfully the North
taxed the South during the Civil War." Hollingworth says such grief "is
not a manifestation of nervous instability. It results from uncommon
insight or intelligence. The very intelligent seldom weep at what moves
the average person, but they weep when the average person perceives
nothing to call forth tears" (p. 129). Hollingworth acknowledges that the
gifted are often strained by the fact that they know so much, yet can do
so little because they are only children. However, she emphasizes that
this frustration is balanced by the fact that they can "do" more than
other children, "and by the fact that they so rapidly grow up in other
respects to a point where the whole organism becomes a competent
servant of the intellect." She concludes, "Perhaps their intellect enables
them to adopt the philosophical point of view to an unusual degree. At
all events, they are as a group less 'nervous' than unselected children,
by all criteria at present established" (p. 130).

This attention to emotional health and other noncognitive dimensions
of giftedness establishes giftedness as an orderly, consistent arrange-
ment of positive qualities. Through this imagery, people are encouraged
to believe that positive qualities suffuse the gifteds' entire being, from
physical health, size, and beauty to character, temperament, and interests. Because these qualities represent upper middle-class idealizations,
and because they conform to, and occur within that culture's "native
tongue," they are recognized and understood by gifted child consumers
who are themselves intimately acquainted with that culture's norms.
Moreover, because whatever work that was done to make gifted children appear beautiful, brave, selfless, well-off, strong, stable, philosophical, and so on is masked or hidden from view, gifted child consumers do
not attribute these qualities to the experts who produced them. Through
the process that Berger and Luckmann (1967, pp. 89–92) call "reification,"
these constructed images are attributed to the gifted children themselves
as facts of nature, as if they represent an innate, objective difference.

2

From Overt to Covert Racism:
New Gifted Child Rhetorics

So numerous are the intellectual gifts that differentiate gifted and regular children that any attempt to find an area of "weakness" or even average development in the gifted is no easy undertaking.

From "Causes and Consequences of Metamemory in Gifted Children"
by Borkowski and Peck (1986)

As already noted, overcrowding in urban public schools at the turn of the century created pressure to separate pupils into ability tracks. Persell (1977, pp. 85–86) argues that this pressure was less a function of the sheer number of students in the school system than of their racial and cultural mix: the greater the representation of minority group students, the greater the utilization of separate educational tracks. Thus, when the need to incorporate large numbers of foreign immigrants subsided in the 1930s and 1940s, ability tracking fell into disuse. However, when southern blacks moved into northern cities in increasing numbers in the 1950s, along with the influxes of Mexican Americans and Puerto Ricans, the popularity of ability tracking surged (Persell 1977, pp. 85–86). Accordingly, although gifted child scholars trace the sudden growth of gifted education during the 1950s to the launch of Sputnik and the mounting sense of competition with the Soviet Union (Tannenbaum 1979; Davis and Rimm 1989), there is another, unacknowledged explanation for the cyclical interest in gifted education. Because ability tracking is most common wherever economically and racially diverse school systems exist (Oakes 1985, pp. 65–67), it may provide the silent mechanism by which some social groups receive superior educations.

The language used to defend and rationalize ability tracking has gone through a cycle of its own since the era of Terman and Hollingworth. After Nazi racial policies and practices became known, eugenics talk "dropped below the horizon in social science" (Degler 1991, p. 204). In the 1950s and 1960s, the legal end to the "separate but equal" concept of educational equity (Oakes 1985) and the growing realization of de facto segregation's persistence (Cremin 1988, p. 265), produced mounting pressure on gifted child scholars and other educators to abandon explicit references to race and class superiority.[1] In large measure as result of this pressure, contemporary scholars portray giftedness as more heterogeneous, flexible, and broadly based than did their forebears. As expressed in a recent *Gifted Child Quarterly* editorial (Dettmer 1991, pp. 165–166), "Educational services for highly able and talented students must be determined according to a philosophy of inclusion—'who will benefit at this time from these services?'—and not a philosophy of exclusion." Although psychologists from the 1920s conceptualized intelligence as singular, as "the ability to see and learn the truth" (Thorndike 1924, p. 232), contemporary scholars refer to the multidimensionality and variety of intelligences. Thus, according to Renzulli (1978, p. 181), "Multiple talent and multiple criteria are almost bywords of the present day gifted student movement, and most educators would have little difficulty in accepting a definition that includes almost every area of human activity that manifests itself in a socially useful form."

Perhaps the most graphic illustration of the present effort to portray contemporary gifted child education according to a "philosophy of inclusion" is "Taylor's Talent Totem Poles" (Taylor 1978). This widely reproduced figure (see Davis and Rimm 1989, p. 14; Eby and Smutny 1990, p. 106; Sisk 1987, p. 89) consists of the cartoon faces of seven children stacked on top of each other, forming six columns or "totem poles." Each totem pole is labeled for a different ability, "academic," "creative," "planning," "communicating," "forecasting," and "decision-making." The faces at the top of the totem poles have the biggest smiles, indicating the most ability, and the faces at the bottom of the poles have the biggest frowns, indicating lowest ability. As the child grinning atop one pole can be found grimacing at the bottom of a neighboring pole, the central message is that no child can accurately be described as generically superior or inferior to others. Depending on how they are seen, every child is both gifted and nongifted.

Also in keeping with the new rhetoric of inclusion, gifted child scholars now conspicuously display commitment to cultural pluralism. Contemporary textbooks routinely include a chapter devoted to this theme (e.g., Colangelo and Davis 1991; Davis and Rimm 1989; Eby and Smutny 1990; Feldhusen, Van Tassel-Baska, and Seeley 1989; Sisk 1987; Pendarvis, Howley, and Howley 1990), and journal articles display passionate concern for minority issues (e.g., "Underrepresentation of Minority Students in Gifted Programs: Yes! It Matters!" by Smith, Le Rose, and

Clasen 1991). In one of the most detailed of these statements, 35 gifted child scholars maintained that cultural minorities must be empowered to determine what giftedness means for members of their own groups (Maker and Schiever 1989). As an American-Indian scholar (George 1989, p. 112) put it, "Gifted and talented American Indian students are who we say they are."

Still, what initially appears as an effort to redefine giftedness as something local and culture-specific, falls far short of the anticipated outcome. There are pleas for "culture-fair" and "culture-free" tests and calls to adjust scores on "biased" measures to compensate for the minority child's social "disadvantages," but underneath is the older presumption that once giftedness is located, the identified children share a common attribute whether they are American Indian, black, Cantonese, white upper middle class, and so on. Accordingly, another contributor to the Maker and Schiever collection writes, "Gifted and talented students, regardless of ethnic background, need to associate with each other to share their ideas and experiences. . . . Their chief cause of anxiety is feeling alone and different from other children because of different interests, higher ethical standards, and different concerns" (Kirschenbaum 1989, pp. 94–95). In effect, giftedness is still treated as a child's most defining status overriding considerations of ethnicity, age, and culture.

To further illustrate the similarity between contemporary and nascent gifted child discourse, consider the four tables contained within a collection edited by Maker and Schiever (1989, pp. 4, 78, 152, 210) that describe the cultural variables affecting giftedness among Hispanics, American Indians, African Americans, and Asians. The columns of these tables list "absolute aspects of giftedness," the cultural values of the relevant minority group, and the behavioral characteristics of that minority group. Consistent with the rhetoric of Hollingworth and Terman, not only do these tables display giftedness as something that exists in a pure or "absolute" way, but also the characteristics of minority groups are displayed as often conflicting with these ideals. For example, "absolute" giftedness is described in unremittingly positive terms: as "high expectations of self," "ability to generate original ideas and solutions," "high level of language development," "extraordinary quantity of information," "idealism, a sense of justice, and advanced levels of moral judgment," and "emotional depth and intensity." By contrast, the language used to describe the values and behaviors of minority group members often reflect strikingly different, negative stereotypes. Black culture and children (p. 210), for example, are characterized by terms such as "conformity," "manipulative behavior," "immediate or short-term gratification," "mastery of minimum academic skills," "physical punishment, blunt orders rather than discussion," "parental pressure conduct oriented, rather than task oriented," "acting out," "compliant behavior," and "leadership in street gangs."

NOTHING'S CHANGED

If giftedness in its "absolute" form can be expected to be highly original and idealistic, and blacks can be expected to be conforming and oriented to immediate or short-term gratification, the unstated implication is that blackness and giftedness exist in opposition to one another. This is not to imply that black people are inherently less gifted. In fact, contemporary gifted child scholars repeatedly reject this presumption. It means, rather, that black culture opposes giftedness, that it is an obstacle or disadvantage to the realization of giftedness in the black child. In the words of a gifted child scholar, "Although gifted and talented students can be found in all walks of life and in all racial and ethnic groups, they are more likely to be found in some groups than others. The groups with high incidence of the gifted place a great emphasis on intellectual values and have more extensive opportunities to develop talents and skills already present in the child" (Gallagher, quoted in Greenlaw and McIntosh 1988, p. 50).

It is recognized that gifted children are born into families of cultural minorities, but it is assumed that these families cannot encourage or nurture their potentiality. Accordingly, Davis and Rimm (1985, p. 272) reason that "gifted black children may perform only at an average level in school because of socioeconomic, language, motivational, personal, or cultural handicaps." The implicit message is that blacks can realize the full potentiality of their giftedness by distancing themselves from their culture of origin and assimilating to the dominant culture, a meaning encapsulated by the label "the disadvantaged gifted" (Van Tassel-Baska 1989b).[2] Regina's problem illustrates:

> Regina is typical of many black gifted students; she has difficulty in completing assignments and working independently. Without the stimulating environment and support of her enrichment teacher in a cluster group setting, it is highly possible Regina will not develop her potential ability. Culturally different gifted students have the added difficulty of having to simultaneously function in two cultures. Too often, black students do not know how to react to the highly competitive performance-based educational climate of predominantly white elementary and middle schools, and this problem is intensified in high school. (Sisk 1987, p. 229)

Contemporary gifted child scholars typify the need for "disadvantaged" gifted children to distance themselves from their culture of origin through cautionary tales in which the gifted child appears "held back" by the values and traditions of her ethnic group. For example, Clark (1983, p. 337) shares the story of Rosa, a Mexican-American whose father refused to let her accept a scholarship to Stanford, because it is not right for unmarried women to be away from home. The story ends with Rosa, "who loved her family and loved the marvelous ability of her mind . . . [being] forced to give up one to have the other."[3]

Sisk (1987, pp. 238–239) describes a slightly different conflict involving a disadvantaged gifted child named Malcolm. He comes from a family of nine siblings, has an older brother committed to a state training school, and an "abusive" father known as a "roaring drunk." Although Malcolm's school counselor proposed a career for him in mathematics, it is an "uphill" battle, because "neither the parents nor Malcolm are interested in 'bettering themselves'."

Van Tassle-Baska (1989b, p. 29) sums up the problem of the disadvantaged gifted this way: "while the family collectively as well as individually can be seen as a pivotal positive force in the lives of these successful students from disadvantaged backgrounds, it also serves as a potential contradictory role model. While students may receive encouragement for good grades and achievement in school, future aspirations may be tied to family history."

> I don't want to be a doctor. What I really want to do is cook. My grandmother—my whole family—cooks real well. However, I do like getting recognized for my schoolwork. My family is extremely proud of me and my brothers will brag to their friends about my report card.
> Female Student F (Van Tassel-Baska 1989b, p. 29)

The most interesting feature of gifted child education's new discourse of cultural inclusiveness is that it provides the appearance of radical change, the appearance of an effort to open gifted child education to those who have been traditionally excluded, without compromising the core beliefs that initially made giftedness so compelling. Because the potentialities of giftedness within the white upper classes are never questioned, and because the potentialities of giftedness within minority groups are, the traditional biases of gifted education remain intact.

To illustrate further, in *Educational Psychology of the Gifted* (1982, pp. 247–249), Khatena provides a list of "descriptors for children affected by cultural diversity" that include such negatives as "inability to trust or consider 'beauty in life'," "outer locus of control rather than inner locus of control," "inability to attend to task without supervision," "lack of training and development," "anger and frustration increase animalistic desire to survive," and "a need to use subterfuge in environment to get message across." Similarly, in *Growing Up Gifted*, Clark (1983, pp. 339–340) describes "Japanese, Chinese, and other Asians," as having a "strong valuing of conformity, which inhibits creative activity or divergent thinking," a "quiet manner, which may foster unrealistic expectations and inappropriate assessments," and an "attitude of perfectionism, making using mistakes as learning experiences quite difficult." Jews are described as being "often overly competitive," having a "perfectionistic attitude that causes tension and frustration in learning new material," with "pressure to achieve from family sometimes excessive, especially with males." Blacks are said to have "limited experience with varied or extended language patterns." And Mexican Americans are characterized by "attitudes depreciating education for family after high school" and "attitudes that differ on basic time, space reality."

These negative idealizations stand in sharp contrast to the praise and wonder continually heaped on the gifted.[4] Although some scholars emphasize gifted child virtues that others do not—Davis and Rimm (1985, pp. 24–25), for example, devote more attention to gifted children's "high moral thinking, empathy, and perspective taking" than do Tuttle and Becker (1983)—the specifics of each virtue seem insignificant against the totality, the sheer number, of virtues attributed to gifted children. Taken as a whole, these descriptors make gifted children appear divinely, quintessentially praiseworthy (Tuttle and Becker 1983, p. 34):

THEY
1. Are curious
2. Have a large vocabulary
3. Have long memories
4. Sometimes learn to read alone
5. Have a keen sense of time
6. Are persistent
7. Like to collect things
8. Are independent
9. Are healthy and well coordinated, but some may be delicate
10. May be bigger and stronger than average
11. Sustain interest in one or more fields over the years
12. Initiate their own activities
13. Develop earlier, sitting up, walking, talking
14. Learn easily
15. Have a keen sense of humor
16. Enjoy complicated games
17. Are creative and imaginative

18. Are interested and concerned about world problems
19. Analyze themselves, are often self-critical
20. Like older children when very young
21. Are original
22. Set high goals and ideals
23. Are leaders
24. Have talent(s) in art, music, writing, drama, dance
25. Use scientific methods of research
26. See relationships and draw sound generalizations
27. Produce work that is fresh, vital, and unique
28. Create new ideas, substances, and processes
29. Invent and build new mechanical devices
30. Often run counter to tradition
31. Continually question the status quo
32. Do the unexpected
33. Apply learning from one situation to different ones
34. Problem-solve on a superior level, divergently, innovatively
35. May appear different
36. Enjoy reading, especially biography and autobiography

Gifted children are portrayed as specializing not only in cognitive and academic areas but also as excelling in everything. Thus, for Eby and Smutny (1990, pp. 154–155) a "young gifted child" not only "learns rapidly," "is attentive, alert," and "highly imaginative," but also "is looked to by others for ideas and decisions," "is chosen first by peers," "easily repeats rhythm patterns," "makes up original tunes," "takes art activities seriously and derives satisfaction from them," and "shows mature sense of humor for age."

ASSEMBLING OBLIVIOUSNESS

Because "mundane inquiry constitutes itself and its world by remaining oblivious to its constitutive work, and part of that constitutive work includes that very obliviousness" (Pollner 1987, p. 167), the cultural presuppositions underlying gifted child directives and attributions are never examined. This obliviousness makes it possible for an educator (Kanigher 1977. p. 50) to suggest that gifted children should visit brokerage firms, read the *Wall Street Journal*, and purchase stock, preferably a variety that pays a quarterly dividend, so that "the dividend can be added to the child's bank account four times a year."[5] Through this same obliviousness, another educator (Gallagher 1985, pp. 218–219) shows that the gifted might explore "the range and scope of a concept such as heroes" through exemplars in which the male "hero" is described as "blue-eyed and blond," and in which women appear only as "fair damsels" or a wife who fixes the hero's breakfast and receives his grateful kiss. Similarly, after almost a decade of publishing pictures of neatly dressed white children demonstrating their giftedness by smiling into test tubes or making notations on "award-winning compositions," the *Gifted Child Quarterly* finally published a picture of an African American in 1967. However, the African-American male appearing in this photograph was not portrayed as gifted, but as the subject of a photographic essay on hippies. The writing beside his photograph (in which he grasped a "Haight Ashbury" sign) referred to the "pity rather than contempt" that should be directed toward hippies (Ransohoff 1967, p. 181). The next photograph of an African American to appear in the *Gifted Child Quarterly* (1968, p. 18) was titled "Disadvantaged gifted progress in new residential school."

Depending on one's perspective, one might easily call gifted child scholarship's covert racism and classism a consequence of naivete, forgetfulness, or even stupidity. However, such condemnations not only overlook the meticulous, artful work required to produce this racism and classism, but also suggest that "naivete," "forgetfulness," and "bias" are somehow automatic, requiring no constitutive work of their own. The very opposite is the case. If gifted child scholars were unsuccessful in finding new, increasingly complex ways of shielding from themselves the evidences of their project, their project could not be pursued. Gifted child scholarship renders itself oblivious not through failing to reflect on racism and classism. On the contrary, gifted child scholarship reflects powerfully and deeply on these topics. The reflections, however, are so patterned by the gifted child idiom that no matter how deeply, abstractly, or analytically gifted child scholars strive to move beyond racism and classism, they reproduce an "ontological space" (Pollner 1987, p. 107; Spencer 1982) in which they once again find themselves addressing, exploring, and describing cultural hierarchies.

Consider, for example, how sophisticated Perino and Perino (1981, p. 129) are in constituting themselves as combating inequality in gifted education: "We must be cautious in equating the culturally different with the disadvantaged. . . . Members of the predominant American cultural group seem fond of saying that anyone other than themselves is deprived, which expresses a negative view of ethnicity. Different does not necessarily mean disadvantaged. For example, not all Spanish-speaking people are disadvantaged, but many poor whites are clearly so." Only after they have established this commitment to cultural pluralism and

First photo of an African American to appear in the *Gifted Child Quarterly.* He was
portrayed simply as a "hippie." According to the author of this photographic essay: "They don't know why they are what they are. . . . They
don't think." Reprinted with permission © 1968, vol. 11, p. 18 by the National Association for Gifted Children.

only after they have established their own "caution" in managing that
commitment, can they introduce a formula for sustaining the traditional
hierarchies of gifted child discourses. Thus, in their very next sentence,
Perino and Perino show how it is possible to articulate negative expectations about cultural minorities without losing a democratic gloss: "We
must avoid using stereotypes of cultural groups and instead see that
disadvantage is directly related to social and economic class." By attributing negative idealizations to social class differences and not to ethnicity per se, these scholars find an acceptable rhetoric through which
they can conclude that black and Hispanic

> children do not have as many adult models who would motivate them
> toward academic pursuits and high achievement. Their interests are more

often developed in the streets of big cities where their adult models may
not demonstrate behavior that would be reinforced by the cultural main-
stream. The children are more apt to acquire interests and motivations that
are more immediately gratifying than those offered by schools, where
frustration tolerance and delayed gratification are rewarded. For these
reasons, it is a fact that there are many gifted and talented minority children in the population whose potential may never be identified or developed and who may lack the essentials of even doing average work in
school. (p. 131)

To further illustrate the construction of obliviousness, over 40% of the
cartoon figures represented in Delisle's *Gifted Kids Speak Out* (1987) are
dark-skinned, creating an appearance of commitment to equality and
integration. Yet, that text offers no accompanying references to African-
American, Hispanic, or American-Indian culture. Instead, giftedness is
displayed as an ideal of homogeneity and assimilation. Take, for example, these statements of gifted children's "plans for the future" (p. 104):

I will go to high school, and for college, I will go to the University of
Florida. Then I'll become a real estator or get involved in computers. I will
get married and then go into retirement and Medicare.
—Boy, 10

To either teach children that are mentally handicapped or (most probably)
go to hospitals and dance and sing for them.
—Girl, 9

My future plans are to go to Penn State and play either football or baseball
or both. And whichever one I like best will be my career. I will also take up
some kind of back-up career, like law.
—Boy 10

I would like to be a professor or a scientist. I think I would like to create
things that would help the world. It would also be interesting to pass on
the information I have learned to others.
—Boy, 10

1. Go to college and graduate school.
2. Get married and find a well-paying job.
3. Help my children to become good people.
—Girl, 10

I'd like to be an actress, singer, physical therapist, or teacher. When I'm
about 20, I plan to pursue my career (whatever it is) and find the perfect
place to live and work.
—Girl, 10

As was true 60 years ago, gifted children's career aspirations are explained, defended, and qualified in terms of upper middle-class vocab-

ularies of motive. Male children are still most often displayed as future scientists, lawyers, and surgeons and females as the ones who "dance and sing" at hospitals, the ones motivated to "help [their] children to become good people." Similarly, when contemporary scholars provide examples of gifted children's "exact" thinking, they do not use culturally neutral language. Like gifted child scholars from the 1920s, they call upon the vocabularies, values, and institutions of upper middle-class experience. Consider, for example, the dialogue that one scholar (Silverman 1989, p. 75) offered to demonstrate the thinking of highly gifted children:

The Boy:	Do you always talk in such a strange manner?
Dr. Levy:	What do you mean?
The Boy:	Well, your vocabulary is so limited. I thought you were on the faculty of the University of Pennsylvania.
Dr. Levy:	I thought you were a 4-year-old boy!
The Boy:	I would prefer that you would talk to me as if I were a person.

Gifted children are not taught to think and speak in culture-free language; rather, they are taught to use the vocabulary and codes of the dominant culture. However, gifted child scholars do not proclaim this language as superior *because* it belongs to the white upper middle class. Rather, the cultural origins of this language are portrayed as irrelevant. What matters, according to scholars, is that this language is logically, intrinsically superior. In other words, its dominance is deserved:

The emphasis in our school curriculum is on verbal skills and on the form of English used in the middle class home. This form of language is set up in a logical, sequential fashion, with a beginning and ending and a fairly clear meaning, and it encourages children to think in this fashion. The language is characterized by more questioning and less commanding behavior. It allows children to think more independently and to reach larger numbers of their own conclusions.

In homes of the lower class, on the other hand, whether black, Hispanic, or white, there is more control associated with language. The black, Spanish-speaking, or poor-white parent will offer a child a predetermined solution with few alternatives for consideration. Thus children from these groups, regardless of their innate potential, are at a disadvantage in the development of skills, especially verbal ones. (Perino and Perino 1981, p. 130)

Kaplan (1989a, p. 173) recommends that gifted children be enjoined to use phrases such as "Another point of view might be," "The accumulated evidence indicates that," "The issue germane or central to the point seems to," and "The assumption proposed appears to be that."

The upper middle-class origins of these terms are not acknowledged; instead, this language is described as "the language of questioning, challenging, and verifying information," as if it existed apart from or transcended culture (Kaplan 1989a, p. 173). Thus, the values and beliefs that are expressed are not treated as human constructions representing one group's interests and visions. Giftedness and its features are treated as natural phenomena, as attributes existing independent of time, setting, and culture. Consider these examples.

The *Gifted Child Quarterly* published 32 papers from 1988 through 1991 that used samples of children specifically described as "gifted." This label was used in the same way for all, despite the fact that the children were defined as gifted because of their prior membership in different gifted child programs, each of which had different admission criteria: One program labeled children as gifted exclusively by means of standardized achievement tests; eight admitted children exclusively by IQ, using scores ranging from 120 to 135 as cutoffs; the remaining 16 programs relied on differing combinations of criteria such as IQ, achievement test scores, survey instruments, grades, class rank, references, and nominations. That one sample came from a "pullout enrichment" class with no subject focus, and another from an "accelerated" class or full-time summer program in a highly specialized topic area (e.g., calculus), was not seen as problematic. Nor was concern expressed over the fact that the children enrolled in these programs represented different socioeconomic or cultural backgrounds or were nominated to and accepted by these programs on the basis of highly discrepant information. Thus, despite stated belief in the heterogeneity and variety of intelligences, and despite stated belief in the cultural specificity of giftedness, empirical studies portray giftedness as a single dichotomous variable that exists independently of the conditions of its discovery and occurrence. In other words, what has specific cultural origins is treated as the self-same thing over all past and prospective conditions.

Not only are gifted child samples treated as homogeneous, but also findings are regarded as comparable regardless of the measures and procedures employed. In keeping with, and supporting, a model of continuous, linear knowledge development, studies on the gifted are presented as increasingly refined portraits building on the works of predecessors, whose observations, like their own, are treated as transcontextual and transcultural. To illustrate, a recent study (Wooding and Bingham 1992) examined 30 students enrolled in a Canadian junior high for the gifted to determine how these children might respond to a stressor.[6] The gifted subjects were found to manage stress more efficiently and to recover sooner than a matched sample of nongifted children. The investigators portrayed these findings as comparable to, and supportive of, a host of other gifted child studies (e.g., Ludwig and Cullinan 1984; Reynolds and Bradley 1983; Terman 1925, 1954; Terman and Oden 1940, 1947, 1951) that utilized samples drawn from different countries, eras, and age groups and were based on different selection criteria. For example, the gifted children in Ludwig and Cullinan's study came from a Chicago suburb, were not enrolled in junior high but grades 1–5, and unlike the Wooding and Bingham sample, were not in a school for the gifted, but in a pullout enrichment class. Although the Canadian gifted were selected from their special junior high solely on the basis of IQ, the Chicago group was selected by six criteria, including "teacher referral," "general classroom functioning," and "ability to complete tasks." These groups were displayed as comparable, although no effort was made to assess differences in race, social class, or culture.[7] Through these means, gifted children's other characteristics fade into the background. Giftedness operates as the child's central, even only, feature worth noting.

There are perhaps no better examples of scholars treating giftedness as a transcultural facticity than the three books, *On Being Gifted* (American Association of Gifted Children 1978), *Gifted Children Speak Out* (Delisle 1984), and *Gifted Kids Speak Out* (Delisle 1987), devoted to gifted children's comments about their giftedness. Although these books are comprised of hundreds of interviews of gifted children, the authors make no effort to place them into a cultural context or to explain how these children came to be identified as gifted. Their giftedness is treated as entirely nonconditional, as part of "that universal and publick Manuscript that lies expansed unto the eyes of all" (from Sir Thomas Browne, quoted in Woodbridge 1940, p. 3). Like Santayana's (1924, p. x) reference to "the stars, the seasons, the swarm of animals, the spectacle of birth and death," their giftedness is treated as something self-evidently seen and known, as "the facts before every man's eyes."

What gifted child scholars specifically exclude from inquiry is the ways in which human beings furnish themselves with the children who serve as objects of gifted child research. They treat gifted children as an a priori facticity, as if they, gifted child scholars, had nothing to do with their existence. Through the "retrospective illusion" (Merleau-Ponty 1964), gifted child scholars and the consumers of their reports treat the objects of their perception (gifted children) as if they were the preexistent causes of their perception and, in so doing, gloss the contingent character of what is perceived. That gifted child scholars are continuously confronted by the artifacts of giftedness (labeled children, gifted child programs, parent support groups, journals, books, institutes, etc.)

makes them forget their own and others' essential contribution to giftedness. Having forgotten these contributions, scholars can carry on their
activities as the authors of giftedness.

POSITIVE SOCIAL CONTROL

According to this analysis, the meaning of giftedness is not located in
some special class of children. Nor, to be precise, is this meaning located
in experts' writings on giftedness. Rather, it is located at the intersection
of experts' arguments and readers' understandings. Within this perspective, gifted child experts from the first decades of the century did not
simply offer their readers a definition of giftedness, but also they offered
a definition that made sense within a particular cultural context. This
was accomplished by taking an unknown class of people (gifted children) and systematically relating them to an associated, known class of
people—members of the white upper middle class (cf. Strauss 1959).
Because being gifted, being upper middle class, and being white each
share the predicate of "superiority," the linkage of these concepts appeared reasonable, particularly in view of the fact that gifted child consumers are themselves upper middle class and white. The image of the
gifted as the embodiment of goodness received widespread recognition
at the same time that the image of the feebleminded became recognized
as the embodiment of social evil, because together these images articu-
lated the polar extremes of a moral order that assigns worth to all human
characteristics, particularly social class and race.

Acceptance of these archetypes not only gave gifted child scholars the
capacity to recognize children who were cognitively superior, it changed
the meaning of being upper middle-class and white. Upper middle class
career choices, interests, and motivations, as a result of their identification with giftedness, became sanctified. By portraying giftedness as a
phenomenon of social class and race, experts supported a difference
that, although formerly suspected or believed, gained new legitimacy
through scientific argument. Inadvertently, then, gifted child discourse
from the first decades of the century supported people's general belief in
the naturalness, sacredness, and correctness of white upper middle-
class dominance.

For Foucault, the power of such "positive" social control comes from
its seamlessness, its invisibility, and ubiquitousness: "The judges of nor-
mality are everywhere. We are in the society of the teacher-judge, the
doctor-judge, the educator-judge, the 'social-worker' judge; it is on them

that the universal reign of the normative is based" (1977, p. 304). Although harassment, defamation, and assault are easily named as repressive, efforts to identify people's strengths, to give support and "advantages," appear irreproachable. It goes without saying that programs aimed at recognizing children's "gifts" are not comfortably classed with programs explicitly aimed at exerting hierarchical control and domination. This inability to make positive social control accountable explains its effectiveness, its capacity to quietly infiltrate democratic, egalitarian discourse, and to permeate modern social experience. It also explains why there is a well-developed literature on the social construction of retardation (e.g., Bogdan and Taylor 1982; Ferguson 1987; Mercer 1965, 1973; Smith 1985) without a comparable literature on the gifted.

To this day, when IQ testing is criticized, it is almost always for creating a negative expectation, for identifying members of some cultural group as slow, not for identifying members of other groups as fast (e.g., Aguirre 1979; Beeghley and Butler 1974; Gould 1981; Mensh and Mensh 1991). Thus, when a California Federal District Judge declared IQ tests invalid in 1979, it was for assigning a disproportionately large percentage of black children to classes for the "educable mentally retarded," not for assigning a disproportionately small percentage of black children to classes for the gifted.[8] Similarly, Gould's (1981) outrage in *The Mismeasure of Man* was aimed at psychologists and educators from the first decades of the century for coining negative terms no longer in use: "feebleminded," "high-grade defective," "moron," and so on; however, no mention was made of psychologists' and educators' ongoing selective use of positive terms such as *gifted*. Despite widespread questioning in the academic literature on the various methods used to conceptualize, describe, and identify human intelligence, and despite the markedly unbalanced racial and ethnic composition of gifted child educational programming, use of the term *gifted* remains relatively immune to criticism.[9] For example, among the 408 reference sources listed by Aby (1990) on the "IQ Debate," only three are indexed under the topic heading "gifted children;" 16 are indexed under "mental retardation and race," with no reference sources listed (and, indeed, no topic heading) for "gifted children and race."

This selective attention cannot, of course, fully explain the continuing underrepresentation of blacks, Hispanics, American Indians, and other ethnic minorities in gifted education. However, it may partially explain why this underrepresentation is so resistant to change. Presumably, any imagery that obscures and conceals the connection between giftedness and exclusionary ideology makes such a connection more difficult to address and discredit. Ironically, then, those elements of contemporary discourse that make gifted child programming *appear* democratic and integrated mystify efforts to identify the reasons why such programs are *not* democratic and integrated. To illustrate, as in the days of Hollingworth and Goddard, contemporary textbooks on gifted children are illustrated with photographs of the gifted. However, unlike texts from the 1920s, a large number of the children represented in these photographs are of African-American descent (e.g., Davis and Rimm 1985; Eby and Smutny 1990; Kitano and Kirby 1986; Sisk 1987). Although this display of "inclusiveness" may have a democratic intent—to create the expectation that groups long underrepresented in gifted child programs belong in and are welcomed by such programs—there is a second, unintended consequence. Because this positive imagery masks existing discrimination, that discrimination goes unchallenged.

By portraying gifted education as either integrated or aspiring toward integration, responsibility for social control is concealed. Instead, responsibility for the underrepresentation of minorities is attributed to factors located outside of, or peripheral to, gifted education itself. Most commonly, it is attributed to the excluded themselves, to their "real learning deficits, not just hidden talents" (Tannenbaum 1990, p. 120). It is attributed to the families of the excluded: "These children often come from families with low socioeconomic status and/or educational orientation. Typically these families provide little stimulation of higher level thinking skills through conversation, books, travel, shared problem solving, and educational activities" (Whitmore 1987, p. 147). Responsibility is attributed to "our schools, our attitudes, our values" (Zappia 1989, p. 26), to "minority children slipping through the cracks of a blind system" (Eby and Smutny 1990, p. 120), to the "social and cultural biases in standardized tests" (Richert 1987, p. 151), and to "insensitive" and "biased" teachers (Minner 1990, p. 37). What is conspicuously absent, however, is the suggestion that our very understanding of giftedness —the ways we study, validate, recognize, and describe this phenomenon— reflects and supports discrimination.

Many aspects of the relations between gifted child discourse and social control have changed over time. In the current climate it is impossible for a scholar to write, "The immemorial division of mankind into 'lower,' 'middle,' and 'upper' classes, economically speaking, rests on a biological foundation which guarantees the stubborn permanence with which it persists in spite of all efforts to abolish it by artifice" (Hollingworth 1926, p. 360). Yet, a gifted child education that does not make such statements, that reiteratively displays its commitment to cultural pluralism, continues to exclude minorities.

3

From Objects of Awe to Objects
of Commiseration:
Gifted Children as Victims

I wonder who can be so insensitive as to experience no emotional
appeal in some of the stories . . . of the inhumane treatment of gifted
children.

From *Toward the More Humane Treatment of Gifted Children*
by E. Paul Torrance (1963)

By the mid-1920s although the gifted had become an established part of
educational discourse, there were still very few educational programs
for members of this new social category. In 1930 there were only nine
states and 14 cities with gifted education programs. This represented
75 classrooms with an enrollment of 1,834 pupils. By 1940 there were
still only 93 gifted child classrooms enrolling 3,255 pupils (Froehlich,
McNealy, Nelson, and Norris 1944, p. 207). By 1966, however, gifted
child enrollment had swelled to 312,100 pupils (Renotsky and Green
1970, p. 63). Today 1,978,858 pupils are enrolled in gifted programs
(National Center for Educational Statistics 1992), representing 5.35% of
all-white pupils and 2.44% of black and Hispanic pupils (*New York Times*
1988).

In this chapter I examine the rhetoric behind this phenomenal growth,
specifically, how scholars created demand for gifted education by reiteratively enumerating, describing, and explaining gifted children's
troubles.

35

A NEED FOR GIFTED CHILD PATHOS

During the late nineteenth and early twentieth centuries, several "child-saving" movements were galvanized by images of children's sufferings and deprivations (Ronald Cohen 1985; Cravens 1985). For example, the New York Society for the Prevention of Cruelty to Children was organized in December 1874, only eight months after the *New York Times* reported the maltreatment of "Little Mary Ellen" (Bremner 1971). Although child savers routinely emphasized the "bright eyes" and "quick intelligence" of abused and neglected children (Mary Ellen was called a "bright little girl, with features indicating unusual mental capacity"[1]), it was not until the 1930s that any concerted effort was made to link gifted children to images of pain and hardship. This chapter explores how this linkage evolved in social scientific writings.

Because gifted children are by definition more capable than others and, according to researchers such as Lewis Terman (1925) and Leta Hollingworth (1926), usually better off financially, any attempt at portraying gifted children's vulnerability is bound to be counterintuitive. At first glance, there is little reason to believe that the gifted need special assistance as they already have more than others. Still, unless it is shown that the gifted experience unexpected forms of disadvantage, proposals to improve their treatment almost completely lack emotional appeal. Why should a population that is more successful, stronger, better endowed than others require or deserve special provisions? Accordingly, to justify support for the gifted, a case must somehow be made for their unique neediness and vulnerability.

Prior to the 1930s, gifted child scholars attempted to create sentiment for the gifted by comparing their treatment to that of the feebleminded. Quite simply, they argued how unjust it was to have special classes for the feebleminded with no comparable services for the gifted. Gifted child scholars maintained that if feebleminded children can be segregated and placed in their own classrooms, then not giving equivalent recognition and attention to the best students represented unfair discrimination. This appeal is exemplified in O'Shea's (1926, p. xxi) introduction to Hollingworth's *Gifted Children: Their Nature and Nurture*: "The present writer can easily recall the time when everyone thought that bright children could look out for themselves—as a result of which they were neglected, in the schools at any rate, in order that teachers might devote all their energies to the less able and backward pupils."

No one argued in this vein more passionately than Hollingworth herself (1926, p. vii):

This preoccupation with the incompetent resulted from the natural tendency of human beings to notice whatever is giving them pain or annoyance, taking for granted that which proceeds in an orderly and agreeable manner. It was due also to the wave of uninformed humanitarianism, which rose in the latter half of the eighteenth century, and extended through the nineteenth century. Under this influence, expensive and even palatial institutions were established for the preservation and care of the feebleminded, the delinquent, the crippled, the insane, and others who varied biologically in the direction of social incompetence. Philanthropy, originally meaning love of man, degenerated to mean love of stupid and vicious man.

Gessell's (1921, p. 44) argument that "the superior child is more in danger of retardation than the dullard," represented an ingenious strategy for redirecting some of the sentimental support given the feebleminded to the gifted. In Freeman's (1924, p. 209) words, the gifted's "retardation . . . comes out when we compare their potential progress with their actual progress." Similarly, for Leta Hollingworth (quoted in Harry Hollingworth 1943, p. 125), the gifted "rather than the dull became the 'laggards' and the 'retarded' because the accomplishments expected of them and permitted to them were so woefully below the achievements of which they were easily capable."

Still, comparisons of the gifted and the feebleminded are severely limited as rhetorical strategy, because they do not lend themselves to personal vignettes or testimonials. It is one thing to speak of "palatial institutions" for the feebleminded and quite another to show that Child A who is feebleminded has more advantages than Child B who is gifted. In other words, the claim that the gifted are treated unjustly in comparison to the feebleminded can only be supported by sweeping generalizations, a mode of argument poorly suited to evoking a significant emotional response.

What gifted child scholarship needed was a set of images through which the gifted could be portrayed not only as an oppressed group but as oppressed individuals—individuals whose sufferings and vulnerability were describable in all the detail of time, situation, and action.

However, because the gifted are defined as smarter, stronger, more tranquil, more sociable, "made of finer stuff than the majority" (Goddard 1928, p. 35), their vulnerability could not be attributed to them as a weakness or flaw. To retain gifted children's superiority, their vulnerability had to be located outside themselves. Their capacity to be harmed had to be attributed to an unsuitable environment, to their dependency on a social system that is unresponsive to their needs, to caretakers and peers who are either jealous of their capacities, baffled by them, or inclined to misappropriate them for their own selfish purposes.

If failures are to be discussed, they must be attributed to the nongifted. The case for gifted children's vulnerability thus did not depend on a new, imperfect, version of giftedness, but on a new, highly negative, version of nongiftedness. Three types of negative images were most common: one that emphasized the indifference, scorn, and tyranny of the nongifted toward the gifted, a second that emphasized the nongifted's efforts to exploit the gifted, and a third that emphasized the nongifted's lack of intelligence and sophistication. In the first sections of this chapter, we examine the set of images by which the nongifted appear as the anti-gifted, as a population wracked with envy and hostility toward their intellectual betters. Then we examine the set of images showing the nongifted exploiting the gifted, using them to gratify their vanity and advance their ambitions. The final section examines how the nongifted are pictured as well-intentioned but overwhelmed and confused by the many complexities and subtleties of giftedness.

As the discussion proceeds, we note that the rhetoric of gifted children's troubles unfolded in stages: First, the primary themes and images of this discourse were introduced; second came a flood of discourse directed at changing the perceptions of the collective audience; third came a rhetoric of inclusion, moderation, and compromise resulting from awareness that the cause had been won. We illustrate this unfolding primarily by showing that the more successful gifted child education became, the less extreme were the pronouncements on gifted children's troubles, and the less scholars attempted to arouse public opinion to the rejection and control of gifted child enemies.

THE EMERGENCE OF THE ANTI-GIFTED

From the early 1930s, hostility toward the gifted was traced to envy and jealousy, to a constant, persistent, yet completely undeserved, perception that the gifted are arrogant and competitive. Terman (Burks, Jensen, and Terman 1930, p. 265) was the first to identify this brand of negativity: "There is no scorn like the scorn of older boys for the younger and weaker who aspire to equality with them, especially if they are conscious of their own relative inferiority to the latter in intelligence." He argued that older nongifted children can be expected to pick on younger gifted children to compensate for their own feelings of intellectual inferiority: "The physical and social immaturity of the younger child offers the desired opportunity to even the score."

In Hollingworth's (1931) "The Child of Very Superior Intelligence as a Special Problem in Social Adjustment" and her posthumously published *Children Above IQ 180* (1942/1975), the bully emerged as the nemesis to the gifted, as a creature ceaselessly and mindlessly programmed to persecute his smaller, more intelligent peers. Hollingworth (1942/1975, p. 303) claimed that when the gifted child attempts to socialize with nongifted classmates, they usually respond with the silent treatment. And "if he persists, they become annoyed, hurling at him the dreadful epithet, 'Perfesser.' If he still persists, they pull his hair, tear his shirt from his back, and hit him with a beer bottle." Hollingworth called these encounters a direct penalty of being gifted "for little boys of like age, in the grade proper for their age, do not come into contact with these over-age bullies to anything like the same extent, and hence do not become targets for the latter" (pp. 271–272). Hollingworth added that gifted children are made vulnerable not only because of their younger age and smaller size, but also because of their superior moral development. They are too caring and sensitive to retaliate with sufficient violence to keep the bully at bay: "One young gifted boy thus bullied said, 'I rigged up a sling and was going to hit him [the bully] with a marble, but got afraid I might shoot his eye out'" (p. 272).

For Hollingworth (1942/1975, p. 242), the entire American school system was to blame for its unwillingness to provide segregated programs for the gifted: "At present, compulsory education, with heterogeneous classes, forces upon gifted children situations that would be analogous to those arising if teachers and superintendents were compelled to consort daily, unprotected, with giant thugs and gangsters."

According to Herbert A. Carroll, in *Genius in the Making* (1940), gifted children can expect to be continuously confronted by painful, resentful awareness of their intellectual superiority: "Again and again envy will cause individuals to point out and to emphasize . . . [the gifted child's] faults" (pp. 58–59). The envious include not only casual acquaintances and other school children but even the gifted child's parents. Carroll illustrated with this anecdote from a biography of Marie Curie:

> One morning while Bronya [an older sister] was faltering out a reading lesson to her parents, Manya [Marie] grew impatient, took the book from her hands, and read aloud the opening sentence. At first, flattered by the silence which surrounded her, she continued this fascinating game; but suddenly panic seized her. One look at the stupefied faces of her parents, another at Bronya's sulky stare, a few intelligible stammers, an irrepressible sob—and instead of the infant prodigy, there was only the baby of four, crying through her tears:
> "Beg—pardon! Pardon! I didn't do it on purpose. It's not my fault—it's not Bronya's fault! It's only because it was so easy!"

Manya had suddenly conceived, with despair, that she might perhaps never be forgiven for having learned to read. (p. 92)

Carroll claimed that as gifted children grow older, they are increasingly likely to be ostracized by members of their family. The gifted child "tries to make contact with them by doing the things they like to do, by appearing interested in the things they consider important. Occasionally, he succeeds, but he is much more likely merely to arouse resentment by what they consider to be his patronizing attitude" (pp. 93–94). Marguerite Peachman (1942) provided the example of a mother who continually berated her gifted 6-year-old: "The mother repeatedly stated that the child had a bad disposition, was exceedingly jealous of a younger sister, and that she was ashamed to say he was her son. She seemed chagrined that he did not follow the usual pattern and seemed quite aloof from her. Affection was lavished on the more ordinary child . . . due to her unconscious jealousy of the boy."

Most revealing is Torrance's (1963) analysis of the "flying monkey" image as symbolic of the gifted child's repression and rejection by parents. Torrance claimed that many gifted children's stories utilize a flying monkey as a central character. In these stories, the parents are upset when they learn that their baby monkey is gifted with the ability to fly. They exclude their baby, send it away "or, the mother may have the father give the monkey 'a good talking to' and tell him that the other monkeys will think he is 'crazy in the head' if he continues to fly. They tell him they will fear him and that he will have no friends. They may teach him to hide his wings, or camouflage them so that others will not know he can fly. Or, they may cut off his wings" (Torrance 1963, pp. 143–144). Even when the baby monkey uses its flying skills for the good of others, "such as obtaining the top bananas for the other monkeys or saving their lives by flying them out of the burning jungle," it still risks all kinds of punishment and ridicule (Torrance 1963, pp. 143–144).

According to the "flying monkey" metaphor, parents repress the gifted child not from envy or because the gifted have a competitive edge and so make ordinary people appear inferior. Instead, the gifted excite hostility simply because they stand out: "To be gifted is to discover at first hand the uneasiness of society in the presence of the 'different' individual" (Feinberg 1970, p. 172).

Several writers contend that the American belief in equality jeopardizes the acceptance of the gifted (Mead 1954; Terman and Oden 1954): "From our earliest Puritan origins our attitudes have been of a negative nature. We have a long history of regarding superior endowment with suspicion, for exceptionality has long been correlated with psychological abnormality. . . . The popular stereotype of the gifted is not always a kind one. We are all cognizant of such terms as 'egghead,' 'ivory tower thinker,' 'dreamer,' and many others" (Adler 1961, p. 135). Margaret Mead (1954) argued that success in our culture is only appreciated if it is achieved by those of modest ability who then rise to the top by virtue of courage, hard work, and suffering. By Mirman's (1970a, p. 145) account, "There seems to be a malaise deep within the fiber of the American people that results in the worship of mediocrity as though it were the most desirable state of achievement."

Perhaps the greatest boost to the image of the gifted as languishing in an atmosphere of neglect was the 1972 Congressional Report on gifted education. "We are increasingly being stripped of the comfortable notion that a bright mind will make it on its own," Sidney P. Marland, Jr., the former U.S. Commissioner of Education, wrote to Congress: "Gifted and talented children are, in fact, deprived and can suffer psychological damage and permanent impairment of their abilities to function well which is equal to or greater than the similar deprivation suffered by any other population with special needs."[2] The tragedy here, according to Bernard Miller (1981, p. 6) is that "intellectual potential . . . is like a delicate flower; it cannot survive neglect."

However, the gifted must not only be prepared to be ignored and unappreciated. In addition, "the gifted must be prepared to take blows dealt them both consciously, and unhappily, often unconsciously, in the effort to tear them down, or squash them to the level of the middle of a given group" (Isaacs 1969, p. 35). The editor of the *Gifted Child Quarterly* summarized the penalties that befall the gifted child:

1. He is treated last in importance.
2. He is treated as a curiosity.
3. He is treated as one to be isolated from the others.
4. He is treated as one who needs additional attention (IF time can be found).
5. He is treated with suspicion and skepticism.
6. He is treated with fear.
7. He is treated as an experiment.
8. He is treated as if to be destroyed.
9. He is ostracized.
10. He is denied privileges the more average get.
11. He is handled so as to be disposed of as quickly as possible.
12. He is tolerated only.
13. He is treated as one who should learn that he must be like the others if his total welfare is to be considered. (Isaacs 1965, pp. 169–170)

Carroll (1940, pp. 216–217) included teachers among the anti-gifted: "Any psychologist or teacher with an interest in bright children could tell stories without number of the humiliating treatment accorded by instructors to those who are intellectually superior." Given their intellectual inferiority, nongifted teachers are likely to become defensive and rigid in their dealings with the gifted. Hollingworth (1942/1975, pp. 300–301) illustrated with the case of a gifted boy described by his teacher as "impudent" and "a liar." His crime was that he corrected his teacher: The teacher said that Gutenberg was the "first discoverer" of printing, and he said, "No; the Chinese *invented*, not discovered, printing." After this, "she gave me a raking-over before the whole class."

Hollingworth felt that the only way that gifted children can adapt to such authority figures is to learn that their dullness cannot be changed. She argued that gifted children must learn that "human beings in general are incorrigibly very different from themselves in thought, action, and desire" (1942/1975, p. 299), a point driven home with the story of a gifted 7-year-old who came home from school one day weeping bitterly: "Oh, Grandmother, Grandmother," he exclaimed, "they don't know what's good! They won't read!" According to Hollingworth, it later became known "that he had taken book after book to school—all his favorites from his grandfather's library—and tried to show the other third-grade pupils what treasures these were, but the boys and girls only resisted his efforts, made fun of him, threw his treasures on the floor, and finally pulled his hair" (p. 260). Hollingworth repeats the refrain that the gifted can only avoid these tragedies if they "learn to suffer fools glady—not sneeringly, not angrily, not despairingly, not weepingly—but gladly, if personal development is to proceed successfully in the world as it is. Failure to learn to tolerate in a reasonable fashion the foolishness of others less gifted leads to bitterness, disillusionment, and misanthropy" (pp. 299–300).

Failure to understand and tolerate rejection at the hands of the nongifted may also cause the gifted to deny their own superiority: "Indeed, many teachers and parents of very bright children recall one or more occasions when a child purposely flunked or failed to complete a report so he could be 'just one of the gang'" (Ginsberg and Harrison 1977, p. 11).

According to Friedenberg (1962) in "The Gifted Student and His Enemies," the specific animus aroused by gifted students is best defined by the French term "ressentiment." This emotion is less conscious than the scorn described by Terman and Hollingworth, because it is not focused on specific experiences or events. In contrast to Hollingworth's bully, the ressentient do not acknowledge their hatred of the gifted but instead continuously deny and rationalize, producing an ever-present, vague ill-temper directed at the intellectually superior. As Friedenberg wrote,

Consider the poor mathematician, who manages to salvage enough math to become a high school teacher, or the ninth-grade teacher who hates mathematics and never meant to have any traffic with it at all. Such teachers manage by knowing a set of answers, and a conventional procedure for arriving at them. They maintain their self-esteem by convincing themselves that this is really enough; and the student who really understands mathematics puts them in a dilemma. On the one hand, he may show them up as incompetent. On the other, they don't know that he may be cheating somehow, and laughing at them for being taken in. They dare not commit themselves either way. If they are authoritarian, they bully him into solving the problems 'the way I show you as long as you are in my class.' If they are 'philanthropic,' they respond with studied tolerance and amusement to Johnny's 'attention-getting behavior.' But in either case they try to make sure that he doesn't embarrass them by actually getting up and doing mathematics in front of the whole class." (p. 415)

Although Friedenberg emphasized the subtler, more complex expressions of prejudice against the gifted, his formulation in no way ruled out or replaced a much simpler discourse in which the nongifted were portrayed as crass, priggish individuals, capable of unexpected violence. Especially during the years when Ann Isaacs, the founder of the National Association of Gifted Children, edited the *Gifted Child Quarterly* (1956–1974), overt, unrestrained brutality by the nongifted toward the gifted was portrayed as a normal, everyday occurrence. In this climate, there is no surprise associated with a teacher of a gifted boy declaring, "I'll make him work if I have to break his spirit to do it—and ridiculing and shaming him is the only way with children like him" (Torrance 1963, p. 135). Similarly, descriptions of a gifted child "paddled repeatedly by the math teacher because he likes to do calculus instead of the regular in-grade math" and another gifted child who "has learned to stay out of the teacher's way so he won't get clouted so much" (Isaacs 1971, p. 177), reflected a typical, expected pattern.

One well-used storyline has the teacher stubbornly refusing to believe that gifted children's creative achievements are their own. In 1963, for example, Torrance described how a gifted girl's history teacher unjustly accused her of cheating: "Before the whole class, while pounding on Dee's desk with her hand, she ridiculed Dee by swearing that Dee's homework was not done by her." The teacher said that Dee's report was not in her handwriting; however, her mother later explained that Dee's handwriting was inconsistent because she has the ability to write with both hands—"It's just as natural for her to switch hands when one gets tired as it is to breathe" (pp. 139–140). In 1970, Norman Mirman, the President of the National Association of Gifted Children, shared these accounts written by a former gifted child: "One of my teachers told the class that I was a very poor student and very immature, and that they would just have to learn to tolerate me. Another year, I was punished for 'cheating' on my reading list." His "cheating" consisted of his claiming to read more books than the teacher thought humanly possible (1970b, p. 264). Eleven years later, Sylvia Rimm (1981, p. 43) told the tale of a teacher who held aloft a gifted boy's homework assignment, declaring to the class, "I want this to be an experience for all of you. This is Bob's story. He is nothing but a cheat! He could never write a story like this and cheaters will get what they deserve." The teacher then ripped Bob's homework sheets into shreds.

THE ANTI-GIFTED TODAY

Contemporary images of the anti-gifted, when they appear in gifted child scholarship, are now usually located in poetry, fiction, and letters to the editor inserted between more traditional displays of scholarship. Consider this excerpt from "Chad's Poem" (Curtis 1985, p. 14), published in G/C/T (Gifted/Creative/and Talented Children):

> I sit in a vacuum
> Day after day.
> My brain is turned off
> And wasting away.
> My fingers are writing,
> Who cares what they say,
> Just turn in that paper
> Day after day.
>
> I'm bored and I'm tired
> I'm lonely and sad.
> "No, you're gifted and lazy
> And noisy and bad!"
> "Put him in a private school,
> Send him away,"
> The principal, teachers,
> And counselors say.

"To Be, or Not to Be, Gifted" (Krueger 1981, p. 17), also published in G/C/T, reveals that the image of the anti-gifted survives as a force to be reckoned with:

To be, or not to be, "gifted,"—that is the question:—
Whether 'tis nobler for my mind to suffer
The slings and arrows of misfortune and jealousy,
Or to take arms against a sea of stereotypes,
And by opposing confirm them?—To hide,—to daydream,—
No more; and by daydreaming I end
The heart-ache, and the thousand unnatural stares
That I am heir to, 'tis an escape
Devoutly to be wisht. To conform, to daydream,—
To dream! perchance to think: ay, there's the rub;
For in that state of daydream what thoughts may come,
When I have shuffled through this boring day of school,
Must give me pause: there's my mentor's respect
That makes endurable this long school day;
For who would bear the jeers and scorns of classmates,
The rigid teacher's oppression, the proud teacher's contumely,
The pangs of lost comradery, the administration's delay,
The insolence of peers, and the spurns
That patient merit of the unworthy takes. . . .

Jodie Foster's recent film *Little Man Tate* contained all the sentimental strategies gifted child scholars introduced 50 years earlier: The nongifted kids called the quietly suffering gifted boy "dork" and "freak." The schoolchildren scorned his birthday invitations, scattering them around the schoolyard, and when no one came to his party his mother enrolled him in a school for the gifted whose principal immediately reassured him that she would not let anyone laugh at him again.

Other examples of the anti-gifted image in contemporary discourse include the gifted child "survival" books. For example, Delisle and Galbraith's (1987, pp. 111–112) *The Gifted Kids Survival Guide II* has a chapter that exhorts gifted children, much like Hollingworth did in 1942, to "learn to suffer fools gladly." Also, *The Gifted Kids Survival Guide: For Ages 10 & Under* (Galbraith 1984, p. 9) begins with this question: "When kids tease you for knowing so much or for getting perfect papers, do you ever wish you weren't so smart?" Later on, Galbraith (pp. 46–47) notes that "one of the most bothersome things about being gifted is the teasing that comes with the label. And there are no two ways about it: when you're GT, you are going to be teased." The author then lists some of the names hurled at the gifted: "Mr. Genius, " Ms. Know-It-All," "Hotshot," "Teacher's Pet," "Brain," "Hypo" (short for high potential), and so on.

However, as gifted child scholarship became more established during the 1970s and 1980s, unconditional generalizations about the anti-gifted appeared increasingly awkward within the context of academic journals. In contemporary times, one rarely finds scholars declaring, as Isaacs did

(1971, p. 179), "Anyone killing off the gifted need not necessarily live in fear that his punishment will be severe." Journal articles and editorials no longer proclaim that "it's just as serious a problem to be the mother of the intellectually gifted as the mentally retarded" (Mirman 1970a, p. 144).

While the anti-gifted may still yell, pound on desks, call names, and even hit, they appear to play a significantly smaller role in contemporary gifted child discourse. As gifted child education became more accepted among educators, parents, and scholars, it outgrew its dependency on a bullies-in-the-schoolyard style of rhetoric. The extreme righteousness of this earlier gifted child discourse produced "a dialectical tension growing out of moral conflict" (Cathcart 1972), but its tone of confrontation was unsuited to sustaining a gifted child education that was a success story.

Because of its new broad-based acceptance, the gifted child movement increasingly focused on a series of milder, less polarizing images. Instead of describing those who would harm the gifted as abusive thugs, contemporary scholars increasingly described them as deficient but well-intentioned individuals who could be corrected and controlled through appropriate instruction and counseling. In effect, this new discourse "medicalized" gifted child enemies (Conrad and Schneider 1980). Instead of "bad" or "evil," they were now sick, confused, anxious, or ignorant. As one might imagine, this new conceptual scheme had attractive practical consequences: If the appropriate response to those who threatened the gifted is more therapeutic than punitive, then gifted education's sphere of influence is expanded: more clients are available to professionals newly trained in gifted child counseling and family therapy.

The next section addresses gifted children's vulnerability to the "exploiter," an antagonist motivated primarily by neurotic impulses. These new villains mask their threat by appearing zealously supportive of, and fascinated by, the gifted. Exploiters are not interested in harming gifted children; rather, they wish to live through them vicariously and voyeuristically.

GIFTED CHILD EXPLOITERS

On December 17, 1934, *Time Magazine* reported the "discovery" of an 8-year-old boy whose IQ tested at 230, a score distinctly superior to that of another child described just two weeks earlier in *Time* (December 3, 1934) who had an IQ of 196. The December 17 article chronicled how the director of Brooklyn's Ethical Culture School "could contain herself no longer" and so had to reveal that one of her pupils topped the first boy's IQ by 34 points. "But just as jealous," according to *Time*, was the representative of another school who claimed that the 230-IQ-child was really a "product" of her school since he had been a student at the Ethical Culture School only three months. The 230-IQ-child's parents then stepped forward to declare that they, not any institution, deserved the credit for their boy's distinction.

Paul Witty's (1936) "Exploitation of the Child of High Intelligence Quotient" chastised *Time Magazine* for giving gifted children such "excessive and unwholesome attention" (p. 299). Witty suggested that making "dogmatic prognostications" concerning the futures of very bright children was harmful to them (p. 304). His message: Treat gifted children as children, not as objects to be displayed and compared. Curiously, Witty made no mention of the "exploitation" expressed in the rivalry between parents and schools regarding "credit" for these children or in the "exploitation" implicit in placing two children and their IQs into head-to-head competition.

It was not until 1945, in a paper called "Hazards of the High I.Q." by Douglas Thom and Nancy Newell that these issues were raised. After an examination of 43 children with IQs above 130, Thom and Newell noted "the extreme conceit of [those] . . . convinced of the genius of their child," how "seven parents had gratified their vanity by boasting about their children and exploiting their cleverness at every opportunity" and eleven parents "had pushed and overstimulated their children beyond their capacity to maintain a balanced adjustment" (p. 68). Through such images, the possibility for a new discourse on gifted child vulnerability was introduced in which the antagonists were not playmates or teachers, but almost always the child's parents.

According to Bridges (1973, pp. 40–42), parents often use their gifted children to keep up or compete with their neighbors. For example, working-class parents may push their children into prestigious professions, such as medicine, despite their gifted children's disinterest or objections, so the parents can ascend the social scale.

A biographical vignette published in *Gifted Child Quarterly* (Fabri 1964, pp. 64–65) titled, "Tribulations of the Artistic Child (and of Its Parents)," described the career of a gifted child who was continuously pushed by his parents to develop artistic skills. However, his parents were not social climbers; instead, they were "proud to have a first born child everyone admired at an early age." The problem was that his parents ceased to support his artistic activities at the point when he considered making a career out of them: "It was one thing to be gifted, but an entirely different matter to carry that gift into a lifelong profession. Their son to be an artist! A bohemian! . . . No, a thousand times No!" (Fabri 1964, p. 65). In other words, so long as the artistic activity met the parents' needs, they supported it; but when the son developed needs independent of his parents, the parents objected strenuously.

As the gifted child exploiter image developed in the 1970s, it became increasingly associated with psychoanalytic vocabularies and motivations. According to Marvin Fine (1977), parents of gifted children can be so impressed with the image of their child's giftedness that they lose sight of the real child underneath. This is exemplified by the story of a woman looking at an infant and remarking, "What a pretty child." The parent then replies, "If you think she's pretty you should see her pictures" (p. 496). The problem this emphasis on image creates, according to Fine, is that the gifted child "attempts to conform to the parent's projection, thereby losing touch with his own feelings and needs" (p. 496).

For Diane Schetky (1981, pp. 3–4), the best example of this exploitation is the childhood of John Stuart Mill. His father exercised complete control over his education, cloistering him at home, keeping him separate from all other children, "to avoid the contagion of vulgar modes of thought and feeling." The boy could only associate with his father's friends. Young Mill mastered Greek at 3, and was considered a prodigy in mathematics and logic at 8, but his father was never satisfied. By the age of 20, Mill was severely depressed and suicidal.[3]

In *Giftedness, Conflict, and Underachievement*, Joanne Whitmore (1980, p. 151) argued that many parents unconsciously slip into a pattern in which their gifted children are given little opportunity to play, explore, or act childish. Their right to be children is denied. Instead, they are constantly given homework and other highly structured projects designed to improve and challenge them. Once a gifted child is given a goal, a higher one is then set, so that no success is ever experienced as good enough. Paradoxically, exploitation can also take the form of an overindulgence in which the gifted child is showered with goods and services. Patricia Hollingsworth (1990, p. 4), uses the case of Miriam to show how parents who felt deprived as children attempt to relive their childhoods through their daughter. Accordingly, Miriam's parents believe that, "nothing is too good or too much for . . . [their] gifted child. Miriam rarely has the opportunity to request or earn anything. Miriam's mother often buys clothes, technological gadgets, and toys that Miriam has never requested. Miriam's room is redone as a 'surprise.' Miriam's homework is largely completed by her mother. Miriam's project ideas are vastly changed and 'improved' by her mother. . . . She never needs to take the initiative. All needs are taken care of for her."

The most detailed description of the gifted child exploiter was provided by Alice Miller (1981) in *Prisoners of Childhood*. Using the language of psychoanalysis, Miller described a type of parent whose emotional equilibrium depends on having the child behave or act in a particular way. Although these parents are ordinarily able to hide their own vulnerability behind a hard, totalitarian facade, extremely intuitive gifted children are able to perceive and comprehend their underlying neediness. An unconscious bargain is then struck between the deeply insecure parent and the gifted child in which the child becomes what the parent needs—confidante, comforter, adviser, supporter—if the parent, in turn, guarantees love and security to the gifted child. However, the penalty gifted children pay for this bargain is that they submerge their real selves in favor of an "as-if personality." One day they may wake up and ask their parents: "What would have happened if I had appeared before you, bad, ugly, angry, jealous, lazy, dirty, smelly? Where would your love have been then? . . . Does this mean that it was not really me whom you loved, but only what I pretended to be? What became of my childhood? Have I not been cheated out of it? . . . My abilities—were they simply misused?" (p. 15).

As the image of the gifted child exploiter evolved in the 1970s and 1980s,[4] it increasingly appealed to the expertise of the psychiatrist or psychoanalyst, not the individual trained in gifted child education. Thus the main limitation of the "gifted child exploiter" image is that it offers a nemesis whose motivations are, if anything, too complex, subtle, and unconscious for the gifted child advocate to claim jurisdiction over. Moreover, because the exploiter dynamic portrayed gifted child parents in an extremely negative light, this image threatened to alienate a group whose support is essential to a flourishing gifted child movement. The gifted do not buy or lobby for the services they receive; their parents do. Accordingly, the exploiter image had limited utility as a means of providing roles and recognition for the most important gifted child advocates —parents. Like the anti-gifted, the exploiter image was too harsh to sustain the gifted child movement on a long-term basis.

THE CONFUSED, ANXIOUS, AND IGNORANT

Social movements are complex, continually evolving social dramas, and each stage that unfolds requires both delicate and abrupt changes in language, argument, and imagery (Stewart, Smith, and Denton 1984). Thus the stage of steady and secure growth in gifted education required a new spirit of moderation, a softer, more temperate emotional appeal.

This meant that gifted child antagonists had to be assembled with smaller doses of meanness and psychopathology. Instead of appearing malevolent, petty, and exploitive, they increasingly became misguided and ill-informed. As a gesture of healing, the new rhetoric emphasized that the gifted are mostly victimized innocently.

Hollingworth's *Children Above IQ 180* (1942/1975, p. 278) provided the outlines for this new common sense. According to Hollingworth, we can expect that the gifted child represents a special problem of discipline, because such a child, "while very immature in years, has come to exceed one parent or both in intelligence." When the parent is less intelligent than the child, there is a natural tendency for the child to lose respect for the parents: "Very readily such a child perceives that in comparison with himself his parent is slow-witted and lacking general information." One unfortunate consequence of this state of affairs is that the child may "become the director of the parent's activities," reversing the normal parent-child hierarchy. Because gifted children learn so quickly, they soon figure out what forms of behavior are successful in manipulating their parents (Hollingworth 1942/1975, pp. 278–279).

According to this line of discourse, parenting a gifted child provides special risks, obstacles, and challenges. The first of these challenges is to determine who's in charge: "It sometimes happens that devoted parents, intent on providing an ideal climate for their gifted children, fall into the trap of believing that these little beings, by virtue of their extensive vocabularies and impressive speech and logic, are capable very early of making complex decisions and setting their own goals and directions" (Davis and Rimm 1989, p. 388). When gifted children's demanding behaviors are nurtured or even tolerated by the parents, not only are generational boundaries and lines of authority confused, the gifted are not very likely to learn empathy and sociability skills (Fine 1977, pp. 495–497).

A second, related set of problems, has to do with sibling and other family member relationships. When the gifted child has less talented siblings, parents must learn to assess each child's performance individually and not compare one to another. What parents must specifically guard against is the tendency to "root for the underdog." While this attitude is very American, it deprives the gifted child of recognition of his or her superior performance (Davis and Rimm 1989, p. 404). Other family relationship issues concern marital partners' "lack of communication with each other about expectations and standards for the gifted child" (Dettmann and Colangelo 1980, p. 159). Parents may not only be inconsistent with one another; they may compete to establish a favored position with the gifted child, that is, to establish themselves as the "good" parent and their partner as the "ogre" (Davis and Rimm 1989).

Third, parents of a gifted child must learn to deal with the dissonance between their image of "a child" and "their child" (Ross 1979). Because parenting a gifted child is so different from the normal pattern, parents can be expected to be confused, anxious, and uncertain. Like most parents, they are only prepared to deal with "normal" children, and so lack norms, role models, and information. In their resource guide for parents of young gifted children, Saunders and Espeland (1991, p. 37) describe the special challenge posed by children such as Treesha who could walk and climb out of her crib long before the normally expected ages:

> Every night after Mom and Dad put her to bed, Treesha scaled the walls of her crib, crawled backwards down the stairs, and searched the house until she found her parents. Then she came toward them with a big, proud, nearly toothless grin.
>
> "Go back to bed," her mother would say. "Mommy! Mommy!" Treesha would respond. "To bed," her father would say. "Daddy! Daddy!" tiny Treesha would answer. One of them would haul her back up—and in five minutes Treesha would have made her way back down. Only after she collapsed in exhaustion at her parents' feet (usually sometime around midnight) would Mom or Dad be able to tuck her covers around her for good. The first few times it happened, Treesha's parents bragged to their friends about how precocious their daugher was. Weeks later, Dad was heard to moan, "*Nobody* wants a child like that."

Some typical errors parents of the gifted make include mistaking their early childhood exploration and experimentation for hyperactivity (Vail 1979), assuming they need as much sleep as normal children (Pickard 1976), and getting overly upset with their children's untidiness (Keirouz 1990; Pickard 1976). Moreover, because the gifted always seek to understand and question, "they are unwilling to accept adult explanations that are based on force, age, or lack of logic, such as 'Do it because I say so!'" (Miller 1981, p. 16).

A fourth general issue for parents is their deep concern with the gifted child's achievement. In discussions with parents of gifted children, Hackney (1981, p. 52) noted their "heavy sense of responsibility," their belief that having a gifted child represents "a special duty to see that he/she develops that talent as fully as possible." Consistent with this perception, gifted child parents are admonished "to spend as much time nurturing his or her talents as they would meeting the special needs of a slow or retarded child. The stereotypic statement that 'the bright child will get along fine without any special assistance' is false" (George 1977, p. 556).

The cost of making errors in raising gifted children is not only measured in terms of personal stress and loss of well-being but also in terms of the discrepancy between what the gifted child accomplishes and what that child has the potentiality to accomplish: "For children who have the touch of talent and giftedness, the level of understanding will determine whether they develop their endowments or settle for anonymity and mediocrity" (Miller 1981, p. 14). "Underachievement" is the slogan used to encapsulate this specific gifted child vulnerability. Although any child may theoretically achieve less than what they should, among the gifted "underachievement" is a particularly disturbing possibility, given the enormity of their potential: "One of the greatest social wastes in our culture is that presented by the gifted child or young person who either cannot or will not work up to his ability" (Gowan 1955, p. 247). Parents must understand that what they do or fail to do is critical to warding off underachievement: "Probably the most general area of parental confusion arises out of the notion that potential (which says a child is gifted) and achievement (which can sometimes indicate otherwise) are synonymous" (Nathan 1979, p. 267).

Although gifted children's underachievement is measured in terms of their failure to go as far as their abilities would lead us to expect, responsibility for that failure is not attributed to the gifted themselves. Instead gifted underachievers fail because:

> Inadequate home environment leaves them personally maladjusted and unable to use their intellectual ability.
> Inadequate home environment limits their horizon and fails to stimulate them to use education for vocational achievement, although they are personally well adjusted.
> Inadequate home environment fails to instill in them a deep drive or need for achievement.
> School and home together fail to instill in them an intrinsic love of learning. (Havinghurst 1976, p. 258)

By raising doubts about parents' capacity to manage the delicate operation of raising a gifted child, not only is gifted children's vulnerability reaffirmed but so also is the indispensibility of gifted child professionals, the population uniquely equipped to show parents the specific ways to accomplish appropriate gifted child nurturance.

Above all, parents need professional help to determine whether their child is actually gifted. If parents do not make a correct determination, they may be missing an important opportunity to support their child's special abilities (Dettman and Colangelo 1980). Frieda Painter (1984, pp. 31–32) shows that the capacity to make a positive identification in a child as young as 1 year old greatly reduces the sufferings of both gifted children and their parents:

A health visitor identified a gifted baby when she was calling upon a mother who had just given birth to a second child. The mother was suffering from post-natal depression, which was worsened by the ceaseless demands of her older child, at that time a baby not much over a year old. The child cried and shrieked continuously when the mother did not give him her full attention. As she had no one to help her, she could not do this with the new baby needing a considerable amount of her time. Worst of all, the older child, John, needed very little sleep; he was awake late into evening, again early in the morning and usually once or twice during the night as well, crying and shrieking for no apparent reason and preventing his parents from getting enough sleep. The mother became increasingly distraught and was approaching a breakdown. The health visitor gave the older baby a number of tests which showed that he was very advanced for his age, and then told his mother that she thought he was "gifted."

Once John had been recognized as a gifted child, it was possible to alleviate both the parents' and child's stress. The first thing that was done was to substitute the toys that John was given—a bunny rabbit and a simple rattle—with ones that were appropriate to his giftedness: "The father was an electrician, so he was able to make a game with colored lights for him to play with, and the mother bought him educational toys said by the makers to be for children aged two to five years. . . . The most important acquisition was a typewriter, which the father adapted with an electric battery and complex circuits so that banging on the keys brought on various combinations of coloured lights" (pp. 32–33). From then on, when John awoke in the middle of the night, he did not cry for hours but occupied himself with his new toys and gadgets.

Of course, supplying the baby with appropriately stimulating and challenging toys does not settle matters. New and more complex problems are continually anticipated: "If the typical parent has to ask at least 100 questions, the parent of a gifted child may have to get answers to at least 200" (Ginsberg and Harrison 1977, p. 27). Most importantly, parents need to know how much educational stimulation is appropriate for their gifted child at each stage of development. A spate of "how-to" books (e.g., Smutny, Veenker, and Veenker's 1989 *Your Gifted Child*, Takacs's 1986 *Enjoy Your Gifted Child*, Delp and Martinson's 1977 *A Handbook for Parents of Gifted and Talented*, and Ginsberg and Harrison's 1977 *How to Help Your Gifted Child*) suggest that reading and extracurricular activities should be emphasized and expanded, accompanied by the general admonition that parents should be more involved with the child at home. According to W. C. George (1977, p. 555), "without active help from parents in translating appropriate aspirations into reality, a bright, well motivated youth may turn into an ineffectual, bored, even mediocre student who is unable to live up to his potential." At the same time, parents must be on guard against overstimulating; they must be careful not to push too hard: "Some loss of personal autonomy and sense of self are likely to follow in a child so managed" (Fine 1977, p. 490). Accordingly, parents can err on the side of providing too little academic encouragement or on the side of providing too much.

Parents of gifted children also need to be aware that simply having a warm, friendly relationship with their children is not always helpful. For example, although one study found that high-achieving males need "warm" mothers during the first seven years of life, and high-achieving females need "warmth" from both parents (Groth 1971), another study found that gifted children whose mothers were authoritarian received better grades (Nichols 1964), and still another study found that an excessively "positive" parent-child relationship can be harmful: "While parents of bright achievers evaluated their children in a more positive way than did parents of bright underachievers, the parents of gifted underachievers had a more positive view of their children than did those of gifted achievers" (Ziv 1977, p. 50).

Ironically, Willard Abraham (1958, p. 50) cites John Stuart Mill's father as an example of a parent who knew how to encourage his gifted son's achievement without letting him get a swelled head. Abraham used this excerpt from Mill's biography to illustrate:

> "He kept me, with extreme vigilance, out of the way of hearing myself praised, or of being led to make self-flattering comparisons between myself and others. From his own intercourse with me I could derive none but a very humble opinion of myself; and the standard of comparison he always held up to me, was not what other people did, but what a man could and ought to do. . . . I was not at all aware that my attainments were anything unusual for my age."

Abraham conceded that, "in most cases that would be carrying things too far" but warned that "it is just as dangerous to bend over in the other direction" (p. 50). Again, parents of gifted children are portrayed as walking a fine line between recognizing their child's giftedness appropriately and making either too much or too little of it. The continual message is that raising a gifted child represents unfamiliar territory everywhere laden with pitfalls and uncertainties. Too much or too little authority, stimulation, encouragement, warmth, pressure, and so on may produce boredom, sulkiness, premature burnout, stress, egoism, and a host of other ills. Just how parents might be able to provide appropriate levels of care—"the golden mean"—is portrayed as always problematic as there are so few role models and traditions to guide them. Thus, instead of parents having a clear chance of success with their gifted child, they have but a meager likelihood that has to be checked every step of the way. Instead of giftedness being a resource for disentangling problematic situations, it is a problematic situation itself, and one not easily solved.

In sum, parents raising a gifted child appear to have many more opportunities to fail than parents raising an ordinary child and thus must work harder, invest more resources, and make more adaptations. Above all, they must seek the assistance of experts to make sure that the solutions they contrive will produce the desired effect: The degree to which a gifted child's "superior endowment represents a problem to him and his parents is largely a function of the size of the discrepancy between the intellectual capacity of the gifted child and other members of his family. The larger the discrepancy, the greater the potential problem and the more important the need for professional counseling" (Ross 1964, p. 159). According to this mode of argument, parents who would harm the gifted appear more inept than evil, more in need of guidance than repression. Although a negative judgment is made about these parents' ability to raise gifted children on their own, it is balanced by a positive judgment about their good intentions and capacity to adapt.

A PROGRAM OF PERCEPTION

Scholars created a "program of perception" (Bourdieu 1991, p. 128) that made it possible to discuss gifted children in the language of social justice. Capitalizing on this century's "surge of sentiment" (Shorter 1977) for children, on the new images of children as "priceless, lovable, and vulnerable innocents" (Best 1990, p. 4), scholars dramatized the "plight" of the gifted, made their sufferings credible, and inspired social action on their behalf.

To make a gifted children's movement possible, scholars had to find a way of representing these children as both highly superior and highly vulnerable. Gifted child scholars had to answer the following challenge: Convince people that children "endowed in superior degree with integrity, independence, originality, creative imagination, vitality, forcefulness, warmth, poise, and stability" (Hollingworth 1942, p. 284) require more resources and services than others. According to this analysis, scholars managed to portray the neediness of gifted children while preserving their superiority not by focusing on gifted children themselves but by focusing on the crudeness, brutality, instability, pettiness, naivete, and shallowness of the nongifted. Through this enumeration of the nongifted's vices and deficiencies a moral drama was staged in which one group was portrayed as inferior, so that another could be portrayed as superior. To the degree the nongifted were displayed as envious and exploitive, the gifted were displayed as enviable and virtuous. The more confused and naive the nongifted appeared, in the more complex and subtle appeared the gifted.

We can see, then, why gifted child scholars chose to locate the vulnerability of gifted children within the nongifted and why they describe the nongifted according to a series of negative images. The more effective scholars were in getting images of moral culpability, weakness, and brutality associated with the nongifted, the more effective they were in getting images of moral superiority, strength, and sensitivity associated with the gifted. The nongifted had to be downgraded for the gifted to be upgraded.

Although scholars have never relied on a single set of images to represent gifted children's superiority and vulnerability, gifted child discourse provides a good example of how the language supporting a social movement took on new emphases and modulations as times and conditions changed. The more successful and entrenched gifted child education became, the less was the need for scholars to describe gifted children as participants in an oldtime melodrama with villains lurking about waiting to pounce on innocent victims. A gifted child education that was prospering did not require a language of polarization; it required a language of compromise and inclusion. With success, then, gifted child discourse muted its good guys/bad guys rhetoric, substituting in its place a language of healing, bargaining, and sustaining. Those who hurt the gifted were transformed into figures who were forgiveable, approachable, and available for instruction and guidance. The genius of gifted child scholarship thus consisted of its capacity to portray a type of victim who is without weakness and, also, a type of villain who is fully redeemable.

4

From Gifted Children
to Successful Adults:
The Promise Fulfilled

Intellectually gifted children are among the most valuable assets of a civilized nation. To waste them is to waste the fundamentals of power.

Leta Hollingworth[1]

The gifted children's movement has been incredibly successful at creating the perception that these children are a "national resource," that they are assets to be used in sustaining this country's competitive edge. To illustrate the strength of this association briefly, one need only look at how gifted child education experienced a surge of support immediately after the launching of Sputnik, an event widely interpreted as a shocking defeat, as evidence that Russian brainpower had outperformed ours (Tannenbaum 1979). Reports critical of American education for neglecting the gifted were suddenly everywhere (e.g., "Let's Stop Wasting Our Greatest Resource,"[2] "Untapped Leadership,"[3] "Waste of Fine Minds,"[4] "Young Genius: Our Greatest Waste"[5]). In the immediate aftermath of Sputnik, research on gifted children quintupled: 1957 and 1958 showed 22 abstracts on giftedness appearing in *Psychological Abstracts*; however, 1959 and 1960 showed 109 abstracts. Among all abstracts published on giftedness between 1927 and 1965, more than 90% appeared after the launch of Sputnik (Albert 1969).

The point here, of course, is not that Sputnik launched the gifted children's movement. Rather, the Sputnik crisis revealed a "program of perception" concerning gifted children that was already in place. During a time when Americans were critically worried about losing technological leadership to the Russians, they made evident their belief that neglect of gifted children was the source of the crisis and that providing more resources to the gifted was the answer. These understandings, and

57

the evidence that made them compelling, were not born with Sputnik but developed over the previous 35 years in the research of Terman, Hollingworth, Cox, and other gifted child scholars.

Before examining how scholars assembled the belief that gifted children are a resource to be used in competition with other nations, I briefly consider why such a belief is not entirely self-evident, that is, why there might have been any doubt in the first place.

"EARLY RIPE, EARLY ROT"

On January 11, 1924, the *New York Times* published an editorial that challenged a fundamental assumption of the gifted child movement. According to the editorial, titled "Precocity Doesn't Wear Well," gifted children fizzle out as adults.

Support for this message came from the case of William James Sidis, the most famous child prodigy of the era. Although Sidis was reading and spelling by the age of 2, could type in both English and French by 4, had developed a mathematical formula for calculating the day of the week corresponding to any given date by the age of 5, entered Harvard by 11, and gave a lecture that same year on "Four-Dimensional Bodies" that was celebrated across the nation—he was a has-been by the age of 20 (Manley 1937; Montour 1977).

Perhaps because Sidis was considered to be a very nongifted adult, Henry Goddard (1932, p. 355) felt some need to declare that Sidis had probably never been gifted to begin with: "Our term 'gifted child' does not include so-called 'child prodigies' such as the Sidis boy . . . who are all the products of home forcing and not examples of hereditary ability." Although Sidis was denied the gifted imprimatur on what appear as scientific grounds, there can be no doubt that he was the worst possible advertisement for gifted child education: His life was not "attractive," "merry," or "wholesome" (Coy 1918). Sidis was the exemplar of "early ripe, early rot."

His troubles began soon after his famous lecture. He had what was called a "general breakdown" and was admitted to a sanatorium for treatment. When he returned to Harvard, he was withdrawn and could not be persuaded to lecture again. Although he graduated Harvard with honors at the age of 16, he told the gathered reporters: "I want to live the perfect life. The only way to live the perfect life is to live it in seclusion" (Manley 1937).

On May 1, 1919, William James Sidis's name appeared on the front pages of newspapers once again. He was arrested for carrying a communist flag during a demonstration. A police officer testified that when he asked Sidis why he was not carrying an American Flag, Sidis replied, "To hell with the American flag!" He was convicted of inciting to riot and assault and was sentenced to 18 months at hard labor (*New York Times* 1919; Wallace 1986). After this incident, Sidis drifted from city to city, working as a clerk at minimum wages. He told the reporters who followed his story that he would only work at jobs that required no mental effort: the "very sight of a mathematical formula makes me ill. All I want to do is run an adding machine but they won't let me alone." He argued that he was not a genius and would take intelligence tests to prove it (Manley 1937).

Sidis continued his wanderings until his death in 1944 from a cerebral hemorrhage: "He died alone, obscure and destitute" (Montour 1977, p. 265). His *Time Magazine* obituary was titled "Prodigious Failure"; *Newsweek's* was titled "Burned-Out Prodigy."

It is easy to understand why the publicity surrounding the life of Sidis threatened the gifted child movement: Unless it is believed that giftedness translates to adult eminence, the gifted child is little more than a curiosity, a flash in the pan who is ultimately no better, and possibly significantly worse, than the ordinary child. Unless it is believed that gifted children are intended to become the leaders of the future, there is no justification, no payoff in providing special services for them. They are a bad investment. If, however, it can be shown that the gifted childhood is strongly predictive of the successful adulthood, then it makes sense to identify the gifted early, to nurture, protect, and direct them above what is done for ordinary children.

In the discussion that follows, we shall explore the methods by which gifted child scholars countered the "early ripe, early rot" argument, how they crafted the perception that these children's early promise is not illusory, that the gifted are those who can reasonably be assumed to be "the future problem solvers, innovators, and evaluators of the culture if adequate educational experiences are provided" (Lucito, quoted in Alexander and Muia 1982, p. 11). We look at the "findings"—the authenticated stories, eyewitness accounts, texts, numbers, sequences of events, accomplishments—summoned to support the belief that giftedness, if not sabotaged or neglected, persists and prospers into adulthood. We also examine the activities performed to create these "findings," to make them appear, as social scientists say, "objective" and "rigorous."

THE CONSTANCY OF GIFTEDNESS

If a phenomenon—for example, the flicker of light or a gust of wind—appears for a mere moment, it is seen as having only a phantom reality

(Merleau-Ponty 1962, p. 318). To experience an object as fully real presupposes duration, that the object appear unchanged through the passage of time. Thus, to successfully communicate the reality of giftedness, gifted child scholars had to establish not only that it existed at one moment, but also that it existed at multiple successive moments. This explains gifted child scholarship's peculiar fascination with longitudinal research. For their object of study to be taken seriously, scholars had to establish constancy.

Consider the sequence of studies Hollingworth did on E. (Garrison, Burke, and Hollingworth 1917; Hollingworth, Burke, and Garrison 1922; Hollingworth 1927). In the first of these studies, detailed evidence is provided that E. is gifted at 8 years of age: We learn that this boy had a vocabulary that included 11,520 words—the same as an average adult. Also, he could reverse clock hands three times without error in less than a minute for each trial, he could repeat five digits backwards two out of three times "absolutely without error" before an audience of 30 adults, "his memory span for digits repeated forwards is at least eight [memory for more than eight digits was not examined]," and so on. Five years later, Hollingworth et al. showed that E.'s performance did not wane. Among the evidence assembled was a quotation from a Columbia College official stating that E. ranked number two out of 483 entering freshman, although E. was then only 12 and his competitors about 18. They also note that his IQ, which was measured at 187 five years before, had now increased to 194. Comments from E.'s teachers are also included as evidence: "I consider it a privilege to have had something to do with teaching him," one teacher wrote. Another testimonial noted: "He is a good sport as well as a good scholar, and being both he ought to go far." The third report, titled "Subsequent History of E.—Ten Years After the Initial Report," shows that this gifted child had turned into a gifted adult. This was established first through reference to his scores on intelligence tests that compared favorably to "the best scores yet made by college graduates." Among his academic accomplishments, it is noted that E. graduated Columbia College with a B.A. "within eleven days of his fifteenth birthday," was awarded Phi Beta Kappa membership and, at the age of 18, finished all the requirements for his Ph.D. except his dissertation.

Of course, the most ambitious, expensive, data-producing longitudinal study ever conducted was the 35-year examination of the gifted children Terman first identified in 1921. Shortly before his death, Terman invoked the data he accumulated on these subjects to conclude that "the superior child, with few exceptions, becomes the able adult, superior in nearly every aspect to the generality" (Terman and Oden 1959, p. 143). Intelligence tests from 1927–28, 1939–40, and 1950–52 showed that the majority consistently scored in the upper 99th percentile of the general population. In the decade when less than 8% of their age group graduated college (1930–40), about 70% of Terman's original 1528 gifted subjects received a bachelor's degree, with 40% of the men and 33% of the women winning honors (Phi Beta Kappa, Sigma Xi, cum laude, etc.). By 1959, 31 of the gifted appeared in the *Who's Who*, 70 in the *American Men of Science*, and 10 others in the *Directory of American Scholars*. The gifted subjects published nearly 2,000 scientific and technical papers and some 60 books and monographs. They were credited with at least 230 patents, 33 novels, 375 short stories, novellas, and plays.[6]

However, because Terman demonstrated the successes of the gifted through the analysis of central tendencies, that is, by pointing to what the majority did, he had to acknowledge that many gifted deviated from the mean in a negative direction. Given his examination of large aggregates, Terman had to encounter cases that fell far short of the gifted ideal. Because Terman's goal was to understand the ways giftedness developed, to understand the various turns gifted lives took over the years, he could not deny that some of the gifted knew poverty, divorce, sickness, crime, and so on. What he had to avoid, though, was to frame these negative findings as evidence supporting the inconstancy of giftedness. His specific challenge consisted of recognizing these negative outcomes without at the same time falsifying belief in the unwavering goodness of giftedness.

Terman's solution was to define gifted child failures either as rare exceptions or, at the very worst, as no more frequent than what might be found in the general population. So, although he acknowledged the existence of such problems as mental illness, alcoholism, and delinquency among the gifted, their relative scarcity was always emphasized: "There is no evidence that psychotic tendencies are more common among intellectually gifted than among average people, and there is a great deal of evidence that the incidence of delinquency is much lower among the brightest children" (Burks, Jensen, and Terman 1930, p. 321). Although some of the gifted are alcoholics, there are seven times fewer in this group with this problem than might be expected based on the percentage of alcoholics in the general population (Terman and Oden 1959, p. 46). Similarly, with regard to homosexuality, Terman (Terman and Oden 1959, p. 48) declared that "in contrast to Kinsey's report that homosexuality occurs among 25 percent of males and 8 to 12 percent of females, only 2 percent of gifted men and 1.7 percent of gifted women are known to be presently homosexual or to have had homosexual experiences" (Terman and Oden 1959, p. 48). Above all, many of the homosexual gifted "recover": "Six of the 17 men [with] this homosexual history have recovered and have made a reasonably satisfactory heterosexual adjustment. . . . All but one of the 11 women in the gifted group who have had homosexual experiences have married, and six of the marriages are apparently successful" (Terman and Oden 1959, p. 48).

A second strategy Terman employed was continually to refer gifted failures to a range of mitigating circumstances. In 1930, for example, Terman described five extremely troubled gifted youths—one had "twenty-three counts against him on police records" (Burks, Jensen, and Terman 1930, p. 307); the second was "a disturbed sleeper, argumentative, quarrelsome, and domineering with other children" (p. 309); the third was described in these terms, "If he is not interested [in classroom activities], he will do what he sees fit to do, which may be to crawl on the floor, punch his neighbor, or read" (p. 314); the fourth had "frequent outbursts of temper and periods of silent moodiness, utter rebelliousness against restraint or advice, craving for adventure, fondness for trashy literature, and a vehemently expressed aversion to school work" (pp. 316–317); and the fifth committed suicide "because of despondency over an unsuccessful love affair" (p. 321). Although these cases represented very unfortunate outcomes, they did not support the "early ripe, early rot" argument, because Terman dissociated these children's negative behaviors from their giftedness. He attributed these children's problems instead to external forces, to broken homes, parents' cruelty or mental instability, and "unfortunate heredity and environment at its worst" (p. 310). As Terman explained the behavior of a gifted youth named Blake, "The possession of a high intellectual endowment played little or no part in the unfolding of Blake's brief tragic career. His inherited emotional instability determined the course of his life" (p. 321). Thus, a gifted child's failure is attributed not to the inconstancy or deterioration of giftedness but to the uncontrollable conditions that prevent the full use and realization of giftedness.

Through use of excuses, justifications, disclaimers, and other stigma-neutralizing strategies, Terman found a way to bridge the gap between the promise of giftedness and its performance. As the following example shows, a gifted child who engaged in criminal activity did not necessarily contradict belief in giftedness. Instead, responsibility could be attributed to poverty, to his parents' divorce, his mother's lowly social status, being the eldest and smartest sibling, and so on. Note also how Terman and Oden (1947, p. 117) emphasized the constancy of the gifted IQ while accounting for M 287's untoward behavior:

> M 287 came from one of the poorest home backgrounds in our group. His Binet IQ at ten years was 148, and the retest on the Terman Group Test when he was fifteen showed the same degree of superiority. The parents were divorced when our subject, the eldest of three children, was eight

years old. The children were reared by the mother who did day work as a domestic to support them. By the time our subject reached high school he had become very cocksure about his ability, having been superior not only to his schoolmates but also to his siblings. . . . Soon he began a series of small thefts, then followed with burglaries which eventuated in his arrest, six months in jail, and a three-year period of probation. The shock of this experience served to restore his good sense (his own expression), and so far as we know there has been no further delinquency. He is now married and is holding a responsible position.

That M 287 was only a criminal for a phase of his life, was "shocked" back to his "good sense," eventually married, and took up a "responsible position" not only made his delinquency appear less serious, but also it strengthened belief that the gifted have an underlying goodness that ultimately prevails.

Case M 364's life had a similar plot line. His story begins with the sentence, "M 364 (Binet IQ 152) was sent to reform school for a brief period in his late teens after a number of petty thefts climaxed by a burglary" (1947, p. 117), and ends with these observations, "He has been fairly successfully vocationally, and so far as we can learn there has been no further conduct problem. His 1940 score on the Concept Mastery was well above the mean for gifted men." Similarly, we are introduced to M 408 as one who "spent an unhappy childhood in an extremely unsatisfactory home. . . . [He] ran away and spent the next two years in and out of the juvenile detention home and the foster home in which he was placed." As might be expected, again, the story has a happy ending: M 408 eventually became "quite a leader in the industrial plant where he is employed, and is prominent in employee activities. His Concept Mastery score, despite limited schooling and early environmental disadvantages, was equaled by only 10 percent of the entire gifted group. He has collected a sizable private library, described by our field worker as indicating aristocratic literary tastes."

By emphasizing the unusual brevity or inconsequentiality of the gifteds' failures, their dignity in the face of defeat, their tireless efforts to rehabilitate themselves, followed by their ultimate success, giftedness is again and again confirmed as that attribute that can always be counted on to set the identified individual apart. Although Terman had to acknowledge that the gifted have troubles too, they were always gifted people's troubles. Thus, the only adult in Terman's gifted group who was still in prison by the time the fourth volume of *Genetic Studies of Genius* (Terman and Oden 1947, p. 118) went to press, was not just a prisoner, but "an exemplary prisoner . . . the editor of the institutional publication." Another member of Terman's gifted group was caught stealing some equipment from his school but was no run-of-the-mill

sociopath: his "zeal for scientific investigation led [him] . . . to steal
equipment needed in his experiments, but after his arrest the police
department was so impressed by his ability that it gave him a job"
(p. 119). Other untoward activities such as "disturbing the peace," "dis-
orderly conduct," and "drunken driving" were framed as "college pranks"
(p. 119).

In 1947, Terman noted that four gifted males and five females had
histories of "functional mental disorders;" however, these disorders
were not discussed in the language of symptoms and suffering but in the
language of recovery and renewal: "Thus, all of the 4 men, and 3 out of
the 5 women afflicted with functional mental disorders had recovered,
and a fourth woman gave promise of recovery. The 1945 reports showed
continued progress by 8 of these 9 cases." Far from these cases falsifying
the superiority of giftedness, they documented the gifted's resilience:
"Superior intelligence does not appear to be a causal factor in mental
disorder as found in this group but seems, rather, to have helped those
affected to overcome their difficulties. The insight and intelligent coop-
eration shown by those who become mental patients has almost certainly contributed to the improvement noted in several of the cases"
(Terman and Oden 1947, p. 108).

Perhaps the findings that most threatened the predicted association
between giftedness and adult success concerned gifted women's careers. In 1947, only 48.46% of the gifted women were employed full-time
in comparison to 66% of the nongifted women of similar educational
background (Terman and Oden 1947, p. 177–181). The reason for the
difference is that gifted females were much more inclined to define
themselves as full-time housewives: 41.97% versus 25% for nongifted
women. Thus Terman wrote a chapter on "Achievement of Gifted Men"
but had no comparable discussion of achievement for gifted women. He
rationalized this exclusion on the grounds that "the achievement of
women is difficult to estimate and is often the outcome of extraneous
circumstances" (p. 349). Still, he could not resist casting some positive
judgment on gifted women's careers: "A good many of the women
made their most notable achievement in the selection of a mate. Two
of the husbands are eminent musicians, and several others have won
national recognition in the physical, biological, and social sciences"
(p. 367).

By 1955, only 42% of the women in Terman's gifted group had outside
employment, with only 29% of gifted wives employed on a full-time
basis (Terman and Oden 1959, p. 85). However, Terman did not see the
decline in the percentage of gifted women pursuing careers as a threat to
the presumed association between childhood giftedness and adult success. The reason: Being a housewife could be interpreted as a pursuit
that was possibly as creative and worthwhile as anything women might

do in outside employment (Terman and Oden 1959, p. 145). In 1959, "housewifery" was reframed as a career "preference":

> There are many intangible kinds of accomplishment and success open to the housewife, and it is debatable whether the fact that a majority of gifted women prefer housewifery to more intellectual pursuits represents a net waste of brainpower. Although it is possible by means of rating scales to measure with fair accuracy the achievement of a scientist or a professional or business man, no one has yet devised a way to measure the contribution of a woman who makes her marriage a success, inspires her husband, and sends forth well-trained children into the world.

Terman could not deny that some of the gifted in his group did not become wealthy, eminent, or successful by any standardized measure. But he could deny that this finding was meaningful: "Our position so far has been concerned with the achievement of eminence, professional status, and recognized position in the world of human affairs. But these are goals for which a large proportion of highly intelligent men and women do not consciously strive. Many of them ask nothing more of life than happiness and contentment in comparative obscurity" (Terman and Oden 1947, p. 371). Terman thus neutralized the impact of the gifted's failure by arguing that they were never in the rat race to begin with. They cannot be "blamed for not enlisting in the battle for 'success' in the worldly sense" (pp. 371–372). Although Terman's research was a single-minded effort to determine whether giftedness translates to adult success, in the context of explaining the apparent absence of "success" among some gifted, he argued that "everyone must be conceded the right to tailor his own personal philosophy" and that there is "no yardstick for measuring the intangible achievements that make for contentment" (1947, p. 372).

Apparently, then, Terman and his associates regarded "success" as an elusive, ephemeral characteristic when some suspicion existed that the gifted did not achieve it. However, when assessing positive achievements among the gifted, the capacity to measure success was never doubted. This confidence is quite evident in analyses of the "great" historical figures.

THE TEXTS OF HISTORY DON'T LIE

Gifted child scholars refute any doubt that gifted children will grow into eminent adults by referring to the chronicles of history and the books that record the lives of great people. These records describe the child-

hoods of the eminent in such detail that we feel we have seen the connection between childhood giftedness and adult eminence with our own
eyes. We can see that this or that great person from the past (e.g., John
Stuart Mill, Coleridge, Mozart) was once a gifted child. And how can one
possibly doubt that the great people of history produced great works,
made great discoveries, and forever changed the world? We have the
record of their accomplishments, the documents, monuments, authenticated accounts, and uninterrupted tradition (Schutz 1964, p. 137).

Although Yoder's (1894) "Study on the Boyhood of Great Men" preceded the discovery of giftedness, Hollingworth (1926, pp. 17–18) cited
his finding that the achievements of the eminent were often anticipated
by their childhood interests and activities. For example, many of Yoder's
great men did not engage in childish games as boys but devoted themselves to hobbies and activities related to their future careers: Edison had
his chemicals, Shelley his literature, Darwin his collections, Newton his
machines, Stevenson his clay engines. Of Byron, it was said, "The love
of solitude and meditation is already traceable in the child. He loves to
wander at night among the dark and solitary cloisters of the abbey." And
Emerson never engaged in boy's play, "not because of any physical
disability, but simply because from earliest years he dwelt in a higher
sphere."

The first study to assimilate a "great historical figure" to gifted child
discourse was Terman's (1917) "The Intelligence Quotient of Francis Galton in Childhood." Taking for granted that Galton, the founder of the
eugenics movement and Terman's own intellectual godfather, accomplished great things as an adult, Terman set out to prove that between
the ages of 3 and 8 years, Galton had an IQ of 200, that is, that his mental
age at that time was about double his actual age. According to Terman
(1917, p. 209), "The significance of this will be apparent when we say
that after diligent search in several cities and several counties in California
—a search including many thousand of children in scope—the highest
intelligence quotient we have yet found is 170. The number that we have
found going above 150 can be counted on the fingers of one hand."

Though Galton never took an IQ test, his intelligence was established
by reference to his being able to read and write by the age of 4, as this
letter, surviving from Galton's fourth year, confirmed:

> My
> dear
> Uncle
> we have
> got Ducks. I know
> A Nest. I mean
> to make a
> Feast.

Before his fifth birthday, Galton wrote the following to his sister:

> My Dear Adele,
> I am 4 years old and I can read any English book. I can say all the Latin
> Substantives and Adjectives and active verbs besides 52 lines of Latin
> poetry. I can cast up any sum in addition and can multiply by 2, 3, 4, 5, 6,
> 7, 8, [9], 10, [11].
> I can also say the pence table. I read French a little and I know the clock.
>
> Francis Galton,
Febuary 15, 1827

Terman noted that the only spelling error is in the date and that the
numbers 9 and 11 are bracketed "because little Francis, evidently feeling
that he had claimed too much, had scratched out one of these numbers
with a knife and pasted some paper over the other!" Thus, consistent
with the anticipated giftedness, not only did little Francis have astound-
ing cognitive ability, he was also humble and truthful. And, as the following anecdote reveals, little Francis was also incredibly brave and
resourceful: At the age of 5, "he was found holding a group of torment-
ing boys at arm's length," shouting these lines from Sir Walter Scott:

> Come one, come all. This rock shall fly
> From its firm base, as soon as I.

Confirming the early appearance of every virtue, in his first year at
boarding school, at the age of 8, Francis wrote these words to his father:
"I am very glad that you have left off being a banker, for you will have
more time to yourself and better health." According to Terman, "This
little quotation certainly betokens a degree of filial solicitude by no
means common to children his age. Such altruism does not ordinarily
develop so early."

That Galton's spirituality also matured early is shown in the following
letter, written at the age of 10:

> My Dearest Papa:
> It is now my pleasure to disclose the most ardent wishes of my
> heart, which are to extract out of my boundless wealth in compound,
> money sufficient to make this addition to my unequaled library.

The Hebrew Commonwealth by John	9
A Pastor Advice	2
Hornne's commentaries on the Psalms	4
Paley's Evidence on Christianity	2
Jones Biblical Cyclopedia	10
	27

Terman judged that "it is hardly necessary to comment on the above letter as an indication of the boy's mental maturity. It speaks for itself."

To finally prove the point that "a high correlation obtains between favorable mental traits of all kinds; that, for example, children superior in intelligence also tend to be superior in moral qualities" (1917, p. 213), Terman shared this letter, written by Galton's mother when he was only 8 years old:

> Francis from his earliest age showed highly honorable feelings. His temper, although hasty, brought no resentment, and his little irritations were soon calmed. His open-minded disposition, with great good nature and kindness to those boys younger than himself, made him beloved by all his school fellows. He was very affectionate and even sentimental in his manners. His activity of body could only be equalled by the activity of his mind. He was a boy never known to be idle. His habit was always to be doing something. He showed no vanity at his superiority over other boys, but said it was a shame that their education should have been so neglected.

THEY COMPOSED VERSES IN THEIR CRADLES

In 1926, the grandmother of all such retrospective analyses was published, Catherine Cox's *The Early Mental Traits of Three Hundred Geniuses*. The main conclusion from this 842-page volume is that, "the extraordinary genius who achieves the highest eminence is also the gifted individual whom intelligence tests may discover in childhood" (p. 218). First, Cox found that the IQs of the great did not diminish, as William James Sidis's apparently did, but actually increased with adulthood. As children, the great figures of the past had an average IQ of 135, but as adults their IQ averaged 10 points higher, 145. Thus, at the heading of every biographical sketch, the sturdiness and growth potential of giftedness was demonstrated by displaying the child's IQ alongside the more robust adult IQ.

The sketches of the great reiteratively affirmed that their adult achievements were anticipated by their youthful behavior and interests: "In their reported interests, in their school standing and progress, and in their early production and achievement, the members of the group were, in general, phenomenal" (Cox 1926, p. 217). Voltaire composed verses from the cradle; at 3 Coleridge was reading from the Bible; at 5, Friedrich Wolf "could recall ten to fifteen lines of verse after a single reading" (p. 628); at the age of 7 Mozart published sonatas for piano and violin; in his fourth year, Albrecht Von Haller began preaching to the servants, "reciting the Bible stories from his little arm chair in the living-room"; when neighbors and relatives saw the 4-year-old Ludwig Tieck on his little footstool eagerly reading the Bible, they "would shake their heads doubtfully over his unusual talent, or even refuse to believe that he was actually reading" (p. 625); before he was 7, Berthold Niebuhr heard Macbeth read aloud and filled seven sheets of paper on that play "without omitting one important point" (p. 799).

Special care was devoted to dispelling the myth that some geniuses from the past had been backward in childhood. For example, Oliver Goldsmith, whom a teacher once described as "impenetrably stupid," was shown to have "signs of genius" even before he could write. If a teacher thought young Oliver dull, this was partially explained by Oliver's inclination to keep his gifts to himself: whenever he wrote a verse, he almost immediately threw it into the fire. However, "a few of his efforts, rescued by his schoolmaster, so delighted Mrs. Goldsmith that she induced her husband to educate Oliver for a profession rather than for a trade as had been planned" (pp. 263–264). Similarly, although Sir Walter Scott had a record of inferior accomplishment in school, he could memorize long passages of poetry and use the most exotic words and expressions. For example, when being put to bed one night, he told his aunt that he liked the lady who had discussed Milton with him that day. "What lady?" asked his aunt. "Why Mrs. Cockburn; for I think she is a virtuoso like myself." When asked what a virtuoso is, he replied: "Don't ye know? Why it's one who wishes and will know everything" (pp. 604–605).

These children's words were invariably distinctive, extraordinary: When a servant spilled some hot coffee on 4-year-old Thomas Macaulay's legs, he replied to a show of concern: "Thank you madam, the agony is abated" (p. 689). At about 5, Macaulay's mother told him to learn to study without eating snacks: "Yes, Mama, industry must be my bread and attention my butter" (pp. 689–690). When, at the age of 6, Goethe learned of the Lisbon earthquake, he commented: "After all, it is probably much simpler than they suppose. God knows that the immortal soul can suffer no harm through such a fate" (p. 698). And when a bailiff threatened to strike young Hans Christian Andersen for gleaning in a forbidden harvest field, Andersen exclaimed: "How dare you strike me when God can see it?" (p. 716).

Clearly, the evidence that Cox amassed for the constancy of giftedness was not just any evidence. It was thorough beyond compare, compiled with such attention to detail that readers could only conclude that, were others to study the great historical figures, they too would arrive at the same conclusion: that "youths who achieve eminence are distinguished in childhood by behavior which indicates an unusually high IQ" (p. 216).

Terman emphasized that Cox's study was conducted in accordance with the most scientific criteria: "In the first place, it was necessary to make an unbiased selection of cases for study" (Terman 1926, p. vi), a task accomplished by using James M. Cattell's (1903) list of the 1,000 most important men in history. Cattell developed this list not through recourse to some subjective, personal criteria, but by taking out a ruler and measuring the length of the famous people's biographies: the more biographical material, the greater the person (Shurkin 1992, p. 69). From this list, Cox eliminated the great born before 1450 and those whose fame had nothing to do with their accomplishments (e.g., members of royal families), leaving her with 282 eminent subjects. Six thousand pages of typed material, or about 20 pages for each subject (Terman 1926, p. vii) were generated and used to determine two types of IQ: A1 IQ, representing intelligence of the great person prior to the age of 17, and A2 IQ, representing intelligence from 17 to 26.

The accuracy and validity of these IQs was guaranteed by having five gifted child scholars, including Terman and his closest associates, determine the IQs from the volumes of letters, diaries, poems, and other documents available. Although the psychologists had some difficulties agreeing with one another, consensus was ultimately accomplished by eliminating the two raters who disagreed with the majority (Gould 1981, p. 184). Cox figured that, because one of these raters (G) consistently made lower IQ estimates than the average, and the other rater (St) consistently made higher estimates, eliminating these outliers would make the IQ estimates appear more credible and "stable" and would make little difference in the determination of the final IQ: "It may be inferred . . . that the ratings of G and St, if present, would simply equalize one another and give an average approximating that of T, M, and C. . . . [Thus] the agreement of the means and the established reliability of the ratings of T, M, and C give a certain stability to findings based upon their judgments" (p. 72).

Cox acknowledged another challenge: Raters were extremely doubtful about the correctness of their IQ estimates when little or no information was available to make these estimates. This source of uncertainty was removed by ruling that subjects' IQ should be no lower than 100, the IQ norm for the general population. Thus, even when there was no record of a great person's childhood development and accomplishments, as was the case with Sebastian Le Prestre De Vauban (the "celebrated French Military Engineer and Marshall" [pp. 225–226]), a precise estimate could still be made of childhood intelligence. In other words, although no record existed of De Vauban's childhood interests, reading, school standing, and progress, he could still be awarded a childhood IQ of 100. With IQ 100 as a base figure, each positive item of information surviving from subjects' childhood could then serve as the incremental grounds for enlarging the IQ estimate, thereby making IQ a direct function of the quantity of recorded information available. Accordingly, because only one favorable item of information emerged about Sir Francis Drake's childhood—that the boy Drake was "diligent" in his apprenticeship to a sea captain (p. 231)—an A1 IQ one notch above 100 (105) appeared entirely justifiable. At the other extreme, because Cox knew the precise age at which John Stuart Mill learned Greek and Latin, the year he first read Plato, Aristotle, Thucydides, Sophocles, Euripedes, Demostenes, and Cicero, and the year he took up the study of geometry, algebra, conic sections, spherics, Newton's mathematics, and the like, he could be awarded a childhood IQ as high as 190.

Although Gould (1981, pp. 183–188) criticized this methodology on the grounds that the quantity of information available may have much more to do with social status than intelligence (as the wealthy and nobility are much more likely to record the accomplishments of their young than are the lower classes, and that poorer, less-educated families do not have the resources to support and encourage the kinds of childhood activities that Cox used as evidence of precocity), such criticisms neglect gifted child scholarship's longstanding belief that social position is produced by giftedness. That John Bunyon, son of a tinker, did not have scribes and tutors to record his every move, to teach him to recite poetry and Greek from his cradle, as Voltaire and John Stuart Mill had, was not regarded as an unfortunate accident of fate, but a measure of Bunyon's family's lack of innate giftedness. Their poverty, and their boy's lack of recorded accomplishments, resulted from effects of the same cause: the absence of giftedness. According to this mode of thinking, wealth and poverty, vice and virtue are not causes but only effects: "A man becomes a respectable member of society because he was a respectable man from the start—that is to say, because he was born in possession of good instincts and prosperous propensities. . . . Should a man enter the world poor, and the son of parents who are neither economical nor thrifty, he is insusceptible of being improved—that is to say, he is only fit for the prison or the madhouse" (Nietzsche 1901/1909, p. 268).

CONNECTING STATUS TO GIFTEDNESS

To affirm the belief that wealth and status indicate intelligence, each biographical sketch of the great historical figures was preceded by an account of their family's social status. Thus, readers could see that the few historical figures who had ordinary IQs as children (e.g., Andre Massena, John Bunyan, Miguel De Cervantes, James Cook, William Cobbett, Sir Francis Drake, Michael Faraday), came from families of laborers, tinkers, small farmers, sailors, blacksmiths, and so on. Conversely, they could see that as the childhood IQs of the greats increased, so did the status, wealth, and accomplishments of their parents and ancestors. Thus, the children in Cox's study who had the highest IQs (John Stuart Mill, Leibnitz, Grotius, Goethe, Pascal, Macaulay, Bentham) had fathers in the highest occupational categories (philosopher; professor; jurist; director of a university; imperial councillor; scientist; philanthropist).

In a sense, then, the effort to prove the survival power of giftedness cannot be separated from the effort to establish the survival power of status and wealth, as if giftedness and status are fundamentally related to one another, derived from one another, as elements of a single process. Whether or not giftedness has a true inner constancy, the fact remains that if it is able to make itself recognized by us, if it is not to disappear, if we are to be able to speak of giftedness, it is on condition that the appearances of giftedness behave as though they have an inner principle of unity (Merleau-Ponty 1962, p. 319). This principle of unity is not known as a logical or scientific operation; it is not a matter of objective fact reducible to a certain series of causes and properties. Rather, we respond to a power de jure, a legitimacy that makes us see these diverse properties as rightfully connected to this or that nucleus. If we can say that without a certain set of characteristics this object would cease to be recognizable as this object, so we may say that beyond a certain range of changes this object would cease to be a normal, legitimate manifestation of that object. In this regard, the gifted child is known not only by a series of abilities but by a certain social status, by a specific kind of material and cultural success, and by membership in a particular race and ethnic group that together form a single gestalt.

Although gifted child scholars emphasize that "gifted children can be found in all economic levels, ethnic and social groups" (Ehrlich 1986, p. 65), some expressions of giftedness are portrayed as deviations from the norm, as vaguely illegitimate, mutant manifestations. Thus, Humphreys (1985, p. 355) offers black children an outsider, second-tiered relation to giftedness: "At this point in the nation's history, Blacks are, on average, less intelligent as defined herein than Whites. . . . Black children are found at all intellectual levels, but any objective definition of giftedness will qualify a smaller percentage of Black children as being gifted in the school-age population." As Newland (1976, p. 51) explains, "In those uncommon instances where gifted adults appear to have emerged, largely on their own, out of disadvantaged classes, there invariably has been some influence which has caused (and probably partly enabled) them as children to start to compensate for their environmental limitations." From these statements we can see that, even if the connection between giftedness and social status (and race and ethnicity) lies beyond proof and logical analysis, still the fact remains that we see the connection, that the continual copresence of these properties supports and legitimates our defining the one in terms of the other.

The message delivered by the studies of the great historical figures is the same message hammered home in the gifted child longitudinal studies: Beyond the evidence amassed as to the constancy of the gifted's IQs and their consistently virtuous behavior, we see that children born to upper middle-class homes remain in the upper middle-class as adults. In Terman's longitudinal study, for example, there were almost no laborers among the gifted and their parents, less than 1% of each were classified in "slightly skilled trades," and the identical percentage (21%) of the gifted men and their fathers were in clerical, skilled trades, and minor business. Reproducing the achievement of their fathers (who exceeded the proportion of the general population in the professions by 10 to 1 [Terman 1925, p. 63]), the gifted sons exceeded the proportion of the general population in the professions by 8 to 1 (Terman and Oden 1947, p. 193). Similarly, just as the median family income for the gifted children in 1921 was $3,333, substantially more than twice that of the general population at that time, so by 1954 the median family income for gifted subjects was also more than twice that of the general white urban population ($10,866 vs. $5,069). The constancy of giftedness demonstrated the constancy of social class.

Yet, paradoxically, gifted child scholarship could not (and cannot) argue that worldly success and giftedness are inevitably linked: Why divert resources toward the education of the gifted if they are going to be successful anyway? Instead, gifted child scholarship argues that this linkage should occur, that worldly success is an appropriate and just outcome of giftedness albeit not a necessary one. Thus, translating Cox's research into rhetoric supportive of gifted education required an emphasis on the contingency of gifted child success. In this regard, Goddard (1928, p. 125) argued that, "the simple fact that Dr. Cox is able to pick out from all history only three hundred of these remarkable people must surely indicate that only an insignificant proportion of the high-intelligenced have ever had a chance to succeed. It is believed that with better methods and with better attention being given to the problem, an effort to give every gifted child an adequate educational opportunity will most decidedly benefit all humanity and civilization." Dael Wolfle (1951,

p. 42) also emphasized the uncertainty of gifted children becoming immensely successful: "Not everyone—in fact, scarcely anyone—who has an IQ of 160 goes down in history as a genius." Wolfle argued that if the country is to make good use of the gifted children identified through IQ tests, then "the next step is to give active encouragement to the ones who show the most promise" (p. 44). Sidney Pressey (1955) made a similar argument: Those who develop extraordinary abilities at an early age and go on to accomplish great things as adults usually have many excellent opportunities for their abilities to develop along with encouragement from teachers, family, and friends. The message is clear: The gifted may be a national resource but a national resource that can easily be wasted if not carefully managed.

Through the latter mode of interpretation, problem cases such as William James Sidis can be assimilated to gifted child scholarship as cautionary tales. If Sidis did not achieve great things with his giftedness, this is no longer considered his failure but is now commonly attributed to his domineering, exploitative, publicity-hungry father (Feldman 1986b; Montour 1977). In Montour's words, "It is no wonder that William Sidis deliberately ruined his own life to thwart his father's efforts at making him a perfect man" (1977, p. 274). Instead of attributing his failure to too much education as a young boy, in effect, to his being treated as a gifted child, Montour claimed he was not given enough: "More acceleration, not less, might have helped Sidis" (p. 276).

Accordingly, instead of the worst possible advertisement for giftedness, Sidis's life could serve as the exemplar of the waste that can occur if gifted children are not provided appropriate educational opportunity, guidance, and nurture: "How many Einstein's or Galileo's has the world lost by treating prodigies as unwelcome freaks in their youth. What mountains might William James Sidis have moved had he not been stunned into hiding?" (Wallace 1986, p. 286). To underscore the magnitude of Sidis's loss to the nation, a gifted scholar recently estimated that Sidis had the highest IQ ever recorded, somewhere between 250 and 300: "Nobody begins to approach the intellect and perspicacity of William Sidis. . . . I would honestly say that he was the most prodigious intellect of our entire generation (Abraham Sperling, Director of New York City's Aptitude Testing Institute, quoted in Wallace 1986, p. 283).

Consistent with this mode of analysis, the Jacob K. Javits Gifted and Talented Students Education Act of 1988 provided the following rationales for appropriating $16.8 million for gifted education:

1.   Gifted and talented students are a national resource vital to the future of the Nation and its security and well-being;

2. Unless the special abilities of the gifted and talented are recognized and developed during their elementary and secondary school years, much of their special potential for contributing to the national interest is lost.

(Karnes and Marquardt 1991a, pp. 10–11).

5

From Leadership to Critical Thinking: Pegasus in the Classroom

> To plan any but a flexible curriculum for gifted children would be analogous to putting a saddle and bridle on Pegasus.
>
> From *Education of Gifted Children* by Lulu Stedman (1924)

In most recent discussions of inequality in education, power is considered to be exercised only in relation to lower-class children (Burbules 1986; White 1983). For example, Paulo Freire (1970) argues that education of the poor is organized to reinforce passivity, fear, and low self-worth. He points to students' rigidly dichotomized relationship to their teachers: The teacher teaches, students are taught; the teacher speaks, they listen; the teacher commands, they obey; the teacher judges and selects, they observe and absorb; the teacher disciplines, they are disciplined. In Polakow's (1993, p. 157) words, "Poor children are required to fit the world created for them by school structures that violate their promise and devalue their resilience."

My hypothesis in this chapter is that a "pedagogy of the oppressed" directly implies a pedagogy of oppressors; that there is no power relation involving the poor without a correlative power relation involving the affluent (Bourdieu and Passeron 1977). Moreover, I argue that gifted child education constitutes a mechanism specifically geared toward articulating this power relation on the affluent; that it is a strategy to develop a class of people who lead, direct, and originate.[1]

I begin by showing how the gifted child classroom was originally conceptualized and organized in the 1920s. As we will see, the gifted child curriculum was not and never became focused on core academic subjects (math, science, language arts, etc.) but was instead focused on the phenomenon of giftedness itself. Because the gifted are conceived to have leadership ability, they are taught leadership; because they are

77

creative, they are taught creativity; because they have excellent cognitive ability, they are taught to think; and so forth.

In Kaplan's (1989b) words,

> What we are really saying is that a quality curriculum for gifted children is one that enables them to display, to demonstrate, to exhibit, to show off the same characteristics that define them as gifted. If these are children who are curious; if these are children who are creative; if these are children who can make more relationships and can learn more quickly; if these are children who have a wide variety of interests; if these are children who have the ability for understanding the position of the other sooner in their development—the curriculum has to be the stimulus, the catalyst, that enables them to show off what they are capable of doing.

Whether or not children really learn leadership, creativity, or thinking in gifted education may be beside the point. We will see that what matters is that this pedagogy continually elaborates and affirms our understanding of gifted children. Classroom activities for the gifted are thus not only defined by our perception of who the gifted are but also reflexively affirm and sustain those understandings. If we believe in gifted children, then, it is because we participate in a pedagogy that assails our senses the way waves wash against the shore. That this pedagogy confronts giftedness not as unidimensional—not merely as a giftedness-for-sight or for-touch or for-sound, but as a total reality consisting of a complex series of interrelated capacities and activities— produces the richness and clarity of a true spectacle, something that can be embraced with absolute conviction. Just as Cézanne declared that a successful painting contains within itself even the smell of the landscape (Merleau-Ponty 1962, p. 318), so the success of the gifted portrait is the ceaseless anticipation of a distinctive originality, bravery, beauty, wit, discipline, reasoning, generosity, and so on, within these children: "A thing would not have this color had it not also this shape, these tactile properties, this resonance, this odor, and . . . the absolute fullness which my undivided existence projects before itself. . . . There is a symbolism in the thing which links every sensible quality to the rest" (Merleau-Ponty 1962, p. 319).

THE EARLY GIFTED CHILD CURRICULUM

Prior to the emergence of giftedness, students who performed better than others were advanced more rapidly through the school system.

They were either promoted ahead of their peers or placed in separate rapid-advancement classes (Henry 1920). However, in Goddard's (1928, p. 3) language, neither of these models took into consideration "the nature" of the gifted child: "We spent thirty years trying to adjust him to a promotion system. We spent twenty years trying to rush him rapidly through the grades. A curriculum that is not fitted to the type of mind possessed by the gifted child, we attempted to adjust to his needs by giving him twice as much of it!" What should distinguish the class for the gifted, according to Goddard, is not rapid advancement through the standard, nongifted, curriculum but the development of a new learning environment based on the character and needs of gifted children.

First, gifted children allow for a new understanding and use of time. Because "the gifted child can do all the work required by the curriculum in half the time allotted to it" (Goddard 1928, p. 90), teachers can reduce drill and lecture by 50% (Henry 1920, p. 108; Whipple 1919, p. 120). This means that teachers have time and freedom for class projects, field trips, the exploration of new art forms and technologies, to do such things as "extended supplementary reading of standard literature (mainly for appreciation), dramatization, pageantry, free discussion of the important topics in the news of the day, the collection of newspaper clippings correlating with work in civics and hygiene, the illustration of history and geography with such relics, costumes, utensils, etc." (Whipple 1919, p. 124). Given the greater availability of time, gifted students also have "opportunities to see especially good motion pictures and spoken plays, opportunities to hear eminent lecturers, political leaders, visiting consuls, travelers from foreign countries, or specialists in any line, such as musicians, artists, librarians, scientists, and others" (Stedman 1924, p. 188). In sum, "with these children it is possible to do many of the things that every teacher has longed to do with school children" (Goddard 1928, p. 90).

However, projects and field activities are suited to the gifted not only because their teachers have more time. Rather, "gifted minds are especially amenable to instruction by the *project method*, because they excel in 'thinking things together,' in perceiving the relations between and among all the relevant elements in a given field of endeavor" (Hollingworth 1926, pp. 308–309).

Because gifted pupils are more responsible than others, they can be depended on to organize and direct their own learning (Stedman 1924, p. 10). Thus, the gifted class permits a fundamental redistribution of the responsibility shared by the student and teacher: "It is not an uncommon thing for a class of gifted children to conduct an occasional period successfully with almost no guidance by the teacher. Indeed, *pupil-teaching* is one of the devices most mentioned as a means of developing

initiative and a sense of responsibility in gifted children. . . . Their superior mentality, their powers of self-criticism, their ability to pick out the
essential points in a discussion, and their enthusiasm enable gifted children to conduct a recitation almost independently of a teacher" (Davis
1924, p. 137)."[2]

Because these children are natural leaders, they must be given the
opportunity to lead. Thus, the gifted "are in charge of assemblies, they
escort younger children across dangerous street crossings, they keep
order in the halls during recess and noon periods, they supervise the
playgrounds, they act as leaders and 'safety officers' on class excursions,
and in general look after the welfare of themselves and their classmates"
(Davis 1924, p. 139). The gifted also serve on "police patrols," on committees for keeping order, on committees "for looking after library
books, for maintaining order and neatness in the classroom, for inspect-
ing the health habits of the class, for providing flowers and suitable
decorations for the room, for handling various funds (as, for example,
milk money and thrift contributions) and numerous similar activities"
(Davis 1924, p. 139).

Corresponding to the lessened emphasis on drill and lecture, the
gifted receive fewer problems and exercises in formal subjects (Henry
1920, p. 117). Although gifted education is stereotypically linked to images of scholarship and intensive study, the gifted child curriculum is
not focused on advanced work in particular subject areas such as math
and languages: "To enrich the curriculum of the elementary school by
teaching algebra, geometry, Latin, or zoology to young gifted children is
to render them no genuine service, but is merely to anticipate matters
which would have been presented to them in any case" (Hollingworth
1926, p. 311). Instead, the focus of gifted education is the gifted character
itself. The goal is to enhance the qualities that define these children and
set them apart: "Others can conserve, but only the gifted can originate.
Therefore, should not the education of the gifted be education for initiative and originality" (Hollingworth 1926, p. 313)?

The gifted child curriculum encourages the unrestricted exercise of the
gifted intelligence: "To develop fully, they must encounter situations
which will try their powers to the utmost. Without choice and conflict
there can be no real growth" (Stedman 1924, p. 8). Instead of formal
lectures, gifted pupils have informal, spontaneous discussions. Instead
of memorizing facts, they learn to question. And instead of being seated
in desks that are bolted to the floor and arranged in rows, the gifted face
one another in circular seating (Stedman 1924, p. 10): "There is no for-
mality, no regularity, no silence, except upon very special occasions or
for a very few seconds. There are no straight rows of seats. There are no

repeated commands to 'sit up straight.' There is almost nothing that savors of the old-time schoolroom" (Goddard 1928, p. 76).

Because the primary goal of their class work consists of reinforcing their independence and originality and of sharpening their thinking, gifted children are given wide latitude in the selection and exploration of topics. Hollingworth (1926, pp. 331–332) showed how virtually any subject can serve as grist for the mill:

Are Rugs Furniture?

Child Dor [IQ 167]:   Are rugs furniture or objects of decoration?

Child Th [IQ 171]:   They may be considered either way. In one way rugs are furniture, because they are *useful*. They keep cold from coming up through the floor. However, they are also decorative, for if we wanted them only to keep out cold, we could buy just *plain* rugs. We buy them to be decorative, so people will want to come to our house.

Teacher: Could we divide all furnishings into useful and decorative? What of chairs, beautifully carved? Are they necessities or luxuries?

Child Do [IQ 188]:   They cannot be put under either head absolutely correctly, because they are *both* necessary and luxurious. They are furniture and *necessary*. They are decorative and a *luxury*.

Child M [IQ 156]:   People buy beautiful things because their neighbors do. They try to keep up with their neighbors.

Child B [IQ 150]:   Yes. "Keeping up with the Joneses." [*Class concludes that it is impossible to divide all things into furniture and not furniture, or into necessities and luxuries.*]

Many features of the ideal classroom for gifted children are also ideal for children in general. "However, certain features of equipment are particularly important for the gifted. Chief among these is a special library, which should be selected quite differently from the library for ordinary children of like age" (Hollingworth 1926, pp. 310–311). For example, gifted children require many volumes of poetry and books about nature; they also need a complete encyclopedia, dictionaries in both English and foreign languages, atlases, maps, microscopes, a globe, phonograph, and a round table for discussion. According to Hollingworth (1926, p. 310), the gifted are also in special need of typewriters because of the discrepancy between their intellectual capacities and facility of motor control: "'Oh, do we have to write it out?' is a plea often heard in the special class of young children. It is surprising how many of them learn to use typewriters during the early years of the elementary school."

Among the skills developed in gifted education, the acquisition of specific sets of information is always secondary to the development of the character traits that placed the gifted child in the special class to begin with. Thus, the emphasis is on helping gifted children to develop the ability to think critically, reflectively, objectively, to build a consistent system of values, to see both sides of a question, to state problems as well as to solve them, to enhance self-control, to initiate, and to exercise leadership. The ultimate goal is to prepare the gifted "to take their places in civilization" (Hollingworth 1926, p. 313). To this end, it is particularly important that the gifted study the biographies of the eminent: "For adjustment to life as they are capable of living it, they need information as to how persons have found adjustment, as to how careers are made and are related serviceably to civilization, and . . . they need ideals of sustained effort against odds, of perfection in work, and of self-management which arise from close inspection of the noble" (Hollingworth 1926, pp. 319–320).

In keeping with the emphasis on the gifted child's moral and personal development, the distinguishing traits of the gifted child teacher must also be moral and personal. She is not selected because of her mastery in a particular topic area such as math, science, languages, and so forth. On the contrary, since "gifted children exhibit an unusual range of interests and wealth and variety of mental association" (Whipple 1919, p. 115), their teacher should be a generalist: "Teachers of these classes should be chosen for their humanity and their broad background of human culture" (Goddard 1928, p. 55). "She is not there to impart information as a regular thing" (Goddard 1928, p. 57); her role instead is to inspire, suggest, and encourage.

Because the gifted child embodies all virtues, their teacher must represent a similarly unified gestalt. To develop the powers of the gifted, she "must possess an individuality strong enough to challenge those powers" (Henry 1920, p. 100). Like the gifted themselves, their teacher is characterized by open-mindedness, eagerness to study and learn, to receive new ideas and to try new methods. She also possesses unusual self-control, originality, a happy disposition, and is physically and aesthetically pleasing (Goddard, pp. 54–57). She cannot be ugly either in spirit or appearance but "should do her part to supply . . . beauty in face, figure, and costume as well as in voice, manner, and morals" (Goddard 1928, p. 54).

Although the teacher of the gifted must have an unusually high intelligence of her own, she must also "be free from unconscious jealousy and from unconfessed bias against gifted children. . . . The teacher must, in short, be one who can tolerate being beaten by a child, in intellectual performances" (Hollingworth 1926, p. 307). If gifted education teachers have a single characteristic or pedagogic aptitude that sets them apart, it is the ability to allow the gifted's natural abilities to surface of their own accord. They are distinguished by the fact that they do not impose obstacles to gifted children's learning: "These teachers never give orders; they never scold; they never speak in a loud voice; they never get cross. They are always happy and cheerful. They are always polite to the children; they are always devoted and helpful" (Goddard 1928, p. 57).

NOTHING'S CHANGED

The fundamental philosophy and organization of the gifted child curriculum changed very little over the next 30 years. In the 1950s, gifted child scholars were still saying, "we hope to broaden out, not accelerate" (DeHaan and Havingurst 1957, p. 47) and "a well-balanced personality is the ultimate goal in educating the gifted" (Hildreth 1957, p. 43). Far from abandoning their generalist posture, these educators criticized past efforts on behalf of the gifted as having "been at fault in emphasizing intellectual development, the abstract and the academic, textbook work and classical studies at the expense of the child's social, emotional, and physical development" (Hildreth 1957, p. 47). As these gifted education "objectives" from the *Fifty-seventh Yearbook of the National Society for the Study of Education* show, this mode of education continued to be primarily oriented to fostering feelings of mastery, social competence, agency, and self-worth (Passow 1958, p. 194):

1. To deal competently with themselves, their fellow men, and the world about them as human beings, citizens, parents, and participants in the "good life."
2. To build a sound liberal foundation to sustain the vigorous development of specialized competencies at the higher levels which they can handle.
3. To foster self-direction, independence, a love of learning, and a desire to create and experiment with ideas and things.
4. To provide the self-understanding, inner consistency, and ethical standards to see their own uniqueness in terms of responsibility to society.

5. To stimulate critical thinking and a scientific approach to solving their persistent problems.
6. To nurture an appreciation of the cultural heritage bequeathed by societies through the ages.
7. To motivate the desire to meet the special expectations society has for individuals with unique talents.

A quick perusal of contemporary gifted education textbooks reveals that these "objectives" are still in place today. To illustrate, I surveyed all the gifted education textbooks on the shelves of the Connie Belin National Center for Gifted Education and found only a fractional proportion specifically devoted to standard academic topics. Among the 11 most recent textbooks I found that are used to prepare and train gifted education teachers (*Creative Teaching of the Gifted* [Sisk 1987], *Gifted Students in Regular Classrooms* [Parke 1989], *A Thoughtful Overview of Gifted Education* [Eby and Smutny 1990], *Excellence in Educating the Gifted* [Feldhusen, Van Tassel-Baska, Seeley 1989], *Gifted Education* [Kitano and Kirby 1986], *Toward Excellence in Gifted Education* [Feldhusen 1985], *Schooling the Gifted* [Coleman 1985], *Instructional Strategies for Teaching the Gifted* [Parker 1989], *Education of the Gifted and Talented* [1989 Davis and Rimm 1989], *Teaching the Gifted Child* [Gallagher 1985], *Critical Issues in Gifted Education* [Maker 1993]), only 410 pages (about 11% of the 3,832 pages of text) deal with teaching basic academic subject matter (math, science, etc.).

By contrast, the largest portions of these books deal with the nature and characteristics of gifted children themselves, how they can be identified and assessed, and how gifted child educational curricula can enhance the qualities that define these children as gifted. The table of contents for Kitano and Kirby's (1986, p. ix) Gifted Education illustrates:

Chapter One	Introducing the Gifted
Chapter Two	Concepts of Giftedness
Chapter Three	The Nature of Giftedness
Chapter Four	Characteristics of Gifted and Talented Learners
Chapter Five	The Referral-Placement Process
Chapter Six	Curriculum Development
Chapter Seven	Enhancing Inductive Thinking
Chapter Eight	Enhancing Creative Thinking
Chapter Nine	Enhancing Evaluative Thinking and Affective Development
Chapter Ten	The Arts and Leadership
Chapter Eleven	Selected Academic Content Areas
Chapter Twelve	Special Populations
Chapter Thirteen	Implementing Programs for the Gifted
Chapter Fourteen	Parents and Families
Chapter Fifteen	Perspectives for the Future

We can see that particular emphasis is placed on teaching gifted children to think and on strategies for fostering affective development and creativity. Leadership training is also a central component of this curriculum. In the words of Davis and Rimm (1989, p. 197), "There is little disagreement that leadership is important for gifted and talented students, who often are labeled 'tomorrow's leaders'." Typically, leadership training involves learning "about traits of leaders, leadership styles, group dynamics, and how to be a good leader. . . . Students receive training in component leadership skills, such as communication, creative problem solving, critical thinking, decision making, persuasion, and even understanding others' needs" (Davis and Rimm 1989, p. 197). Parker (1989, p. 3) explains why these strategies are essential: "Differentiated programming for the gifted can no longer be justified exclusively on the basis of one's legal right to an appropriate education. Whereas this right is indisputable, it must be complemented with a second point: society cannot nor will not survive without intelligent, imaginative leadership. Leadership training is therefore mandatory for those members of our population who have the intellectual and creative potential to lead."

Gifted children may be defined as "vastly superior" in creativity and cognitive ability, but this is not a warrant for taking these traits for granted. Rather, it is a warrant for accentuating them. Thus, the central means "of providing differentiated instruction for gifted students is to increase opportunities for engaging in creative and higher-level thinking skills, such as planning, predicting, analyzing, synthesizing, evaluating, and inducing" (Kitano and Kirby 1986, pp. 380–381). It is assumed "that (a) gifted individuals benefit more from such opportunities than do their peers, (b) gifted individuals require instruction and/or practice in such thinking processes to be productive, and (c) nongifted individuals can be successful without added opportunities to engage in creative and higher-level thinking."

Perhaps the clearest illustration of how the gifted child curriculum is derived from the concept of giftedness is found in Clark's (1983) *Growing Up Gifted*. That text provides a series of tables listing gifted children's "differentiating characteristics" in the left-hand column with adjacent columns specifying the educational needs and classroom strategies best fitted to them. For example, next to the gifted characteristic "flexible thought processes," Clark (p. 198) lists "to be allowed to solve problems in diverse ways" as an educational need and "teacher acceptance of unusual products; open-ended assignments; opportunities to examine and/or alter existing patterns physically and mentally," as classroom strategies. Next to the gifted characteristic "early ability to delay closure" is the recommendation that the gifted student "be allowed to pursue ideas and integrate new ideas without forced closure or products de-

manded" (p. 198). For the gifted student's "heightened capacity for seeing unusual and diverse relationships," it is suggested that they need
"to 'mess around' with varieties of materials and ideas." For their "early
involvement and concern for intuitive knowing," they should receive
"opportunities to converse meaningfully with philosophers and others
on these ideas" within "an environment of trust and acceptance" (p. 209).
For their strong "self-actualization needs" they require "opportunities
to follow divergent paths and pursue strong interests" within "a trusting
environment where self-esteem is supported and self-exploration valued
and actively facilitated" (p. 212).

What should be specifically noted in all the recommendations is that
they always connect the characteristics of giftedness to strategies for
enhancing students' freedom, their sense of prerogative, and entitle-
ment. Above all, the gifted must learn that what they conceive and
initiate is desirable and important. If the "pedagogy of the oppressed"
(Freire 1970, p. 57) is defined by the active teacher (the subject) related to
the passive, listening student (the object), in gifted education this narra-
tive is reversed: Here the patient, listening teacher is the object, and the
narrating student the subject. The rationale for this strategy is explicit.
In Clark's (1983, p. 212) words, it is anticipated that, "gifted children will
function in society as change agents, innovators, and reconstructionists.
We believe that our societal problem solvers will come from this group."

To adapt the gifted to their future station, their teachers must be
distinguished not by proficiency in any academic area but by their recognition that the gifted require freedom, self-determination, acceptance,
and support. To illustrate, a recent survey (Whitlock and Ducette 1989,
pp. 17–18) of gifted education educators concluded that the outstanding
gifted education teacher "allows student to use own style of work to do
assignment in own way; adapts or changes own plans or lessons to
follow-up on students' interests or on students' suggestions; . . . is willing to be corrected by a student; . . . insists that students make key
choices about how to complete their assignments or projects." Elizabeth
Drews (1976, p. 28) sums up: "Let us all recognize that gifted children
have great insights from the beginning and that our task as teachers is
the Socratic one of leading out the creative and letting them be
where . . . they can discover what in truth they already know."

Consistent with a curriculum in which the primary goal is the release
and enhancement of giftedness, certification and masters degree requirements in gifted education do not specify preparation in math, science, or any other academic subjects.[3] Instead, the following knowledge
and skill areas are essential (Karnes and Wharton 1991; Sisk 1987,
p. 196):

Knowledge of nature and needs of gifted
Skill in developing higher cognitive thinking abilities
Knowledge of affective/cognitive needs of gifted
Ability to develop creative problem solving
Ability to develop materials for the gifted
Ability to utilize individual teaching strategies
Ability to demonstrate appropriate techniques and materials for the
  gifted
Ability to guide and counsel gifted students and their parents
Ability to carry out action research in the classroom

Similarly, the National Association for Gifted Children (Karnes and Whorton 1991) does not require any course sequences in traditional academic content areas. Only these courses are specifically recommended for certification in gifted education:

Nature and needs/psychology of the gifted
Assessment of gifted students
Counseling of gifted students
Curriculum development for the gifted
Strategies and materials for teaching the gifted
Creative studies
Program development and evaluation
Parent education and advocacy training
Special populations/problems of gifted students
Cognitive and affective processing
Supervised practicum in gifted education

As we shall see, gifted educators are sometimes quite frustrated by the vagueness, generality, and overall emptiness of the gifted child curriculum. Still, their efforts to make it more academic and rigorous are not successful. One reason is that gifted education teachers are not trained to provide academic specialization. However, there is a more fundamental explanation.

WHY NO CHANGE?

In 1988, Robert N. Sawyer published a paper in *The Journal for the Education of the Gifted* that anticipates and supports the central argument of this chapter, that is, that the classroom activities commonly labeled "gifted education" are more focused on defining and supporting a class

of people than on advanced academic preparation: "Our corporate concern seems more often gifted children than their education. We narrowly
define our task by those who benefit from our labors rather than the
benefit we wish to give academically talented children" (p. 13).

Sawyer documents his argument by referring to a brochure of a gifted
and talented program. First, he notes that, although the admissions
policies appear selective and rigorous, after more careful reading this
program is in fact open to anyone with "interest" and tuition: "Appli-
cants must be in the top 5% of their class in academic performance or in
the 95th percentile on a tested area of a standardized test administered
in the school. Also, students who have been identified as gifted by their
school districts are invited to apply. If a student has a strong recommendation from a teacher as being potentially gifted in one of the above
categories, then that student is also welcome to apply. In addition, any
interested student is welcome to apply" (p. 6). Then, he notes, this
program offers a "fluff" course in "bears" described like this: "Learn
about real and imaginary bears, from Koalas to Paddington. In addition
to studying the habits of bears in the world, activities will include the
history of the Teddy Bear." Another course described in the brochure
concerns Homer's *Odyssey* but appears to have been written by someone
who had not read the *Odyssey*. The course summary reads: "The basis of
this course will be Homer's *Odyssey*. Traveling with Odysseus, we will
find out what it is like to go to war and then try to come home. As war
correspondents, we will send home reports. As Greeks and Romans, we
will try to arrange a cease fire. In short, we will live the *Odyssey* for
our three weeks together." Apparently, the teacher who organized this
gifted program did not bother to check that Homer's *Odyssey* is set long
after the Trojan war, and that there were no Romans.

Sawyer provides more evidence in the form of a "learning center kit"
marketed by a widely respected gifted child organization. This kit is
devoted to the study of gnomes: "Students may opt to decide whether
gnomes would be better Santa's helpers than elves, to cover the gnome
olympics as a reporter for the 'Gnome Gazette,' or to act out a skit
entitled 'The Gnome Who Came to Dinner.' *Gnomes* also contains two
mazes, two do-it-yourself Gnomie-toons, and a word search puzzle"
(p. 7). Another gifted child workbook deals with "future studies," which
includes such tasks as "creating perfect space pets, developing a zero
gravity sports activity, designing a space chores robot and more, more,
more!" (p. 7). Sawyer's point is simple enough: these "kits" and playtime
diversions may be justified on the grounds that they teach gifted children how to "solve problems" or "learn to learn," but they have no
academic content. These activities have no specific connection to the
basic sciences, social studies, languages, or mathematics.

Still, Sawyer is not fundamentally pessimistic. Although he questions gifted education's practices, his problem is never with giftedness itself. For Sawyer, as well as the other inhabitants of this subuniverse, giftedness has an "insidious presence" (Merleau-Ponty 1962, p. 41) that cannot be questioned. Thus, Sawyer concludes his attack on gifted education not by contemplating its essential absurdity. He refers instead to its "flowering": "Finally, the cause of academic rigor in gifted education is the flowering of gifted education. We can make a difference in the lives of our students and even in the life of our society as a whole, once we resolve to return to the things that matter in academics" (p. 19).

Apparently, Sawyer believes that gifted education need only "resolve" to become more academic and rigorous for it to become so.[4] What he glosses is the theoretical and practical inconsistency between a commitment to "academic rigor" and belief in the identification of gifted children as gifted education's defining act. This conflict is easily illustrated by imagining how gifted education might react to two contrasting students. One excels in calculus but is not remarkable in anything else. This individual appears to have only ordinary "general" cognitive ability, creativity, leadership ability, and so on; that is, this individual appears to have none of the many general abilities that define membership in the class of gifted people. The second student performs poorly in each academic specialty but displays the kind of general abilities that define giftedness. Which student is gifted education most likely to embrace as one of its own? Although the first student excels in calculus and the other excels in nothing specific, gifted education must select the latter. The slogan "gifted underachiever" exists for the specific purpose of repairing and explaining the gap between this student's promise and performance. However, if gifted education were to select the student who *merely* excels in calculus, it would be in the strained position of treating giftedness as unnecessary to gifted education. In effect, it would be undoing itself. These injunctions are not secret or implicit. In Richert's (1991, p. 94) words, "The purpose of identification and programmatic provisions for the gifted is not to label or to reward achievement or conformity to school expectations, but to find and develop exceptional potential." Thus, students who perform particularly poorly in one or more subject areas may be embraced by gifted education (gifted "under-achievers"), whereas students who excel may be excluded (the implicit corollary term, nongifted "overachievers" applies here).

To gain admission to a gifted child program, you have to be identified as gifted by whatever criteria and procedures that program regards as valid. Although some gifted programs treat proficiency in a specific subject (e.g., calculus) as an indicator of giftedness, the candidate is ultimately admitted to the gifted program not because of calculus performance, but because the calculus performance indicates (either in whole or in part) the presence of giftedness. Because membership in the gifted program is determined not by a student's academic achievement but by the belief that the gifted student has "potential," those who work hard and perform well are not guaranteed entry. In fact, once a student is defined as nongifted, no amount of diligent and successful performance will get that student into the program. Conversely, gifted children with low motivation and poor performance are "in" no matter how poorly they do (Weiler, 1978).

After identification is made and the gifted label affixed, the child is then enrolled in a preexisting class appropriate to children of that type. There, educational strategies address general concepts of what gifted children are presumed to need to learn—thinking skills, creativity, independence, leadership, self-worth, and so on. This education becomes a "set piece" for all the "identified" children placed in it (Birch 1984, p. 159). Thus, even if the child who excels in calculus is admitted to this program, the ready-made, generalist character of the gifted program is not the place where calculus skills can be developed.

Although 12 states now require an individualized education program (IEP) for each student enrolled in a gifted class (Karnes and Marquardt 1991a, p. 20), this is not necessarily a method for ensuring that a child's enthusiasm and interest in calculus can be recognized and nurtured. In fact, the opposite is true. As Sisk (1987, p. 58) shows in her IEP for a gifted boy named Mark, a child's obsessive interest in computer electronics can easily be interpreted as a liability within the culture of gifted education. Thus, the lead recommendations on this sixth grader's IEP represent an effort to redirect him from his academic specialty: "Mark should be encouraged to broaden his interests to areas other than science and electronics. Physical activity outside of school would make it easier for him to work out his need for constant movement. Interaction with other young people in a club or organization might help him mature and develop socially. He should be encouraged to seek out a sport and an organization that might interest him, either at school or in the community."

To locate gifted education's discomfort with academic specialization, we need merely consider the number of pages gifted education textbooks devote to discussing procedures for identifying and understanding these children and how little attention is devoted to identifying and understanding academic achievement in particular topic areas. Because gifted education has never focused on academic topics such as mathematics, biology, English literature, computer technology, and so forth, it would need to reinvent itself as something entirely new for it to change course in so fundamental a way. Gifted education would cease to exist as gifted education if it became, in Sawyer's words, "academically rigorous."

Of course, this mode of education makes the gifted appear far more like the oppressed than oppressors-in-training. As Aimee Howley (1986, p. 122) put it: "By systematically diminishing the importance of relevant academic instruction, schools are able to cultivate a class of students who *feel* privileged but who are denied the privilege of fulfilling their academic potential." Still, *feeling* privileged—even when that feeling has no apparent substance—should not be dismissed as illusory or insignificant. Bourdieu and Passeron's (1977, p. 130) comments on what goes into a pedagogy of privilege are instructive:

> Consider, for example, the primacy of manner and style; the value attached to naturalness and lightness; conceived as the antithesis of pedantry, didacticism or effort; the cult of the "gift" and the disparagement of apprenticeship, the modern reformulation of the ideology of "birth" and contempt for study; the disdain for specialization, trades and techniques, the bourgeois transposition of contempt for business; the pre-eminence conferred on the art of pleasing, that is, the art of adapting oneself to the diversity of social encounters and conversations; the attention devoted to nuances and imponderables, perpetuating the aristocratic tradition of "refinement" and expressed in the subordination of scientific to literary culture, and of literary culture to artistic culture, still more conducive to the indefinite niceties of the games of distinction; in short, all the ways, declared or tacit, of reducing culture to the relation to culture, in other words, of setting against the vulgarity of what can be acquired or achieved a manner of possessing an acquirement whose whole value derives from the fact that there is but one way of acquiring it.

The last few lines of this passage are most interesting: The critical element of the pedagogy of privilege is not what is actually learned or acquired through this pedagogy but how what is "acquired or achieved" is perceived. And the perception that matters most is "the fact that there is but one way of acquiring it." To transpose this mode of analysis onto gifted education, what gifted children are actually taught—whether it is leadership or the history of teddy bears—makes no difference. What matters is that these things are taught through gifted education. The prestige, power, and privilege thus derive not from the content of what is taught, but from where it is taught and who is taught.

Because these recognitions threaten the very existence of their subuniverse, gifted child scholars gloss their possibility. Although scholars have no difficulty recognizing gifted education's "universal assumptions," (that "giftedness exists and is recognizable," that "identification plus programming nurtures giftedness," a "commitment to identification," "the system is reliable," and "the child becomes the adult" [Coleman 1985, pp. 59–60]), what they cannot recognize are the meanings and implications of these assumptions.

Pollner (1987, p. 164) suggests that there is a sense in which we are all "ontological dopes," because we are oblivious to the ways in which our routine practices either sustain or contradict our fundamental beliefs—our ontology.[5] So it is with gifted education. Like Don Quixote, who when told that Dulcinea is actually a farmer's daughter, declared that he will nonetheless continue to think of her as "the greatest princess in the world" (Cervantes, quoted in Schutz 1964, p. 146), so scholars' faith in gifted education cannot be shaken by the revelation that it is not a direct route to academic excellence. Nor can it be shaken by evidence that it legitimizes social hierarchies.

6

From the Golden Chromosome
to Gifted Behaviors:
Preserving Giftedness

To Don Quixote there is really a fortress with towers in shining silver, a
dwarf's trumpet announcing the approaching knight, beauteous maidens
taking the air at the castle's gate, and a castellan. Only to the observer
there is an inn, a swineherd blowing his horn, two women of easy virtue
and an innkeeper.

From "Don Quixote and the Problem of Reality"
by Alfred Schutz (1964)

Gifted child scholars are reflective. They criticize their projects, show
concern about objectivity, worry over racism and elitism. They are not
stupid. Yet, in the end they always represent themselves as confronting
real gifted children. Whether it is gifted children of concrete events such
as "how many scored above 135 on the Stanford Binet," gifted children
of symbolic events such as "underachievement," or gifted children of
abstract theoretical properties such as "the practices through which the
gifted potential is supported and nurtured," scholars reflect on, experience, and describe gifted children as independent of their reflecting,
experiencing, and describing (Pollner 1987, p. 127).

Their stubborn belief in giftedness is essentially practical. On the one
hand, without gifted children there can be no gifted child scholarship;
and on the other, gifted child scholarship has no language with which to
speak, think, or question that does not rely on giftedness as a foundational assumption. This does not mean, of course, that gifted child
scholarship is different from any other subuniverse of knowledge. As
Evans-Pritchard (1937, p. 338) described the Azande, "They reason excellently in the idiom of their beliefs, but they cannot reason outside, or
against, their beliefs because they have no other idiom in which to

express their thoughts." To provide an example from the world of academics, when experimental social psychologists examine the experimental method, they do so by running new experiments (Pollner 1987, p. 114). And so it is with gifted child scholarship. Problems with the procedures and assumptions that organize this domain are examined only to the extent to which they adequately retrieve the presumably real gifted children who form the topic of this domain.

Gifted child scholars' belief in gifted children is much like the mathematician's belief in certain unquestioned and unquestionable axioms. According to Gasking (1955, quoted in Mehan and Woods 1975, p. 9), such axioms are "incorrigible," because they are nonfalsifiable regardless of what happens: "The truth of an incorrigible proposition . . . is compatible with any and every conceivable state of affairs. (For example: whatever is your experience on counting, it is still true that $7 + 5 = 12$.)" Although at times you may add $7 + 5$ and get 11, this is not an occasion for revising the system: rather, it is an occasion for managing the discrepancy between the expected and the observed: "Either 'I have made a mistake in my counting' or 'Someone has played a practical joke and abstracted one of the objects when I was not looking' or 'Two of the objects have coalesced' or 'One of the objects has disappeared,' etc." (Gasking 1955, quoted in Mehan and Woods 1975, p. 10). Thus, for any belief system, foundational threats must be converted into standard, typical, problem-solving issues; hard-to-obtain answers must be replaced by comfortable truisms;[1] uncertainty must give way to well-determined goals and well-proved means to bring them about. To survive, the subuniverse must find ways of dealing with innumerable challenges.

NEW CHALLENGES

By the 1960s, just as it was becoming increasingly awkward to link giftedness to talk of racial and ethnic superiority, it was becoming more and more difficult to portray giftedness as some sort of "golden chromosome," as an absolute—"something that exists in and of itself, without relation to anything else" (Renzulli 1980, p. 4). This changed perception was not merely a result of the new pressure to acknowledge cultural diversity but also came from social science studies that questioned the premises of gifted child education as originally conceived in the 1920s.

For example, in developing a scale to determine how a child's aptitude becomes differentiated, a group of researchers (Davis, French, and Lesser 1959) found that aptitude in any one of five areas—vocabulary, numbers, reasoning, science, and space—is only loosely correlated to the others. Also, Guilford and Hoepfner (1967, 1971) found empirical support for a model of intellectual functioning involving three different and independent ways of processing and analyzing information. More recently, Feldman (1980, 1982, 1986a, p. 302) concluded that "giftedness is relatively domain specific" after observing that precocious learners who advanced rapidly in a specific area (e.g., chess, music, math) did not show marked advancement in other areas of learning. Similarly, only 39% of the eminent adults studied by Goertzel, Goertzel, and Goertzel (1979, pp. 255, 282, 345) appeared to have been all-around good students as children.

The potential threat such findings pose to gifted education is clear enough: If special aptitudes can be differentiated sharply and operate independently of one another, it becomes meaningless to identify children who presumably possess potential in everything. Why organize a program of education around general giftedness when achievement in one domain (e.g., mathematics) is only weakly correlated with achievement in other domains (e.g., in psychology, music, language arts, basketball, etc.)? Moreover, why must the child who performs excellently in math be denied the "gifted" label for failure to persuade test makers of general aptitude?

The notion of providing general "enrichment" to generally "gifted" children also risks absurdity in the light of research showing that learning is sequential and developmental (Bayley 1955; George, Cohn, and Stanley 1979; Keating 1976; Keating and Stanley 1972; Hilgard and Bower 1974; Hunt 1961; Robinson and Robinson 1976). According to this research, effective teaching depends on students mastering material in a particular order, that there be "an appropriate match between circumstances that a child encounters and the schemata that he/she has already assimilated into his/her repertoire" (Hunt 1961, p. 268). In the words of Julian Stanley (1980, p. 10), "if Susan reasons extremely well mathematically and is eager to move ahead faster and better in mathematics, her most pressing intellectual needs will not be met well by even the best imaginable special course in social studies, French conversation, or even computer science or chess. She needs the appropriate level and pace of mathematics now." From this point of view, recognition of Susan as "gifted" (as a person who has a series of interrelated abilities) is a distraction to the critical question of assessing her actual achievement levels in particular domains of learning.

A third threat came from a spate of studies (Bloom 1963; Harmon 1963; Helson and Crutchfield 1970; Hudson 1960; Mednick 1963; Parloff, Datta, Kleman, and Handlon 1968; Richards, Holland, and Lutz 1967; Wallach 1976; Wallach and Wing 1969) showing that the relationship between performance on standardized academic tests and real-world accomplishments is extremely tenuous. What standardized tests do predict, according to Wallach's (1976, p. 57) review of this literature, "are the results a person will obtain on other tests of the same kind."

Two of the most dramatic examples of how academic skill assessments show little correlation with real-world achievement are the careers of Werner von Braun and Albert Einstein: von Braun, who developed the principles of rocket propulsion, failed ninth-grade algebra and Einstein failed the admission exams to Zurich Polytechnic (Csikszentmihalyi and Robinson 1986, p. 276). Moreover, using the life stories of extraordinary achievers as evidence, Gruber (1986) showed that qualities not measurable in standardized tests (e.g., passionate and prolonged involvement with a particular subject) determine actual achievement.[2]

The questions raised by this research are fundamental: What is the justification in supporting gifted education programs if passing the entrance requirements posed by these programs has only a limited relationship to both immediate academic achievement and more remote career creativity and productivity? Does membership in a class of people distinguished by standardized test-taking ability have any practical significance either in the near or distant future?

What we now show is that gifted child education managed to survive these challenges, not by refuting them, but by assimilating them. To use the language of Thomas Kuhn (1970), these challenges were redefined as "puzzle-solving" issues, as "insider" problems that could be resolved by improving the procedures and methodologies already in place. The gifted child paradigm itself was not questioned. In other words, the threats were nullified by assimilating them into the standard dialogue by which gifted child scholars ongoingly discuss new and better ways of identifying and nurturing gifted children.

ANSWERING CHALLENGES

To illustrate how this assimilation was accomplished, let's examine two papers by Joseph S. Renzulli (1978, 1986)—"What Makes Giftedness? Reexamining a Definition" and "The Three-Ring Conception of Giftedness"—that address some of the new challenges to the gifted child paradigm. These papers are significant not only for sustaining gifted education in the face of numerous subversive possibilities but also for their widespread influence. Between 1972 and 1988, "What Makes Giftedness" was the most frequently cited gifted child study listed in the *Social Science Citation Index* (Carter and Swanson 1990).

Renzulli (1978, p. 182) begins by acknowledging that "studies clearly indicate that vast numbers and proportions of our most productive persons are not those who scored at the ninety-fifth or above percentile on standardized tests, nor were they necessarily straight-A students who discovered early how to play the lesson-learning game." However, this is no reason to scrap the notion of standardized cutoffs. Because "more creative/productive persons come from below the ninety-fifth percentile than above it," Renzulli (1978, 1986) reasons that we could include more of these persons in gifted programs if the "talent pool" available to these programs was widened from the top 5% of students to the top 15% or 20%. Accordingly, rather than creating a new way of enlisting gifted children, we manage with the old way—standardized cutoffs—by adjusting it in some fashion.

Second, if standardized tests of ability and academic performance are only marginally correlated with career success, it would appear that gifted education needs to consider new criteria for discriminating candidates. Because "popular maxims and autobiographical accounts to hardcore research findings [show that] one of the key ingredients that has characterized the work of gifted persons is the ability to involve oneself totally in a problem or area for an extended period of time," then "task commitment" would appear an appropriate criterion for defining giftedness (pp. 182–183). Also, because "as one reviews the literature in this area, it becomes readily apparent that the words 'gifted,' 'genius,' and 'eminent creators' or 'highly creative persons' are used synonymously," Renzulli recommends "creativity" as a requisite of giftedness. However, a seemingly unavoidable problem surfaces: "the haunting issue of subjectivity in measurement" (p. 184). Apparently, "task commitment" and "creativity" themselves require standardized instruments and procedures for "defensible identification systems" (p. 261). Thus what begins as an effort to redirect the field of gifted education away from identifying gifted students on the basis of standardized tests comes full circle by subtly asking scholars to develop new and better instruments (see Jarrell and Borland 1990, p. 303). In fact, Renzulli soon introduced instruments of his own: One is called the *Learning Styles Inventory* (Smith and Renzulli 1984), and the other is the *Student Product Assessment Form* (SPAF), an instrument that Renzulli (1986, p. 81) described as having a high degree of "validity and reliability" in determining whether children identified as gifted demonstrated appropriate levels of "general ability," "task commitment," and "creativity."[3]

Third, what began as an effort to emphasize specific performances in specific contexts (e.g., task commitment was described as the "energy brought to bear on a particular problem (task) or specific performance area" [1978, p. 182] and creativity as the "ability to set aside established conventions and procedures when appropriate") ended by reverting to gifted education's standard language of contextless, general abilities. Instead of the focus being children's actual accomplishments, we are once again hearing about a series of stable, nonconditional traits that belong to a particular class of people. This oscillation between performance-talk and ability-talk is particularly striking in Renzulli's (1986) "The Three-Ring Conception of Giftedness." There, Renzulli (p. 60) flirts with radical reformulation: "I believe that a term such as *the gifted* is counterproductive to educational efforts aimed at identification and programming for certain students in the general school population. Rather, it is my hope that in years ahead we will shift our emphasis from the present concept of "being gifted" (or not being gifted) to a concern about developing *gifted behaviors* in those youngsters who have the highest potential "for benefiting from special education services." However, the awkwardness of the term "gifted behaviors" is a dead giveaway. What is really going on is a kind of ruse in which gifted child scholars acknowledge a problematic practice (e.g., the reification of giftedness), so that they can continue to engage in that practice. That is, only by acknowledging distaste for treating gifted-ness as a "golden chromosome," as a trait people either have or don't have, can they legitimately continue to treat giftedness in this way. Interestingly, Renzulli (Renzulli and Reis 1991, pp. 182–183) is at least partially aware of the rhetorical significance of this language shift: "In this regard, we should judiciously avoid saying that a young person is either gifted or not gifted. It is difficult to gain support for programs when we use as a rationale statements such as, Elaine is a gifted third grader. It is precisely these kinds of statements that offend many people and raise all the accusations of elitism that have plagued our field."

Nonetheless, Renzulli (1986, pp. 73–76) appears unable to resist sum-moning the traditional language by which gifted children are described in terms of a complex series of abilities. This is particularly apparent within the subsection of the "Three-Ring Conception of Giftedness" dealing with a "taxonomy" of the "behavioral manifestations" of each "cluster of giftedness." We can see that these clusters (general and spe-cific ability, task commitment, and creativity) are never in fact described in terms of specific behaviors, performances, or accomplishments. In-stead, they are consistently portrayed as general abilities existing within people, as absolute traits that occur apart from specific situations and cultural expectations:

Well above-average ability
General ability:
High levels of abstract thinking, verbal and numerical reasoning, spatial
  relations, memory, and word fluency.

Adaptation to and the shaping of novel situations encountered in the external environment.

The automatization of information processing; rapid, accurate, and selective retrieval of information.

Specific ability:

The application of various combinations of the above general abilities to one or more specialized areas of knowledge or areas of human performance (e.g., the arts, leadership, administration).

The capacity for acquiring and making appropriate use of advanced amounts of formal knowledge, tacit knowledge, logistics, and strategy in the pursuit of particular problems or the manifestation of specialized areas of performance.

The capacity to sort out relevant and irrelevant information associated with a particular problem or area of study or performance.

Task commitment

The capacity for high levels of interest, enthusiasm, fascination, and involvement in a particular problem, area of study, or form of human expression.

The capacity for perseverance, endurance, determination, hard work, and dedicated practice.

Self-confidence, a strong ego and a belief in one's ability to carry out important work, freedom from inferiority feelings, drive to achieve.

The ability to identify significant problems within specialized areas; the ability to tune in to major channels of communication and new developments within given fields.

Setting high standards for one's work; maintaining an openness to self and external criticism; developing an aesthetic sense of taste, quality, and excellence about one's own work and the work of others.

Creativity

Fluency, flexibility, and originality of thought.

Openness to experience; receptive to that which is new and different (even irrational) in the thoughts, actions, and products of oneself and others.

Curious, speculative, adventurous, and "mentally playful"; willing to take risks in thought and action, even to the point of being uninhibited.

Sensitive to detail, aesthetic characteristics of ideas and things; willing to act on and react to external stimulation and one's own ideas and feelings.

Like Terman, Hollingworth, and Goddard 60 years earlier, Renzulli recognizes that the gifted child is one who not only has "high levels of abstract thinking, verbal, and numerical reasoning, spatial relations, memory and word fluency," but also sets high standards, has endurance, perseverance, originality, openness, self-confidence, and so forth. This child shines in all ways. Renzulli's argument that the gifted gestalt should represent a convergence of general and specific ability along with ample doses of "task commitment" and "creativity" fully mirrors the very definitions of giftedness this "new" conceptualization was intended to replace. Apparently, then, gifted child education survives critical challenges first by agreeing with them and then by proceeding to find new ways to adjust, represent, and keep on doing what it has always done.

By acknowledging that performance always depends on context, that it always depends on the culture and setting in which it occurs, that it cannot be predicted by standardized tests and defined in terms of some stable personality traits, gifted child scholars do not have to acknowledge to themselves or anyone else that their practices depend on the very beliefs they reject. Thus they do not have to defend or discontinue these practices. They can go about locating, studying, nurturing, and teaching gifted children as always.

According to Davis and Rimm (1985, p. 13), it is possible to acknowledge that giftedness is nondefinable in some standard, all-purpose way without experiencing any breaches, interruptions, or inconsistencies at the level of practice: "As a final solution to the definition challenge, we repeat that (1) there is no one final and agreed-upon definition of gifted and talented, (2) the specific definition that a program accepts will determine the selection instruments and procedures, and (3) for any program those instruments and decision criteria will actually define who is gifted'." As Borland (1989, p. 166) put it, "Giftedness should be defined differently in different settings, but in a manner that is logical and consistent with the realities that obtain in each of those settings."

This solution makes the selection of giftedness nonproblematic at the program level, because whoever fits a specific program's criteria would be seen as "gifted." Still, if there are as many definitions of giftedness as there are instruments and programs to measure them, then general statements about the "the gifted" appear logically impossible. Indeed, because new instruments and gifted programs can always be anticipated, one can easily argue that giftedness as a concept can never be circumscribed by its operationalizations and that the accumulation and transfer of gifted child knowledge across settings is impossible. However, that argument is never made. At the level of practical action the logical possibility of continuing or discontinuing the study of gifted children is irrelevant and uninteresting.

To say gifted child scholars are not "interested" in theoretical or logical consistency is not to point to their error or to the opportunities they miss (Garfinkel 1967, p. 8). What it means is that the capacity to identify gifted children, to train gifted child teachers, to conduct gifted child classes, and to make general, nonconditional statements about them is of such singular relevance to the survival of gifted child education that all other considerations are nonexistent.

PRESERVATION THROUGH SELF-REFLECTION

I have referred to gifted child scholars' "obliviousness" to the methods by which their faith in gifted children is sustained. But what appears as a profound sort of carelessness or naivete is itself an artful, subtle accomplishment without which gifted child scholarship could not continue. Although the creative accomplishment of gifted child education may be said to rely on the construction of its own obliviousness, that obliviousness is never total or complete (cf. Hilbert 1977). Ironically, obliviousness to the possibility of a world without gifted children is sustained and supported by reflective activity. Put another way, gifted child scholarship· conserves itself through continual self-examination, the identification of uncertainties, and the recognition of failure.

If, according to Austin (1962, p. 70), an object's reality is most effectively established not through positive assertion of that object's characteristics, but by excluding the possible ways it is *not* real, then the elaboration of what gifted education is not and should not be implicitly affirms what gifted education is and must be. Because "talk of deception only *makes sense* against a background of general non-deception" (Austin 1962, p. 11), the continual discussion of deceptive practices within gifted education supports and sustains the constancy and validity of gifted education's underlying principles. Like Descartes (1641/1960) in the *Meditations*, continual doubting leads to an indubitable truth.

To illustrate, Robert J. Sternberg (1982) wrote a paper called "Lies We Live By: Misapplication of Tests in Identifying the Gifted" that attacked several practices associated with identifying gifted children. He questions, for example, the practice of treating exact-sounding test scores— e.g., "an IQ score of 119, an SAT score of 580, a creativity score in the 74th percentile"—as accurate predictors of giftedness. Sternberg (p. 160) backed his claim with this anecdote:

> A teacher's college in Mississippi required a score of 25 on the Miller for admissions. The use of this cutoff was suspect, to say the least, since 25 represents a chance score on the test. (There are 100 items with four answer options per item, and no penalty for guessing is subtracted for wrong answers.) A promising student was admitted to the college despite a sub-25 Miller score, and went through the program with distinction. When it came time for the student to receive a diploma, she was informed

that the diploma would be withheld until she could take the test and receive a score of at least 25. I am pleased to say that she did in fact retake the test and receive the requisite chance score. But I am less pleased with the logic behind the readministration: The predictor had somehow come to surpass the criterion in importance! The test had become an end rather than a means.

Although this story's explicit message is that standardized tests are often inaccurate, the story's implicit message is that giftedness (and nongiftedness) represent constant, discoverable realities against which the accuracy of intelligence tests can always be assessed. Sternberg's paper thus creates the outward appearance of undermining gifted child education but on another level preserves gifted education by isolating sources of trouble and labeling them exceptional. Analysis of the deceptiveness of standardized tests implicitly supports the inherent accessibility and knowability of giftedness. Put somewhat differently, Sternberg shows that tests of giftedness lie but giftedness does not.

To further illustrate how self-criticism sustains the reality of giftedness, let's examine a paper Richert (1991) wrote for the *Handbook of Gifted Education*. In this paper, she condemned a host of practices associated with gifted children:

1. Elitist and distorted definitions of giftedness
2. Confusion about the purpose of identification
3. Violation of education equity
4. Cosmetic and distorting use of multiple criteria
5. Exclusive program design (1991, p. 81).

The net result of this display of indignation is that gifted child education is distanced from these questionable practices. The more strident the condemnations of elitism and inequity within gifted education, the less appropriate it becomes to blame gifted education itself.[4]

Richert argues that "many states and districts are using elitist definitions of giftedness that include only certain kinds of gifted students, most often those who are white, middle class, and academically achieving" (p. 81). However, these failures are not attributed to gifted education but rather to the practitioners who "distort" gifted education's ideology: "Some state or local definitions distort the intention by inappropriately distinguishing between gifted and talented, creating a hierarchy by using the former for general intellectual ability . . . and the latter for other gifted abilities" (p. 81). Although Richert abhors a reality in which "some gifted students are consistently being screened out by present prevalent practices" (p. 83), the fault is not with the concept of screening students for giftedness. Instead, the fault is attributed to the misapplication of this concept: "Tests are being used in ways that test makers never intended, sometimes to measure abilities that they were not designed to determine" (p. 83). Richert (p. 85) calls programs that serve only 2% to 5% of students "elitist." Again, however, the blame is not attributed to the underlying premise by which the gifted are selected from the multitude but to the manner in which this premise is operationalized: "While programs for the gifted, by definition, cannot serve all children, serving fewer than 25% of students will exclude too many students with gifted potential."

Through this mode of argument, the failures of gifted education do not challenge its foundations but are elaborated in such way that they reflexively affirm them. In other words, failures are used as resources for organizing, identifying, and explaining the "core meaning" of gifted education (cf. Hilbert 1992, pp. 93–95). Furthermore, by displaying passionate outrage at deviations from these core assumptions, they are implicitly removed from consideration as possible topics in their own right. Thus what begins as condemnation is not only transformed into affirmation but an affirmation that curtails mindful attention to the premises of its arguments.

Richert (pp. 93–94) concludes with the reassurance that gifted student programs can be equitable and nonelitist if practitioners recognize "that the purpose of identification and programmatic provisions for the gifted is not to label or to reward achievement or conformity to school expectations, but to find and develop exceptional potential." An outsider reading this statement out of context might wonder why students who achieve at high levels and do what is expected ("conform") shouldn't be labeled and rewarded. Why is it more equitable to label and reward those who show "potential" for high achievement while passing over those who actually achieve? However, readers of Richert's paper, themselves members of the gifted subuniverse, never ask these questions. These concluding statements are glossed as self-evident truths. After continually reading about the "wrongness" of practices that contradict the core meaning of giftedness, readers presumably have renewed confidence that the core project, the identification and nurturance of "exceptional potential," is essentially unquestionable.

Ironically, then, gifted child scholarship preserves itself not by overlooking the "errors" of its practices but by continually reflecting on them. "Error" discourse within gifted child scholarship represents a never-ending process of affirming the "correctness" of gifted education's core assumptions. By continually noting inconsistencies between these assumptions and actual practice, gifted child scholars have new evidence of the fundamentally consistent and reasonable character of those assumptions. Because the examination of "error" within gifted child practice depends on the belief in gifted children as a real, "out there" entity, that belief is taken for granted and disattended during "error" discourse. Thus, gifted child scholars always find themselves confronting a world that is problematic in its particulars: Is "task commitment" really a component of giftedness? Should a gifted child program recruit from the top 5%, 10%, 15%, or 25% of students? Does culture have a major impact on giftedness? Should minority group students be recruited into gifted programs in a different way? But, at the level of its fundamental assumptions, there are no such questions. Gifted children remain an incorrigible truth.

7

From Giftedness to Nongiftedness: Assembling Ordinary Children

> How many times has it occurred to me that the quiet of the night made me dream of my usual habits: that I was here, clothed in a dressing gown, and sitting by the fire, although I was in fact lying undressed in bed! It seems to me now, that I am not looking at this paper with my eyes closed, and that this head that I shake is not drugged with sleep, that it is with design and deliberate intent that I stretch out this hand and perceive it. What happens in sleep seems not at all as clear and distinct as all this.
>
> From *Meditations* by René Descartes (1641/1960)

To know the meaning of wakefulness, we must know the countermeaning of dreams. Our understanding of one phenomenon depends on our understanding of the other. So it is with giftedness and nongiftedness. Although gifted child educators may appear to speak only of the "superiority" of the gifted and say nothing overtly negative about the nongifted, it is impossible to make the gifted's "superiority" happen or appear without a conceptualization of a comparison group.

To imagine how perception of the superior depends on perception of the inferior, we might look at the contrasts by which Jodie Foster displayed the gifted boy in her film *Little Man Tate*. She made us believe in Tate's giftedness not only by portraying his sensitivity and erudition but also by constantly treating us to images of the nongifted's stupidity, brutality, coarseness: Here an ordinary child is picking his nose; here another is hitting a child over the head; we see two boys fighting with pencils; still, others are teasing and calling names. While Tate examines a Van Gogh still life, the nongifted students are sitting impassively, rocking, tapping, staring blankly. Against such backdrops, Tate's alertness and sophistication are striking. Conversely, in comparison to Tate, the nongifted appear as a lower life form.

The most general consequence of this linkage between giftedness and nongiftedness is that we always have nongiftedness at the same time as—and precisely because—we have giftedness (cf. Douglas 1970, p. 4). Going further, we may even say that the more intense the belief in giftedness, the more intense will be the belief in nongiftedness: "An age of saints . . . will also necessarily be an age of satans or demons and vice versa" (Douglas 1970, p. 4). And just as individuals strive for goodness to the same degree they strive against evil, so we can expect gifted child advocates to hold ordinariness in contempt in direct proportion to their admiration of giftedness. The most positive affirmations of giftedness always occur alongside the most negative characterizations of the nongifted.

ASSEMBLING ORDINARINESS

According to gifted child scholarship's rhetoric of inclusion, the gifted are not more special or unique than anyone else. They are not worth more. They do not deserve more. Gifted education does not foster and support social hierarchies. Sandra Kaplan (1989b) elaborated this position at the Alberta Colloquium on Giftedness:

> We know that the real definition of giftedness is to possess certain degrees and dimensions of characteristics to a greater extent than do others. We're talking about the fact that all of us are curious but we know that some of us have more curiosity more highly developed than others. We know all of us have a potential for creativity. Some of us have greater degree and more kinds of dimensions to that creativity than do others. So when I talk about gifted children, I'm not talking about those who are different. I'm talking about those who differ. I could be certainly not-gifted and still be curious and creative. You could be not-gifted and be curious and creative. But there are those who are gifted whose curiosity and creativity, as an example, exceed the expectations in degree and dimension that we anticipate the norm to be.

Kaplan and other gifted child scholars deny that gifted child discourse assumes a two-tiered caste system with the gifted representing the good and deserving, and the "not-gifted" representing the negative. On the contrary, says Kaplan, *both* gifted and nongifted children can be curious and creative. The distinction is one of degree, not kind. These children differ but are not different.

To clarify this issue, we briefly consider Wittgenstein's (1953, p. 194) "duck-rabbit":

When one looks at Wittgenstein's "duck-rabbit," one does not see an amalgam of a duck and a rabbit; one sees either a picture of a duck or a picture of a rabbit. They are not seen simultaneously. Nor do the duck and rabbit pictures shade or melt into one another. Although we may speak of these pictures as having commonalities, we perceive each in strict either/or fashion. The same goes for giftedness and nongiftedness. Like the duck and the rabbit, gifted and nongifted children have several characteristics in common. Just as the duck and the rabbit have the same dot for an eye and the same double lines for a neck, both gifted and nongifted children may be curious and creative. And just as we do not perceive the duck and the rabbit differing "by degree," so child x who is defined as gifted is not seen as partially gifted and partially nongifted. Child x is not 75% gifted and 25% nongifted. Child x is simply gifted. Accordingly, although there are many ways to designate commonalities between giftedness and nongiftedness, and any one of these commonalities can be expressed in terms of a continuum, the gestalt of giftedness and nongiftedness can only be identified in absolute or categorical terms.

This is perhaps clearest when comparisons between the gifted and the nongifted are conducted in a straightforward, explicit fashion. Consider, for example, our previous discussion of how Hollingworth (1942/1975, pp. 259–260) continuously elevated the gifted by portraying the nongifted as a mob of violent, unruly fools. For example, a 10-year-old gifted boy

> wishes to discuss with his own likenesses the events of medieval history, but he finds they make him no reply. And if he persists, they become annoyed, hurling at him the dreaded epithet, Perfessor. If he still persists, they pull his hair, tear his shirt from his back, and hit him with a beer bottle. (I am speaking of *real* life.)

Similarly, when Davis (1924, p. 134) observed that gifted children needed to be told only once not to chew gum for that behavior to cease, whereas "in a class composed of normal children, exposed to the same suggestion, no fewer than fifteen pupils in the period of one week were asked to remove gum from their mouths," the contrast is between fundamentally different categories of people. To Davis, the gifted are unique in terms of their standards and truthfulness, their ability to govern themselves, assume responsibility, and respect the rights of others.

Newland (1976, p. 42) provides another example of an explicit contrast between giftedness and nongiftedness. The focus here is on a categorically different type of thinking ability:

> Central to the matter of the non-gifted's "picking up" the gifted's learnings or strategies is his basic capacity to do so. The story is told of the girl who expressed considerable frustration in finding out what "x" was equal to; she said she had kept a full record of the different numbers she had found for "x," and they didn't agree at all! Hers was a failure of conceptualization. For one to learn "osmotically" from any group, he must possess an adequate armamentarium of whatever symbols (words, signs, and other notations) are contributive to that learning, must be able to abstract and generalize, and must be capable of seeing less-frequently recognized and understood relationships that are involved in that learning. This, of course, is the forte of the gifted—the characteristics that most clearly differentiate them from their slower-learning classmates.

And here we can see how the nongifted appear dull, helpless, and inefficient when directly compared to the gifted:

> The mentally gifted can learn to perform any kind of work, at will or at need, through the whole gamut of occupations, for as a group they are physically as well as mentally superior. At need, the gifted man can even perform his professional tasks and do his own manual work also. The millions at and below mediocrity cannot do likewise. They cannot carry on their manual tasks and at the same time serve their own needs in the fields of thought, such as medicine, surgery, law, education, chemistry, international diplomacy, religion, and the management of commerce. (Hollingworth 1926, p. 361)

Still, I do not wish to suggest that explicit contrasts between the gifted and nongifted are common. The contrary is true. Texts on giftedness routinely describe these children without direct reference to the nongifted. Because the purpose of this discourse is not the lowering of the nongifted but the elevation of the gifted, the nongifted rarely assume center stage in gifted child texts and research studies. Consider, for example, that among the 32 papers published in the *Gifted Child Quarterly* from 1988 through 1991 that examined samples of gifted children, only seven used samples of nongifted children to assess contrasts empirically.

The favored method for displaying the nongifted does not consist of direct description of their failures and inadequacies. Rather, the portrait of the inferior group is most commonly elaborated implicitly and indirectly through description of the gifted's superiority. In this regard, every expression used to describe gifted students has an implicit reverse meaning for the nongifted. To illustrate, Hollingworth's (1926, p. 145) assertion that the gifted "are temperamentally more disposed to fair play, sympathy, kindliness, and honesty than are children at large" also means that the nongifted are temperamentally *less* disposed to fair play, sympathy, kindliness, and honesty. Similarly, "the composite impression . . . of a population which values independence, which is more task- and contribution-oriented than recognition-oriented, which prizes integrity and independent judgment in decision-making" (Martinson, quoted in Newland 1976, p. 82) creates the "composite impression" of another population who values conformity, is not task- and contribution-oriented, a population who does not prize integrity and independent decision making.

Consider the phrases most commonly associated with giftedness (Terman 1919, p. 260): "Has such keen powers of observation," "shows a passionate desire to learn," "asks endless questions," "is interested in everything," "is ambitious to excel," "writes such wonderful examination papers," "has such a fine command of language," "has fine reasoning powers," "answers always to the point," "has a keen sense of humor," "is more dependable than other children his age," "conscientious to a fault," "such a lovely child," and so on. These phrases only make sense alongside the belief that the nongifted do not have keen powers of observation, do not show a passionate desire to learn, do not write wonderful examination papers, do not have a fine command of language, fine reasoning powers or keen sense of humor. Thus, the phrase "such a lovely child" can only be called a gifted child descriptor if we treat it as exceptional for the nongifted.

Here we might use another Wittgenstein (1953, p. 207) drawing—the "double cross"—to illustrate how discussion of the gifted's superiority defines the nongifted as inferior.

The black cross and the white cross can be discussed in isolation from one another; however, they cannot be perceived or understood in isolation. Unlike the duck and the rabbit pictures, which are not recognized simultaneously and which do not imply one another, the white and black crosses are perceived together, and every angle and line in the black cross necessitates the specific dimensions of every angle and line in the white cross. The outlines of one cross define the other. As a result, any description or understanding of the one, silently defines the other. It is in this regard that all talk about the gifted necessarily elaborates a sense and appearance of nongiftedness. However, just as "you could teach someone the idea of the black cross on a ground of a different colour" (Wittgenstein 1953, p. 208), there is a sense in which the specific colorations of the nongifted remain unclear when we speak only of the gifted. In other words, when we speak of the gifted's superiority, when we say, for example, "the gifted think better," we see an outline of the nongifted's inferiority, but they are otherwise undifferentiated.

Accordingly, through positive discourse on giftedness, the feeble-minded, the dull, and the average are lumped into a single colorless, undifferentiated mass. They are so joined not in order to suppress or malign them. Rather, the purpose is to recognize the gifted who themselves are portrayed as the suppressed population: "Children of superior ability are often submerged with the masses simply because they are not recognized" (Terman 1919, p. 165).

Differentiating the gifted from the nongifted is thus explained as a rescue operation organized by caring people with good intentions. This social control is unremittingly positive: "Educational programs for the gifted are not part of a plot for the elite to take over the world, but rather a desperate attempt on the part of parents and caring educators to try and create a better learning environment for these students" (Gallagher 1993, p. 20). Far from an effort to deny resources or recognition to the nongifted, this pedagogy seeks to provide superior children the recognition and resources due all children: "Every child, whether subnormal, normal, or supernormal, has a right to the kind of education which is best suited to his powers and his needs. . . . It is just as important for the bright child to acquire correct habits of work as it is for the dull or average child to do so" (Henry 1920, p. 9). Far from being elitist, this pedagogy is the only truly democratic way of treating gifted children: "There is a difference between providing an equal *education* for all students and providing an equal *opportunity* for all students to acquire an education commensurate with their abilities. The gifted program provides them with opportunities to exercise their potential that often would not be possible if there were no such school program" (Olstad 1978, p. 188). In Kaplan's (1989) words, "All I want is for them to have their fair share of the opportunity for an appropriate education."

What goes unsaid, however, is that the belief that one group has extraordinary potential is based on the presumption that a contrast group has a conspicuously different sort of potential. Nowhere is this clearer than in the discussion of the gifted's leadership training. For the gifted to lead, the nongifted must follow. If, according to Plowman (1981, p. 15), the gifted leader "figures out what is wrong," "shows others how to solve problems," "handles abstract ideas and sees a broad perspective," and "plans and follows through," then the nongifted are those who are told what is wrong and are taught how to solve problems; they are the ones who have the narrow perspective and need to have someone make plans for them. In Lindsay's (1981, p. 10) words, "It would appear that the [leadership] quest is not the domain of the masses; to the contrary, it is most likely the domain of the gifted, and in particular the gifted in leadership. Not only must they know the way, they must be able to show the way."

We can see that, although gifted child scholars might argue that "all human characteristics, from intellectual abilities to personality traits, can be seen as occurring in individuals somewhere on a continuum that ranges from little potential or capacity to highly developed ability in the given characteristic" (Schiever 1993, p. 207), they always end by treating giftedness as a dichotomous variable representing a difference in kind rather than degree. And we can also see that whatever is treated as the opposite of giftedness is reconstituted as negative by virtue of this comparison. The nongifted may be called by different names—the mass, the mediocre, the dull, the average, the normal or ordinary—but they always have the same negative valence when their existence is invoked in comparison to the gifted.

Here (Hollingworth (1942/1975, pp. 274–275) makes it clear that nongifted 6-year-olds cannot play or even speak the same language as gifted children of the same chronological age: "Children of six years old are ordinarily incapable of becoming interested in long-sustained, complicated games which lead to remote goals, but are, on the contrary, characteristically satisfied by the kind of random activity which bored this child of 187 IQ. The playmates of ordinary intelligence naturally resented persistent efforts to reform them and to organize them for the attainment of remote goals. Furthermore, they did not have in their vocabulary words that the gifted child knew well, used habitually, and took for granted. Literally, they could not understand each other" (Hollingworth 1942/1975, pp. 274–275).

Apparently, the child who thinks, speaks, and acts better is seen as fundamentally different. What remains to consider is how the ceaseless elaboration of a two-tiered caste system harms those on the lower level.

THE EFFECTS OF ORDINARINESS

Whether the continual contrast between the gifted and nongifted actually has an adverse effect on the nongifted is largely answered in a study Dewey Cornell (1983) did on gifted children's family experiences. Using a sample of 42 families with children ages 6 to 11, 22 of whom have children attending gifted programs, Cornell found that having a gifted child is associated with greater feelings of pride and closeness by parents. The gifted child is the focus of this pride and has the highest status in the family. By contrast, the nongifted siblings of gifted children are significantly less well adjusted than other nongifted siblings. Cornell describes the nongifted siblings of gifted children as less outgoing, more easily upset, and more shy and restrained. They were also more excitable and impatient and more tense and frustrated.

Eleanor Fisher (1981, p. 50) noted that parents appear more accepting of their gifted child's unusual requests and behavior: "Parents inferred that their gifted children were 'entitled' to be given wider berth, more opportunities, more allowances." Requests for "secret places," "hundreds of rocks in the playroom," "yards of string to make a magic web," and to "paint his room black," were suddenly understandable once the child was labeled gifted. "I hate those slimy things he collects and I don't think it endears him to all his teachers, but who knows, he might turn out to be a great scientist," was one parent's assessment. Another parent explained how giftedness made a difference: "My sister said we were foolish to spend all our leisure time in museums with a six year old, but we knew it was important to him." Still another said, "I'm glad now I didn't fight him every time he made some weird request."

In particular, fathers appear more engrossed in their gifted child: "I look at his homework every night and if he doesn't have any, I give him half a dozen problems to do. It's my way of being close with him and sharing something I'm good at" (Fisher 1981, p. 50). Fathers spend more special time with gifted children: "I take them on special outings. Her to the ballet, him to Yankee Stadium. I know that sounds sexist but it's their choice. I take them where they want to go. It's a special treat for both of us." When asked if he would do these things with his children if they were not gifted, this father replied: "I really can't answer that, but I can tell you I get a charge out of being with these special kids." A different father said: "I'm not ashamed to say I take her to work with me to show off. I figure if she's gifted she can afford to miss a day and she'll learn more in court with me than she can possibly get in one day at school. My wife doesn't complain so much now that she's in the gifted program."

Having a child labeled gifted has almost the universal effect of legit- imizing parents' rights to demand special services and programs from the school (Fisher 1981, p. 50). This finding is summarized by one parent who claimed: "Labeling my son gives him and me the credentials we need. Now I am no longer seen as just another pushy mother. Now hopefully he will get the special attention he needs."

In my own observations of gifted children in family therapy (dis- cussed in detail in the next chapter), I was struck by how listless and detached the nongifted were in comparison to their gifted siblings. Whether this difference is a result of giftedness or represents a reaction to what goes on at home or is simply a reaction to family therapy at a clinic for gifted children, I cannot say. However, I did note that the nongifted were rarely addressed or noticed during the family thera- py sessions. They were treated as entirely peripheral to what was going on. Reflecting their secondary role, a few of the nongifted dozed during the family therapy sessions. Others attempted to get some attention for themselves by protesting their secondary status but in the end were passed over or ignored in favor of the gifted sibling. For example, one nongifted sibling whispered something to her mother, prompting the mother to say, "She has felt very left out that we really haven't involved her and that she really didn't need to be here and she's been very vocal about why do I have to go." The therapist appeared somewhat confused by this comment, repeated the question, "Why do you have to come?" then after a moment said, "Well, that's something for me to learn too." Then, turning her attention to the gifted sibling, asked, "What about you, R?" The gifted brother assumed center stage with assurance, saying "I don't know . . . I guess I gained a little more responsibility out of all um a little more awareness of what everyone around me thought. . . ."

Perhaps the most dramatic event in the assembly of nongiftedness is rejection by a gifted child program. Just as the symbol that most specifi- cally characterizes giftedness is admission to a gifted program, so the most distinguishing symbol of nongiftedness is the failure to get in.

> I received a letter from my son's school stating that, because of one test result, my son was "not an exceptional student" and thus, would not be admitted to the local gifted program called "Search." Knowing that my son had been doing extra work in school for two years, that every one of his teachers had recommended him for the program, and that test scores are not always accurate, I asked the principal if my son could monitor the program. The principal refused, while the psychologist became upset that I questioned the test result. The principal said monitoring "would make more work for me" while the psychologist stated that my son's presence

would "dilute the magic" found in the group of gifted kids. (Karnes and Marquardt 1991b, p. 39)

One family expressed its outrage over their children's rejection from gifted programs through a series of court battles that lasted several years (*Lisa H. v. Board of Education* [1983]; *Doe v. Commonwealth of Education* [1984]; *Roe v. Commonwealth of Education* [1987]). As plaintiffs, they argued that rejection from the gifted program denied them a proper education, and that the expenditure of funds on gifted programs denied them their fair share of educational resources. The plaintiffs also argued that their exclusion from the gifted program violated their freedom of speech under the First Amendment. It was not a question of thwarting their speech, but rather that they were denied access to the ideas disseminated in the gifted programs (Karnes and Marguardt 1991a, p. 49). Each of these arguments was dismissed by both state and federal courts.

Because the large majority of gifted students spend all but two or three hours per week in regular classrooms (Archambault et al. 1993), comparison or differentiation between members of the gifted and nongifted populations is not an exceptional, one-time only event. If most gifted education occurs among the ordinary and "a quality curriculum for gifted children is one that enables them to display, to demonstrate, to exhibit, to show off, the . . . characteristics that define them as gifted" (Kaplan 1989b), then ordinary children can be expected to routinely bear witness to these displays. In fact, without ordinary children serving as audience and contrast group, the exhibition of giftedness would not be possible. Weiler's (1978, p. 185) study of gifted and nongifted students' interactions in regular classrooms illustrate:

> A teacher of second grade assembled her six MGM [mentally gifted minors] children at a table to build a gingerbread house from graham crackers, candy and icing. The rest of the children, who were seated in the same room and had been assigned math workbook exercises, watched the fun the MGMs were having. (The work-book exercises were not remedial; some of the nonMGMs were, in fact, achieving far better in math than some of the gingerbread builders).
>
> Later the principal explained that the gingerbread house was a culminating activity for the MGMs' "qualitatively different" study of geometric shapes; to use his words, "They couldn't *all* make a gingerbread house!"

Other examples include the time the gifted from the second through sixth grades went to a computer center and played videogames: "The children also named favorite colors, friends, pets, and pastimes; using this information, the computer printed out a personalized story for each child. When they returned to school, the children shared the excitement of their trip with classmates who had not been able to go" (Weiler 1978, p. 185).

According to Weiler, the nongifted participate in gifted activities, too, but as the audience: A movie made by the gifted (a soap opera entitled "As the Stomach Turns") was presented at a school open house ostensibly so that all could get some benefit from gifted children's activities. Similarly, the gifted interested in space travel built and launched model rockets with funds set aside for the gifted program. Again, the role of the nongifted was that of observers: "The launchings were performed during P. E. class so that all children could watch what gifted children . . . do" (Weiler 1978, p. 185).

Although gifted children are mixed with ordinary children in regular classes partly to make their special education less conspicuous and to avoid the appearance of elitism, the gifted are routinely pulled from these classes so that they can receive their "qualitatively different" educational experience. Indeed, some of the field trips they are pulled out for are quite costly, appear inexplicably like vacations or rewards, and are clearly appealing to both the gifted and nongifted: "MGMs flew from Northern California to Palm Springs for two days to study the terrain. Another trip was a flight to San Diego for a two-day boat trip out of La Jolla. I understand that the purpose of this trip was to study whales and marine ecology. (I have since been told that MGMs from another junior high enjoyed a three-day trip to Yosemite to study biology and geology)" (Weiler 1978, pp. 185–186).

No one says that gifted children are more deserving. And no one argues for a first-class education for the gifted and a second-class education for everybody else. Yet, if ordinary children do not get to build gingerbread houses, make films, visit computer centers, launch rockets, go on boat trips, and study whales when they would enjoy and prefer to participate, they can only conclude they are undeserving. If ordinary children are not provided a clear rationale for their exclusion, their exclusion feels unjust.

CONSULTING THE ORACLE

How do gifted child scholars conceal from themselves the possibility that their treatment of the nongifted is unjust? How do they eliminate any doubt that a separate and unequal education is beneficial? These questions are answered by examining a ritual gifted child scholars perform over and over again. Whenever they have doubts, doubts about their practices, doubts about the nature of giftedness and how to differentiate gifted children, they consult an oracle. They prepare for these consultations by following a strictly prescribed set of procedures. They begin by formulating a question about gifted children that can be answered in a yes or no fashion. Then they select groups of gifted and nongifted children and administer measures or instruments that are specifically designed to produce signs that can be interpreted as an answer to the original yes/no question.

From start to finish, the ritual requires the demonstration of complete impartiality, of openness to any verdict, of painstaking commitment to ensuring that the oracle is interpreted correctly. To cite one example, when Rick Shade (1991, p. 137) attempted to learn whether gifted children have a superior sense of humor, he did not use just any sample of children: "To assure certain subgroups were represented in the sample, a stratified sampling technique was employed. All fourth grade students in each district were divided into one of the following four groups: gifted (GT) boys ($n = 38$), GT girls ($n = 42$), general population (GP) boys ($n = 475$), and GP girls ($n = 525$). Subsamples of ten subjects each were then selected at random from each of the four groups." Similarly, not just any measures and instruments were used, but only those that have a history, that have been tested and, as scholars say, "validated": "Humor response was assessed using a measure known as the Children's Mirth Response Test (Zigler, Levine & Gould, 1966) adapted from the Mirth Response Test (Redlich, Levine & Sohler, 1951). . . . The CMRT has been used in other studies (Cupchik & Leventhal, 1974; Klein, 1985; Masten, 1986; Pickering, Pickering & Buchanan, 1987; Prentice & Fathman, 1975; Shultz & Horibe, 1974; Zigler, Levine & Gould, 1967)" (Shade 1991, pp. 137–139).

To ensure impartiality, those who administered the Children's Mirth Response Test were not told in advance who the gifted and nongifted children were. Moreover, reading ability and word recognition played no part in the outcome, because the various items on the Mirth Test (the jokes that were used to elicit the Mirth Response) were played on audiotape. Here are some examples of CMRT items (jokes):

> Tim: "What geometric figure is like a lost parrot?"
> Sue: "Polygon!"
>
> Once Democratic politician William Jennings Bryan, finding no stage at a country meeting on which to stand, climbed up on a manure spreader and said to the crowd, "Ladies and Gentlemen! This is the first time I have addressed an audience from a Republican platform!"

Responses to these jokes were also judged in accordance with a pretested, prevalidated scale:

0 = Negative response (grimace, etc.)
1 = No response (blank stare, etc.)
2 = Half or slight smile
3 = Full smile
4 = Laugh

When all the results were in, the answer to the yes/no question was unequivocal: "in spontaneous mirth response and comprehension of verbal humor, gifted students performed to a significantly higher degree than students from the general population" (Shade 1991, p. 145).

The question that we bring to this, based on our portrayal of gifted education as a cultural phenomenon, is that jokes and the ways people respond to them, have different meanings to every social group. A half smile for the members of one cultural group cannot be judged as equivalent to a half smile for members of a different population. Accordingly, the finding that the gifted were more likely to break into a full smile rather than a slight smile on hearing any CRMT joke may have more to do with the social and ethnic groups to which these populations belong than with giftedness and nongiftedness. This does not mean, of course, that gifted child scholars did something wrong, that their methodology is incorrect—that they should control for social class and race in their ANOVAs or use different control groups. Rather, I am saying that the oracular consultation is a ruse. Whereas gifted child scholars conduct their studies under the pretense that the oracle could conceivably answer their questions with either a yes or a no; in fact, only one answer ever occurs: there are no verdicts coming from the oracle that conflict with belief in gifted children's superiority. In every instance, ordinary children appear inferior.

Similarly, in every instance, gifted children appear more likely to benefit from gifted child programs than do their nongifted peers. This is because when scholars assess gifted child programs, they frame the inquiry in such way that only one verdict is possible. For example, when scholars test whether a gifted child program works, they examine the program's effects on the gifted students who participate (either through a before and after study design or through use of a gifted child control group). What they do not do is examine the benefit that might be derived from using the same or equivalent resources with the nongifted. Because they do not ask whether program benefits given the gifted are important or worthwhile relative to the needs of the nongifted, the nongifted are seen as having only a phantom existence.

To illustrate, when assessing the efficacy of an enrichment program for gifted learning disabled children, Susan Baum (1988, p. 230) noted an improvement in the gifted subjects' self-esteem. She concluded: "Perhaps the major reason this program was successful was that, for the first time, these students were singled out for their special abilities rather than their disability." All of this was well-intentioned, but is it any surprise that a group of children—any group of children—would respond this way to large doses of positive attention and support? By limiting the inquiry to the gifted, however, a program that could reasonably benefit all children was treated as if it was only suitable to the gifted. The conclusion that "gifted learning disabled children require a supportive environment which values and appreciates all individual abilities" (Baum 1988, p. 230) appears justified based on the way the question was framed. But if we now believe that "gifted learning disabled students must become aware of their strengths and weaknesses and be helped to cope with the wide discrepancy between them" (Baum 1988, p. 230), then, implicitly, nongifted learning-disabled students do not have to become aware of their strengths and weaknesses. What is conspicuously vital for the gifted is conspicuously less vital for the nongifted.

From 1988 through 1992, I located 13 studies in *Gifted Child Quarterly* and the *Journal for the Education of the Gifted* that assessed the efficacy of various programs on gifted children. Because only one of these studies compared the effects of such programs on both the gifted and the ordinary,[1] we are left with the impression that gifted education is irrelevant to the ordinary, that it has no effects on them. We are left with the impression that excluding the nongifted is normal, reasonable, justifiable. And because we have these beliefs, the resources that go into gifted education are not seen as resources that are pulled from general education but are only considered a net gain for the gifted.

THIS IS NOT A CONSPIRACY

Despite appearances to the contrary, gifted child educators are not engaged in a conspiracy or plot against the ordinary. Whatever power is operating here is lighter, more subtle, and less self-conscious than anything describable as a "conspiracy" or "plot." In fact, gifted child educators seem completely unaware that the various questions asked of the oracle, and the various rituals employed to elicit signs, are designed in such way that they determine the nature of the answers. They cannot acknowledge the ruse, because they enact it on themselves. Because gifted child scholarship is threatened with absurdity and ultimate dissolution if it were to ever become aware that gifted children are constituted by scholars' own activities, scholars must continually struggle to obscure their own constitutive work. Put another way, gifted child scholarship survives by hiding from itself its own control over the accomplishment of oracular verdicts.

When we speak of power, then, we need to remind ourselves that gifted education does not function in a single direction. It is in fact a "double-entry system" (Foucault 1977a, p. 214): Power is enacted on the children who are included and excluded from gifted child programs but also on the people who run the apparatuses of inclusion and exclusion. This is what Foucault (1977a, p. 170) had in mind when he described discipline as "the specific technique of power that regards individuals both as objects and instruments of its exercise." This is a power, in other words, that acts on itself and also exists apart from an external system of domination that could be used to explain it (Foucault 1977a). Because the subjects of this power double as its objects, and because no one is aware that power is operating, no one is to blame. In the language of Foucault (1978, p. 94), "the logic is perfectly clear, the aims decipherable, yet it is often the case that no one is there to have invented them."

8

From Power to Knowledge:
How Discipline Makes
Gifted Children

> We must cease once and for all to describe the effects of power in negative
> terms: it "excludes," it "represses," it "censors." . . . In fact, power pro-
> duces; it produces reality; it produces domains of objects and rituals of
> truth. The individual and the knowledge that may be gained of him belong
> to this production.
>
> From *Discipline and Punish* by Michel Foucault (1977)

In this chapter I take one comparatively boundaried domain—a social
agency devoted to the treatment and assessment of gifted children—to
consider how disciplinary power "makes" gifted children (Foucault
1977a, p. 170).

Following Foucault (1977a, 1980), I define discipline as a power that
separates, evaluates, and ranks special populations, a power oriented to
the meticulous observation of detail, to gaining compliance through
induction and seduction rather than coercion, and one that utilizes continuous surveillance. In parallel fashion, we can see that naming gifted
children involves the assembly of social hierarchies; it depends on the
assumption that specific types of responses, abilities, and natures are
more desirable than others; and it involves a system of ranking achieved
through repetitive testing, observation, and comparison. Because people willingly have their children labeled and processed as "gifted," this
social control is not repressive or negative; instead, all the beliefs and
methodologies associated with giftedness involve positive expectations
and terminologies.

In keeping with the approach used in the earlier chapters, I attempt to
locate the gifted identity not in giftedness per se but in discourse. Given
the goal of determining how qualities are attributed to gifted children, I

121

pay particular attention to descriptions of gifted children, statements saying they are one thing and not another, statements with openings such as "The gifted are known to . . . " or "Since your son is gifted we can expect. . . ." However, to integrate the concept of "disciplinary power" into the analyses, I am not only concerned with the artful production of these attributions but also with how they cannot be withdrawn or proven false given the constraints under which this discourse is conducted.

This chapter assumes, then, that discourse on the gifted is not free or self-generating. We assume that accounting practices are inseparable from power relations: "Power and knowledge directly imply one another . . . there is no power relation without the correlative constitution of a field of knowledge, nor any knowledge that does not presuppose and constitute at the same time power relations" (Foucault 1977a, p. 27). The relations between power and knowing, therefore, are analyzable in terms of the ways power produces ways of knowing, talking, and acting, and how what is known, said, and done supports and affirms power.[1]

This chapter also assumes that discourse on giftedness is controlled according to certain external conditions that give rise to the discourse and fix its limits (Foucault 1969, p. 229). To illustrate, we might consider the way Foucault linked discourse on leprosy to the institution of the leprosarium. When Foucault (1965, p. 3) asserts, for example, that "at the end of the Middle Ages, leprosy disappeared from the Western World," he is referring to the termination of a particular mode of discourse caused by the closing of the leprosariums at the end of the fifteenth century. Although Foucault identifies leprosy as a social phenomenon, as something whose existence is defined through discourse, the demise of this discourse is attributed to something external to it, to a specific technology (the leprosarium) responsible for separating, recognizing, and understanding leprosy: "In every society the production of discourse is at once controlled, selected, organized and redistributed according to a certain number of procedures." (Foucault 1969, p. 216).

Following Foucault, I now examine how discipline makes giftedness appear, how the apparatuses of surveillance and accountability within a social agency devoted to assessing and treating gifted children are structured in such a way as to create and control knowledge of giftedness. We note that what appears as spontaneous recognition of giftedness should not be taken at face value but should be seen as an organized achievement, a display sanctioned and produced by a specific institutional order.[2]

Instead of only examining how therapists created "family therapy with a gifted child" as a rational, typical, patterned activity, we inquire into the social structures that direct and inform this process. Thus, instead of focusing exclusively on the methods whereby a range of assumptions and contextual features are mobilized to sustain the coherency and determinateness of "family therapy with gifted chidlren," we note how the conditions governing the discourse compel the formulation of some accounts rather than others.

THE GIFTED CHILDREN'S CENTER

The Gifted Children's Center[3] is a clinic specializing in the treatment and assessment of gifted children and their families. The fact that all family therapy sessions occurring at this clinic are videotaped for the purpose of providing supervision suggests a contemporary realization of the Panopticon's[4] "faceless gaze" (Foucault 1977a, p. 214). In this mode of observation, the see/being seen dyad is dissolved: One group is totally seen but does not see; the other sees everything but is unseen (Foucault 1977a, p. 202). This asymmetry creates disequilibrium among the observed, not only because persons who have power are behind the screen, but also because power is produced by the presence of persons behind the screen. The omniscience of video observation not only guarantees supervisors' capacity to intervene and control any dimension of family therapy deviating from agency policy, but also it means that supervisors have infinite opportunities to reward conformity. A phone connecting the unseen observers to those engaged in therapy mirrors this asymmetry in that calls only go one way: from the observers to the observed. Approximately two calls are made during each therapy session and usually result in the therapist introducing a new interpretation or topic for discussion. Although the phone messages appear supportive and encouraging, they remind the observed that intervention can occur at any moment. As a result, therapists are under continual pressure to appear as if they affirm and support the Gifted Children's Center's ideologies, policies, and rules.

Therapists are required to review their family therapy tapes after each session in preparation for a private meeting with the therapy supervisor during which the contents of the therapy session are reviewed. Consistent with Garfinkel (1974, p. 120) who noted that clinic records "are assembled with regard to the possibility that the relationship [between the clinician and patient] may have to be portrayed as having been in accord with expectations of sanctionable performances by clinicians and patients," therapists' anticipation of the review of the family therapy

tapes and their own accountability in supervision places them under
continual pressure during family therapy to produce the appearance of
"good work," to suppress their idiosyncratic responses to families in
favor of responses that are defendable displays of competence. In this
manner, "a relation of surveillance, defined and regulated, is inscribed
at the heart of the practice of teaching, not as an additional or adjacent
part, but as a mechanism that is inherent to it and which increases its
efficiency" (Foucault 1977a, p. 176).

Because therapists are graduate students, and their clinic supervisors
are also their professors, supervisors have double the capacity to compel
adherence to agency norms. However, in keeping with the expectation
that the workings of power must be concealed, therapists never appeared as if their performances were compulsory. Accordingly, whenever a supervisor calls during a family therapy session, directing the
therapist to talk about something different, the therapist never portrays
this as an order from a person in power. Instead, the supervisor's command is portrayed as a request from a "team": "The team feels we
should take another look at. . . ." Of course, there never was a "team."
The people behind the screen consist of three or four graduate stu-
dent/therapists, and their professor/supervisor. The decision to deliver
specific phone messages at specific times is not determined by some
consensus but is always determined unilaterally by the supervisor. The
only way in which one could account for calls as a "team" phenomenon
is that they never take place contrary to other members' wishes. If there
is disharmony or dissent in the observation room, it is unseen.

Thus, although the supervisor has direct, hierarchical power over the
conduct of therapy, that power never appears as direct or hierarchical.
Consistent with Foucault's (1977a, p. 177) description of "disciplinary
power" as "absolutely discreet," as "normalizing," no orders or overt
expressions of power are required to organize therapy sessions and to
divide them into discrete segments: (1) the first 45 minutes of each
session are devoted to conversation between the family members and
therapist; (2) at the expiration of the 45-minute interval the therapist
invites the family members to take a "break" and then goes into the
observation room to talk with the supervisor and other "team" members; (3) during the "team" consultation, which lasts 10 to 15 minutes,
the therapist often asks for assistance in formulating questions and interpretations to introduce to the family but, in any case, always obtains a
prescription concerning what to ask and say; (4) the therapist then re-
turns to the family and in the interval of five to ten minutes asks the
questions and articulates the interpretations obtained in the consultation with the "team."

Similarly, the language of supervision was not one of dominance and submission but of help and assistance. According to one of the supervisors, the most common problem student/therapists' express during "team" consultation (stage 3) is the "loss of therapeutic maneuverability; they don't know what to ask; they're stuck." To complicate matters, "some students don't know when they're stuck." The supervisor said he does not respond to this "stuckness" by telling the student/therapists what to do; instead, he makes "suggestions" or, more commonly, helps them "overcome their resistances to developing their own questions."

At the time I examined the therapy tapes, the ones that were available contained the recordings of therapy sessions with 23 families conducted by nine therapists. Before any filming occurred, family members, including children, signed a form that affirmed that they agreed to be filmed. Therapy sessions were recorded by three therapy supervisors (working separately) occupying an adjoining room with a one-way screen. As they filmed sessions, supervisors routinely talked to ("trained") the student therapists who watched the therapy with them. Thus therapists' and family members' performances were each scrutinized by multiple audiences: therapists by clients, supervisors, and other agency personnel; families by therapists and the unseen, unknown gifted child experts behind the one-way screen. According to Foucault (1977a, p. 202), "The more numerous those anonymous and temporary observers are, the greater the risk . . . of being surprised and the greater . . . [the] anxious awareness of being observed" (Foucault 1977a, p. 202). Because supervisors are observed by their own students and vice versa, power is not in the hands of any one person who could exercise it alone over others (Foucault 1980, p. 156). Supervisors too are under surveillance.

As we will see in the examination of family therapy tapes, the giftedness of the identified child was treated by therapists as an ascribed characteristic, existing independently of what occurred before, within, or after family therapy. Agency norms constrain therapists to treat each child's giftedness as a given. Moreover, the absence of standardization in the processes used to label gifted children and therapists' lack of information on how each gifted child came to be defined as gifted combined to make therapists' recognition of giftedness a matter that not only should not be questioned but also, based on the absence of information, a matter that could not be questioned. To illustrate, the Gifted Children's Center accepts any family for therapy within its catchment area so long as one of the children has been identified as gifted by a local school. The Gifted Children's Center does not identify gifted children on its own, and makes no effort to refute local schools' labeling decisions. These policies were adopted to implement the goal of serving existing gifted child educational programs and in recognition of the fact that there is no universally accepted, or even dominant, criterion for designating giftedness. Accordingly, each school has its own way of labeling gifted children: Some children are labeled because of their scores on achievement tests; some for their scores on IQ tests; others because they received excellent grades in one or more subjects; still others because they display some form of musical or artistic ability, and so forth.

Therapists usually do not know how or why each "gifted" child seen in therapy came to be labeled as such by his/her local school. First, the school records sent to the Gifted Children's Center usually arrive after family therapy has begun; second, they are often not read by therapists; third, even when the records are read, the information they contain is not organized to reveal what criterion or process was used to designate the child as gifted. Family therapists, then, have to assemble the appearance of knowledge despite the fact that such knowledge is either ambiguous or unavailable. Although therapists usually do not know how or why any given child came to be identified as gifted prior to therapy and any manifestations of giftedness within therapy are at best vague, they must still find some coherent appearance of giftedness, given the mandate to make inferences and recommendations about gifted children during therapy.

That therapists have no knowledge how or why any given child is gifted—either because the records are not available, are not read, or are incomprehensible regarding the determination of giftedness—guarantees that therapists' accounts of giftedness are global and absolute. Ironically, the absence of knowledge mandates that accounts appear unequivocal. Because knowledge is required for questions to become accountable, for questions to appear coherent, rational, and planful, therapists do not have the resources to reasonably display their uncertainty about giftedness. Moreover, because therapists cannot say whether a child's giftedness is demonstrated this way or that way, to this degree or that degree, whether it is specific to math, music, or chess, or whether the child is slightly, moderately, or extremely gifted, only one way of identifying giftedness is possible: as a duality. Each child is either gifted or nongifted. Because giftedness cannot be defined by specific acts or specific potentialities, the sum total existence of the gifted child becomes the object of inquiry. Within the theater of family therapy, every aspect of the child's life becomes relevant to the conduct of this demonstration.

Although it is assumed that therapists employ artful practices to create and sustain a world in which it is possible to talk about gifted children, we also note that these practices cannot deviate from rigidly defined goals and boundaries. Above all, under the camera's eye therapists cannot question their own authenticity as therapists, the agency's authenticity as a gifted child agency, or the child's authenticity as a gifted child. Even though student/therapists commonly ask other student "team" members away from the camera, "Did I look like I knew what I was talking about?" this question is never spoken out loud during family therapy.

Because gifted child therapists' adherence to agency norms cannot appear to be mandated by some external power, therapists' submission is always masked or hidden from view. Thus, therapists do not announce their submission but, rather, display it through a sense making that appears improvisational and spontaneous. Here are some illustrations.

DOING GIFTED CHILDREN

Although therapists can easily find reasons to redefine the identified gifted children as nongifted, that is, as erroneously labeled, they do not make use of potentially insurrectionary information. Instead, unsatisfactory or incongruent manifestations of giftedness are either forgotten, passed over, reframed as a paradoxical expression of giftedness, or covered by imputing special understandings and experiences to the gifted child. The identified child's giftedness is always given the benefit of the doubt. Thus, when a gifted child's poor academic performance becomes known in therapy, it is explained as a symptom of boredom or lack of motivation. As one therapist told a gifted boy who did not do his homework, "If it's challenging, you'll do it." Feelings of social isolation are also reframed as sequelae of giftedness:

> Therapist: You're obviously a very very bright young girl, which is a positive thing to be, a positive thing to have. But you're stuck there because there are some negative aspects to it. OK? That you're bright, you want to fit in, OK? The more you achieve
> Gifted Girl: the less you fit in
> Therapist: and the more you're worried about the possibility that you might not fit in.

In one instance, disobedience was treated as a manifestation of giftedness: When a parent complained that her gifted child doesn't obey, the therapist observed, "With gifted kids quite often there is a tendency for them to test boundaries, to challenge. It's a way for the gifted kids to stay sharp." Physical aggression too was reframed as part of the gifted gestalt: When a parent mentioned her son got in trouble in school for tripping a boy he felt insulted him, the therapist interpreted, "Gifted kids tend to have a real strong sense of justice . . . and um that sense of justice is something they're willing to fight for. That's something they are never lazy about."

In many cases, behavior that can be construed as inconsistent with the gifted gestalt is simply "unnoticed." To illustrate, as a father and therapist were discussing whether a gifted boy would perform up to his potential in junior high school or, for the sake of acceptance, act like ordinary children, the gifted boy kicked his younger brother. The father responded by scolding his son in a stage whisper, "You're kicking him and not seeing that . . . Listen, listen, that's not responsible. Turn around. . . . You almost missed his head and you're kicking him around his face and glasses, OK?" The important point is that neither the father nor the therapist attempted to integrate, or even acknowledge, the gifted boy's negative behavior in their dialogue. As if oblivious to the kicking episode, the therapist addressed these comments to the father while the father was scolding his son: "Let me ask you this. If P. had to choose at sometimes as he goes through junior high and so forth as to whether he wants to be accepted or gifted and creative, if it were polarized right there, what do you think would be the most important thing at that moment in his life?" The father, for his part, made no further reference to his gifted son's kicking, and answered this question without hesitating: "I don't think, seeing clearly now, I don't think being gifted or talented is something he's going to lose."

Sometimes behavior that appears inconsistent with the gifted pattern is openly recognized but not treated as disconfirming the child's giftedness. As the next vignette illustrates, even when a child was acknowledged to exhibit concrete or slow intellectual activity, the underlying giftedness was not called into question:

> Mother: Last summer we went to one of those water parks and the price was $13.95 or something like that. But kids under three go in free. R. [the gifted child's younger sibling] was
> Therapist: three and a half.
> Mother: He just turned.
> Father: Two days before. So we weren't going to pay for him.
> Mother: We weren't going to spend $13.95. When S. [the gifted child] found out, we were in line. He became livid.
> Father: He went crazy. . . . He was going to go back to the car for the afternoon. He didn't want to be with us. . . .
> Mother: As a parent, another 14 dollars for a little person who you have to be with constantly isn't
> Father: R. wasn't going to use the facilities at this place.
> Therapist: Yeah, but his [the gifted child's] thinking really isn't abstract enough to understand that.
> Mother: Right.
> Therapist: His sense of justice is very concrete.

This sequence reveals general recognition of a gifted child's concrete thinking, but at no time during or after is his giftedness doubted. Indeed, at no point is there even recognition of the possibility of questioning his status as a gifted child.

The infallibility of giftedness within this context is not the result of a system of logic that permits no disconfirming evidence (Pollner 1987, pp. 56–57); it results rather from a rigidly enforced system of inspection, a continuous gaze, that allows no deviations from agency policy. Because the Gifted Children's Center demands that children predefined by their schools as gifted be portrayed as such, therapists continually make reference to target children's brightness or intelligence as part of the production of actions that maintain those children's "giftedness" as the dominant interpretative framework for family therapy. One therapist, for example, asked if a gifted girl talked to anyone in school about a family problem. When she responded, "I talked to this one teacher . . . I needed to get it off my mind," the therapist replied, "Smart kid that does that." When a mother said her gifted daughter overreacts to punishment in a way that "doesn't fall into my realm of normal," the therapist interjected, "She's bright enough that she has assessed what your realm of normal is." A gifted child mentioned she did her homework before she spent time worrying about family problems. This prompted the therapist to comment, "An application of intelligence." After a father told the therapist about some illness in the family, the therapist intervened with, "It's interesting. Instead of M. [the gifted child] joining on unhealth, he's pulling you toward health and intelligence and all this sort of thing." Another therapist waited till the gifted boy and his sister exited at the close of a session, then turned to his parents and said, "He's a bright kid." In assessing these utterances, it is important to consider that therapists make little or no effort to identify comparable behavior in the gifted child's siblings as "bright" or "intelligent." Thus, in keeping with the agency's mandate to treat only the identified child as gifted, such statements serve the function of setting the identified child apart from other family members, and of singling out giftedness as the identified child's "master status" (Hughes 1945), as that attribute given the highest priority in the ongoing determination of the social pecking order.

Given the institutionally defined omnirelevance of giftedness, a gifted child engaged in virtually any activity was held responsible for the performance of that activity as a gifted child. Like the blind person "whose most ordinary deeds—walking nonchalantly up the street, locating the peas on his plate, lighting a cigarette—are no longer ordinary" (Chevigny, quoted in Goffman 1963, p. 15), everything the gifted child did was treated as potential evidence supporting his or her giftedness. Under the mandate to continually locate evidence of giftedness, even behavior that the gifted child "might" do was treated as supportive of the underlying pattern. In the following dialogue the therapist's unbroken musings on a gifted boy's "sensitivity" was not based on this boy's actual behavior but on his imagined responses to hypothetical situations:

> Therapist: My impression of B., in talking to you, is that there is a part of you that is very very sensitive and you know I just want to talk about that a little bit. . . . That sensitivity is positive in that you'll know, I mean you can probably guess when someone starts getting picked on. You know how they feel. You know if something starts to happen and a person feels real bitter about it, feels real bad. You know exactly how they're feeling. Now the downside.
>
> Gifted Boy: Experience.
>
> Therapist: Yeah, experience. You know it. And also the sensitivity is positive because you are sensitive. In fact, I'd bet you know, like if you came home and know your mom and dad had a disagreement. They wouldn't have to say a word because you could probably sense it kind of, like radar.
>
> Gifted Boy: Beep.
>
> Therapist: There's a positive side in there cause, believe me, a lot of people work a long time, for example therapists and so on. They work a long time to develop sensitivity when there's a conflict between two people, and that's something you already have.

The therapist did not appear to be pretending to see the gifted boy as extraordinarily "sensitive" because she backed her assessment with evidence. She documented the gifted boy's sensitivity by imagining how he would react if his parents came home with a disagreement. And with the appearance of conviction concluded he would understand without a word being spoken—"like radar." Thus, not only is the underlying giftedness confirmed and elaborated by individual examples of this phenomenon, but also the individual examples, in their turn, are pieced together on the basis of what is expected from a gifted child (Cicourel 1973, pp. 85–86; Garfinkel 1967, p. 78). We add only that this sense making operates in a field of continual visibility. Under these circumstances, sense making does not arise from conversation alone; instead, the anticipation of what the camera can see becomes the operational standard for "good therapy" and correct behavior. This recognition makes it understandable why interactants always appear so ready and willing to affirm and support the coherence and rationality of "family therapy with a gifted child."

For their part, parents "go with the flow" in gifted child discourse. They attend to professionals' judgment, seek and require only minimal supporting evidence, and suppress or deny disconfirming beliefs and suspicions, not only because they gain prestige by having one of their own singled out this way, but also because positive qualities in the identified child are consistently emphasized and behaviors ordinarily construed as negatives are reframed as positives. Moreover, the halo of gifted child idealizations is routinely extended to the parents themselves. To illustrate, when the topic of a gifted boy's adoption was introduced, a therapist commented,

> Therapist: I'm glad he's with you guys.
> Father: We are too.
> Therapist: It's like you picked a properly intelligent family so you can match.

Another therapist interpreted family members' avoidance of emotionally laden conversation as a function of their shared smartness: "When you have a family that has a lot of real smart people . . . when people are good thinkers, the way you are, sometimes that other part of you, that emotional part of you doesn't get to show." When a therapist mentioned that gifted children often challenge their parents' authority, the mother asked, "What happens when you have very average parents?" The therapist replied, "I don't believe that for a moment . . . that you're very average parents."

There were few breaches and misunderstandings between therapists and family members during the assembly of giftedness. Although one mother complained to her husband, "Can't she [the therapist] tell us in plain words what is a gifted child?" this complaint emerged only after the therapist exited to consult with her supervisor. Apparently, the mother who asked this question was unaware that the camera was still running. This suggests how surveillance creates the appearance of continual agreement, the appearance of continual fit between questions and answers. Because family therapy sessions are being observed and taped, interactants are oriented to creating a harmony that can be seen from without, not necessarily experienced from within. For both therapists and family members, showable and performable communication takes precedence over felt and sensed communication.

To summarize, according to this analysis, giftedness is not merely an accomplishment of the way people talked about, reacted to, and interacted with those defined as gifted. It is also a function of the procedures that guarantee that agency personnel and clients conform to institutionally sanctioned modes of talk. As a result of these procedures, once children are defined by the agency as gifted, then all who know this definition appear to affirm it by noticing, suggesting, interpreting, and

emphasizing the traits belonging to it (Rosenhan 1973). Moreover, behavior and utterances that appear incompatible with the gifted gestalt
are routinely discounted, unnoticed, or reframed as paradoxical expressions of this underlying pattern. Therapists, parents, and even the
gifted children themselves, appear to make imputations about giftedness spontaneously, improvisationally, as if a system of domination was
not a part of this process. The main giveaway that power is operating is
the compulsivity of gifted child attributions. Consider the sustained creative effort one therapist used to convert "lying in the snow" into a
resource for displaying the reality of giftedness:

> Therapist: Tell me about lying in the snow yesterday.
> Gifted Boy: I don't know. I was just thinking. I was tired, you know. The
>   snow was really heavy so I just sat down in the snow pile.
> Therapist: (laughing) Made a chair for yourself.
> Gifted Boy: Uh huh.
> Therapist: Did you stare at the sky?
> Gifted Boy: Yeah.
> Therapist: What do you think about when you stare at the sky?
> Gifted Boy: I don't know. I just start thinking about movies, books that I've
>   read, and about space.
> Therapist: Do you wonder where space leads?
> Gifted Boy: Yeah, I thought about that before.
> Therapist: What do you think?
> Gifted Boy: It's really confusing because there really can't be anything that
>   doesn't end.
> Therapist: Why not?
> Gifted Boy: Just impossible.
> Therapist: Maybe the limits are in our minds.
> Gifted Boy: It's hard to imagine something that doesn't end.

As if closing in on a target, the therapist structured the ongoing dialogue to convert behavior bearing no literal or logical connection to
giftedness ("lying in the snow") into a resource for displaying giftedness
as pregiven, as something "always already there" (Pollner 1987, p. 106).
Thus, after carefully editing, arranging, and interpreting what the gifted
boy said, the therapist was able to tell his parents: "One of the things
that G. is telling me and that you have told me are things that are
common among gifted children. To lie in the snow and stare at the sky
and wonder at things is very common with gifted children. They wonder about things that other children don't always wonder about."

Consistent with Foucault's (1977a, pp. 197–199) vision of power as a
ceaseless partitioning of people into categories such as mad/sane, dan-
gerous/harmless, normal/abnormal, gifted child family therapy functions

not only to display and confirm giftedness but also to display and confirm nongiftedness. Like the leper "caught up in a practice of rejection, of exile-enclosure . . . left to his doom in a mass among which it was useless to differentiate," the nongifted were treated according to a single ritual: exclusion. Thus, when it was learned in one case that a child participating in gifted child family therapy had been mistakenly identified as gifted, that his school had not identified him in the proper way, he and his family were immediately and abruptly discontinued from therapy.

In contrast to the predisposition to treat conversations as self-ordering, self-producing (Heritage 1984, pp. 280–290; Hilbert 1990, p. 800; Whalen, Zimmerman, and Whalen 1988; Wilson 1991), a condition existing outside of family therapy talk, the existence of a permanent record regarding who is and who is not gifted, plays a part in the cessation of family therapy talk. Although a school record cannot speak for itself, it assumed critical importance because of the anticipation of surveillance and accountability. Moreover, the compulsion to assimilate the boy's records for use in family therapy cannot be inferred solely from an examination of the accounts made in front of the camera, because such accounts can be expected to mask and deny the existence of surveillance and accountability —this power operates "discreetly."

GIFTEDNESS AS CREATIVE ACTIVITY

Although belief in a "technology of power" that exists independently of the methods employed in its discovery suggests a return to a Parsonian view of social interaction—a return to the view that people are "cultural dopes" mindlessly reproducing the norms and values that constitute the settings in which they live (Heritage 1984, pp. 75–84), we should consider that gifted child therapists' affirmation of their institutional order is never automatic. It is never a simple "matching procedure" between the relevant rule and the specific type of compliance required (Cicourel 1973 pp. 11–41; Mehan and Woods 1975, p. 75). Although gifted child therapists' act as if the identified child's giftedness cannot be withdrawn or proven false if certain things happened, as if it is "compatible with any and every conceivable state of affairs" (Gasking, quoted in Mehan and Woods 1975, p. 9), the manner in which this compatibility is displayed is always a subtly organized achievement. The maintenance of the gifted child identity requires continuous creative effort: Anomalies have to be interpreted; inconsistencies have to be concealed or reframed; and methods have to be found to identify, highlight, and fit evidences of giftedness into the anticipated pattern.

Similarly, the masking activities used to cover the existence of this process, the constitutive work whereby therapy activities appear normal, spontaneous, and noncontrived, result from constant anticipation and judgment. Thus, therapists are not like homunculi or puppets; rather, their submission is a reiteratively developed and sustained construction. That their discourse operates in a field of continuous visibility reinforces therapists' motivation to support the policies of the Gifted Children's Center, because individuals who are being observed and who know it assume responsibility for maintaining their own conformity. Accordingly, the seamlessness of therapists' submission, its subtlety and invisibility, result from the creative effort with which they exercise it over themselves. As Foucault (1977a, pp. 202–203) put it, "he inscribes in himself the power relation in which he simultaneously plays both roles; he becomes the principle of his own subjection."

This is not to say that opposition or resistance are impossible. According to Shumway (1989, pp. 161–162), the reason Foucault depicted disciplinary power in the first place was to alert those who exist within these domains that power, not truth, is being exercised. For Foucault, resistance cannot occur unless we question our own responses to the normalizing judgment that is being made over ourselves. What his research provides, then, is the warrant for asking why, if we wish to treat people as equals, there need to be agencies devoted to separating, evaluating, and ranking special populations. The central paradox of Foucault's analysis, however, is that any resistance will inevitably fail. As we can see in the case of gifted children, family members have everything to gain from having one of their own defined this way, so there is no continuing motivation to raise questions, point out incongruities, or call attention to inequities. For family members, this is a discourse in which intellectual passivity appears to be the most rewarding of all possible postures. Although therapists appear tireless in their efforts to locate evidences of giftedness, they cannot choose an alternative course. Within the framework of family therapy, the identified child's giftedness is not a proposition that can be withdrawn or proven false if certain things happen. It is compatible with any and every state of affairs.

9

From Christianity to Democracy:
Giftedness as Virtue

Genealogy . . . operates on a field of entangled and confused parchments, on documents that have been scratched over and recopied many times. . . .

It must record the singularity of events outside of any monotonous finality; it must seek them in the most unpromising places, in what we tend to feel is without history—in sentiments, love, conscience, instincts.

From "Nietzsche, Genealogy, History" by Michel Foucault (1977)

Gifted child discourse is multidirectional and multilayered. There is no linear development. There is no single motive, no clearly definable subject or object, no exact essence, no primordial truth or fixed relationship. Although we can say with certainty that belief in giftedness arises from the passion of scholars, their fanatical and unending research, we still must consider the secret and ardent origins of that obsession. We still must ask what could possibly be gained from believing that gifted children exist.

Nietzsche (1880/1964a, p. 50) provides a clue: Giftedness fulfills the need to accomplish Christ's commands or, perhaps more accurately, the need to believe that Christ's commands can be fulfilled. If the Christian God can only demand the fulfillment of a perfection that is attainable and often attained, then belief that a class of people can satisfy the command "Be perfect as your Father in heaven is perfect," sustains the possibility that Christ's injunction can come true. In a sense, then, Christ's existence is confirmed by evidence that there are 10-year-olds of whom it can be said:

His open-minded disposition, with great good nature and kindness to those boys younger than himself, made him beloved by all his school fellows. He was very affectionate and even sentimental in his manners. His activity of body could only be equalled by the activity of his mind. He

was a boy never known to be idle. His habit was always to be doing
something. He showed no vanity at his superiority over other boys, but
said it was a shame that their education should have been so neglected. (A
description of Francis Galton, quoted in Terman 1917, p. 213)

Ironically, Nietzsche (1881/1911, p. 36) also provides the outlines for
the most cynical and least Christian of explanations: Belief in giftedness
is based on thirst for class distinctions. We all wish to awaken our neighbor's envy, to awaken feelings of impotence and degradation: "we endeavor to make him taste the bitterness of his fate by dropping a little of
our honey on his tongue, and while conferring this supposed benefit on
him, looking sharply and triumphantly into his eyes."

What needs to be emphasized now is that the Christian and nonChris-
tian explanations of giftedness are in no way incompatible, because
living up to the expectations of Christ, being "perfect as your father in
heaven is perfect," can easily be used as the means of asserting the joys
of superiority. Who could be more deserving of envy than the person
who lives according to Christ's doctrines? Nietzsche (1881/1911, p. 37)
reminds us how the nun flaunts her chastity: "with what threatening
eyes she looks into the faces of other women who live differently from
her! what a vindictive joy shines in those eyes!"

Let us hypothesize, then, that gifted child discourse achieves its passionate following, inspires devotion from scholars, because of its peculiar capacity to join the themes of Christianity with the themes of social
class dominance. In this regard, the most cunning feature of gifted child
discourse—what makes it so compelling, so exotic and attractive, yet, at
the same time so calming and reassuring—may be the way it mingles a
justification of power and privilege with a mood of Christian virtue.
Consider, for example, how the characteristics of giftedness are woven
with and through the threads of the Protestant ethic:

1. *Asceticism* and *piety* in portraying how hard these children work,
their discipline, abstinence, thrift, sobriety, humility, maturity: "While
others get to sleep, play bridge, golf, vacation in exotic lands, eat foods
which heighten their taste buds, and perhaps as much as any of these
envious pursuits, put time in loafing, doing just plain nothing other
than relaxing, the gifted are at work on projects of benefit to others."
(Isaacs 1971, p. 176)

2. *Good works* in emphasizing the beneficial practical consequences
of giftedness: "Individuals of surpassing intelligence create national
wealth, determine the state of industry, advance science, and make
general culture possible." (Hollingworth 1926, p. 297)

3. *Rationalism* and *empiricism* in assuming that "only a life guided by
constant thought could achieve conquest over the state of nature" (We-

ber 1930, p. 118), and that the secrets of giftedness are to be discovered and mobilized through systematic observation.

4. *Individualism* in locating the sources of giftedness in character traits originating in the individual: "To take intelligence alone, we now know that there are idiots, imbeciles, morons, dull normals, average normals, bright normals, and geniuses. We have also learned that the kind of educational treatment that fits the average normal child does not fit the moron; neither does it fit the bright child." (Goddard 1928, p. 37)

5. *Capitalism* and *competition* in assuming that gifted children succeed only because they have the wit and stamina to outperform all others: "A competitive social-economic system does, so far as we can infer from present data, foster the interests of the intelligent through making it possible for them to obtain economic goods by the exercise of their powers. . . . Abolition of existing artificial restraints upon differential reward would, of course, further the interests of the gifted." (Hollingworth 1926, pp. 358–359)

6. *Grace* and *calling* in stressing, on the one hand, that "choseness may be equated with being gifted" (Isaacs 1968, p. 98) and, on the other, that "the gifted are subject to the same temptations of 'anyman' . . . but as leaders of men, they need to realize that extra effort on their part is needed to enable them to present modes of behavior which typify the ideal, and represents that which they would like to see others emulate." (Isaacs 1968, p. 101)

Within this system, social class differentials in wealth and privilege are not the result of exploitation or subjection but appear rational, equitable, a part of the natural order. Accordingly, gifted child discourse survives and prospers not only because it provides a language through which the aristocratic, the powerful, the high-stationed and the high-minded are continuously distinguished from the low, the low-minded, the vulgar and the plebeian, but also because it provides accounts of these distinctions that quietly and subtly affirm our central values and beliefs. Gifted child discourse succeeds because it supports a system of rank and privilege that is fully consistent with our culture's dominant virtues. Nowhere is this clearer than in gifted child education's appropriation of the concept "democracy." "If democracy stands for one thing more than another," Goddard wrote in 1928, "it is equality of opportunity. This is exactly what the gifted child never has in school until he gets into the class for gifted children. In the regular class he never has an opportunity to show what he could do. Instead of the special class for gifted children being undemocratic, it is the only truly democratic procedure—the only plan that gives the bright child a chance" (pp. 28–29).

GIFTED CHILDREN'S DEMOCRACY

From the earliest days of the gifted children's movement, these scholars argued that the only truly democratic curriculum was not one that provided an equal education for all children nor was it one that provided all children an equal opportunity to acquire an equal education; rather, democracy, as gifted child scholars defined it, recognizes that all students should receive "an equal opportunity to acquire an education commensurate with their abilities" (Olstad 1978, p. 188). In a paper titled "The Democratic Idea and the Education of Gifted Children," Harvey Townsend (1924, p. 147), argued that this understanding of democracy was fully anticipated by Rousseau, who wrote that "each individual is born with a distinctive temperament which determines his genius and character. There is no question of changing or restricting this temperament, only of training it and bringing it to perfection." And, in the language of Nicholas Hobbs (1951, p. 170), this model is the only way to

> avoid the deadening mediocrity that arises when equality is interpreted to mean that people must all be alike. There are enough leveling influences in our machine-stamped, scheduled, and routinized civilization as it is without adding an ideological restriction to human development. Not only must we avoid this leveling tendency, we must actively seek full expression of the differences between people, with a deep respect for the right of people to be themselves. Full realization of the unique personality of each citizen is surely the highest aim of democracy. Full equity in the pursuit of self-realization seems to be the profound aspiration captured in the phrase about equality in our Declaration of Independence.

Although Hollingworth (1920, p. 207) shares this understanding of gifted children's democracy, she contends that this is a radically different version from the one handed down by the authors of the Declaration of Independence. New times and technologies require new principles: "When our forefathers believed that men were created free and equal, no psychological laboratories had been established. During the past century we have learned that all men are, as a matter of biological fact, created unequal. All that a democratic society can do is to equalize opportunity; it cannot equalize men. All that a democratic school can do is to equalize opportunity; it cannot equalize the children."

The central point is that gifted education appropriates "democracy" in order to disguise or conceal power and also to create a system of beliefs within which power can operate. By taking as a given what is in fact highly problematic—the availability and accessibility of every student's idiosyncratic ability level—gifted education's conception of democracy becomes not only the principle for recognizing differences, but also an imperative for accentuating and preserving them. To illustrate, Kitano and Kirby (1986, p. 5) argue that "equal opportunity" does not necessitate providing the same education for every child, but requires instead that every child should have the means to meet his or her educational potential: "It would be unfair and unrealistic . . . to have the same educational expectations, standards, methods, and materials for both a moderately retarded child and a child of average intellectual ability. In this case, the retarded child would not be receiving an equal opportunity to meet his or her potential. By the same token, a child of superior ability would suffer if given the same education as an average child." The distinguishing characteristic of this line of reasoning, then, is that it treats each child's capacity to learn—each child's "potential"—as part of public experience, as something that lies expansed before the eyes of all to see. The presumption is that educators as well as ordinary folk have no doubt about such questions as: Who is moderately retarded? Who is average? Who is gifted?

For those who might doubt our ability to answer these questions, gifted child scholars point to the fact that we continuously go about our daily lives making judgments about people's abilities. It is almost always taken for granted that "some can repair cars better than others, some can get out more votes than others, some can do better at raising money for causes than others, some dentists can fill teeth better than others, some can see relationships among phenomena better than others, and so on" (Newland 1976, p. 35). So if we are going to question the concept of separate education for the gifted, then gifted child scholars want to know why we do not also question the fact that in sports some students are on the first team and others are on the second, some "make" the band and others don't, some are first violinists, and some "come in first in races, art contests, or in competition in essay writing about our democracy" (Newland 1976, p. 35). In the words of Sidney Hook:

> There are some who mistakenly believe that because a democracy must repudiate the notion of a ruling social or political elite, it must therefore be hostile to the idea and existence of an intellectual elite defined by excellence or performance. There is a danger that the cult of conformity will make the pursuit of excellence seem educationally subversive. . . . We recognize that in a just or fair arrangement everyone should have a right to try out for the team, but not everyone has a right to be on the team regardless of his capacities. (quoted in Olstad 1978, p. 188)

So even if the concept of giftedness is abstract, global, changeable, and changing, and even if giftedness is not directly observed or measured, we may still think of it as seeable and knowable as other, simpler, and more specific categories of behavior where ability is also judged (car repairing, violin playing, football playing, racing, etc.). Accordingly, so far as educating children in the democratic way is concerned, identifying which children are "moderately retarded," "average," or "gifted" is not a problem. Nor is it a problem to determine what the "potential" is for children so labeled. Just how much a moderately retarded child can be expected to achieve is considered a knowable, answerable question. Just how far an average or gifted child can go is also nonproblematic. What is problematic is whether the members of these categories receive the specific resources required for them to achieve the specific future deemed appropriate for them. Thus, we might conclude that the distinguishing features of gifted education's concept of "equality of educational opportunity commensurate with abilities" is, first, that it takes our capacity to estimate children's potential as a given; second, that it accepts as a given the child's expected future at each level of ability; and third, that it seeks to ensure the specific future appropriate to that ability level. This is the mission. This is the specific issue to which the gifted children's movement is addressed. In the manner of Plato's *Republic*, this discourse seeks to match children of a certain type to a future of a certain type.

We have discussed how the virtues of integration, pluralism, inclusion, and multiculturalism were appropriated by gifted child discourse. Although I hypothesized that this rhetoric masked an agenda of social inequality, I now wish to consider this discourse as something more than just a camouflage, more than just a method of obtaining obliviousness to the project's underlying meaning. Now I consider that virtue provides the very framework of power, its enticements, seductions, legitimations, key arguments, and methods of deflecting criticism. Virtue not only represents the familiar, the reassuring, the unquestioned and unquestionable—"a set of traditions, habits, institutions, timetables for activities of all kinds" that can be use to master the problems of daily life (Schutz 1945, p. 370), it represents a vision, an ideology that energizes the project and makes it worth doing. Attributions of virtue thus create a sanctuary from uncertainty, a place where critical analysis appears out-of-place and illegitimate; moreover, they are responsible for the individual psychological mechanisms, the specific beliefs and arguments that enable members to take action in behalf of the movement. In short, virtue is more than the thing that makes power appear natural and normal; virtue is the imperative behind power:

> The essential thing . . . in a good and healthy aristocracy is that it should not regard itself as a function either of the kingship or the commonwealth, but as the *significance* and highest justification thereof—that it should therefore accept with a good conscience the sacrifice of a legion of individ-

uals, who, *for its sake*, must be suppressed and reduced to imperfect men, to slaves and instruments. Its fundamental belief must be precisely that society is not allowed to exist for its own sake, but only as a foundation and scaffolding, by means of which a select class of beings may be able to elevate themselves to their higher duties, and in general to a higher *existence*: like those sun-seeking climbing plants in Java—they are called *sipto Matador*,—which encircle an oak so long and so often with their arms, until at last, high above it, but supported by it, they can unfold their tops in the open light, and exhibit their happiness. (Nietzsche 1885/1964b, p. 225)

It is completely inaccurate to trace gifted child scholars' passion to some evil impulse, say, to a desire to dominate others, to exclude, deprive, hierarchize, diminish, squash, suppress. Nor is it accurate to ask, as Jeannie Oakes (1985, p. 4) did, how well-intentioned gifted child educators could participate in a process that turns out to affect many students in ways contrary to their intentions: "How can they be part of a process that turns out not to be . . . in the best interests of the students they work with?" First, this question assumes there is some absolute way of determining the "best interests of students." In fact, goodness and virtue—people's "best interests"—are always conditional. Specifically, they are constituted from the standpoint of those who have the capacity to make these attributions and enforce them: "it is permissible to look upon language as the expression of the power of the masters: they say 'this is that, and that,' they seal finally every object and every event with a sound, and thereby at the same time take possession of it" (Nietzsche 1887/1910, p. 20).

The question is also inappropriate, because it assumes that the system operates *despite* gifted child educators' good intentions. The opposite is true. The system operates *because* of their good intentions. Like all social movements, gifted child education originated because of its sense of mission, because of a sacred calling. And if it has grown and prospered, it is only because these good intentions, these cherished beliefs, have been ceaselessly rekindled, born out, affirmed.

Again, consider gifted education's discourse on democracy. Because gifted children are seen as vastly different from other children with a markedly superior capacity to perform and achieve, they are separated into different learning groups and provided with vastly different kinds of knowledge and with markedly different opportunities to learn. All this springs from good intentions, because "a child of superior ability would suffer if given the same education as the average child" (Kitano and Kirby 1986, p. 4). And any doubt that these children should be separated in this fashion is quickly dispelled when we see that gifted and nongifted children do indeed learn at different levels and rates.

How could we expect otherwise? How could we expect that children who are provided with vastly different kinds of knowledge and markedly different opportunities to learn would not learn different things, at different rates and levels? How could there be any doubt that the children who are taught in ways thought appropriate to the gifted would reveal gifted-type responses?

We might sum up by saying that the creative accomplishment of gifted child education's discourse on democracy is that it demands our adoption of the very educational practices and structures that retrospectively prove the premises of its own arguments. The belief "that equal educational opportunity does not mean identical opportunity," that "differentiated programs are essential, both to maximize student abilities and to fulfill the democratic credo" (Nelson 1982, p. 63), mandates that gifted students be provided the very educational experiences that affix to them the different gradations of ability that necessitate the "democratic credo" in the first place.[1]

And when the gifted do in fact perform and achieve in a manner consistent with these initial expectations, this is never seen as a result of the special educational opportunities provided for them. Thus, for example, although the school creates the possibility of giftedness in the sense of formulating the traits that define it and developing the learning opportunities that display and confirm it, nowhere is it assumed that these traits are not built into the gifted children themselves. Nowhere is it assumed that the properties of giftedness originate outside of giftedness. Instead, gifted children's achievements are always seen as a function of a stable, pregiven, knowable ability that existed prior to any act of knowing.

Notes

Introduction

1.   As early as 1951, Edwin Lemert suggested that the behavior of the gifted and renowned "should be given the same systematic analysis as that which is applied to the criminal, the pauper, or sex delinquent" (pp. 23–24). However, that recommendation has rarely been followed, notwithstanding periodic complaints that sociological, research is "over-negativized," too focused on "the objectionable, the forbidden, the disvalued" (Dodge 1985, p. 18), on "nuts, sluts, and preverts" (Liazos 1972), and so forth. Daniel F. Chambliss's (1988) "The Mundanity of Excellence: An Ethnographic Report on Stratification and Olympic Swimmers" is a wonderful exception to this pattern and should be read by anyone wondering what a "positive" sociology looks like.

2.   *Gifted Child Quarterly, Journal for the Education of the Gifted, Gifted Child Today, Gifted Education International, Roeper Review, Creativity Research Journal, Exceptional Children.*

3.   The earliest use of the term *gifted child* I can find is in J. H. Van Sickle's (1910) "Provision for Gifted Children in Public Schools" (*Elementary School Teacher* 10:357–366).

4.   See, for example, "An Infant Prodigy," *North American Review*, April 19, 1907 (184:887–888), and "The Boy Prodigy of Harvard," *Current Literature*, March 1910 (68:291–293).

5.   On March 12, 1906, the Superintendent of New York City Public Schools, William J. Shearer, made these comments in the *New York Times*: "The most important problem of the day in school administration is to get the older pupils who are cumbering the lower grades into the higher grades. Their presence in the lower grades is detrimental to the younger children, because they take much of the teacher's time and attention that belong to the children of normal age. . . ."

"Why should 500,000 children be placed upon intellectual treadmills and compelled to move at the same pace for the whole of their lives? Who will dare to defend the plan which compels the poor teacher, by holding back some and driving forward others, to try to keep all moving at the same pace. . . . It means that many thousands are being held back by the slow ones and drilled in habits of inattention and idleness by the senseless, unnecessary marking time, waiting for others to catch up. Is it any wonder that so many lose interest and stop school?"

6. This is a term used by Jeremy Bentham to describe the Panopticon as a solution to the problem of surveillance (Foucault 1980, p. 148).

7. Spector and Kitsuse (1977) and Gusfield (1981) provide detailed discussion of social scientists' role as social problems players.

8. Terman and Hollingworth were both academic psychologists, the former located at Stanford University, the latter at Columbia. Unlike Terman, whose concerns were focused on research, Hollingworth was very involved in the practice of gifted education. She initiated the first course on the nature and needs of gifted children at Columbia and ran a program for gifted children at the Speyer School in Manhattan. Goddard was director of research at the Vineland Training School for Feebleminded Girls and Boys in New Jersey.

There is an extraordinary volume and range of materials on gifted children. For example, as early as the 1920s (Henry 1924), the National Society for the Study of Education published a "Bibliography on Gifted Children" with 453 entries. To gain an overview of this literature's themes, origins, continuities, and discontinuities, I examined all the citations under "gifted children" and "child prodigies" in the *New York Times Index* from the late nineteenth century to the present. I also went through all the issues of the *Journal of Educational Psychology* (from 1910 through the 1930s), and the leading gifted child journals, including the *Gifted Child Quarterly* and *Exceptional Children* (from the first volumes to 1993).

Chapter 1

1. Hollingworth (1926, p. 257) introduced the passage as follows: "The traits of character most frequently ascribed to C by those who know him well are honesty, reliability, bravery, loyalty, and precision. He is a stickler for the exact. No statement is right unless it is exactly right."

2. Kingsley Davis's (1938) "Mental Hygiene and Class Structure" appropriates the Protestant ethic to explain the success of the mental hygiene movement in much the same way I do (here and in Chapter 9): These social movements were richly expressive of a wide range of puritan beliefs and values.

3. In 1943, C. Wright Mills published an analysis of textbooks in the field of social pathology that closely parallels this analysis of gifted child scholarship ("The professional ideology of social pathologists," in the *American Journal of Sociology* 49:165–180). Note Mills' reference to the sentimentality of social pathology rhetoric, the masking of social and moral elements, and the focus on individual-level responsibility.

Chapter 2

1. Although it has become increasingly unacceptable to treat the "middle-class way of life" as superior, explicit references to that superiority were still quite common in the 1960s and 1970s. Consider this passage from *Caring for the Gifted* (1970, p. 63) by Rita M. Dickinson: "Some people sneer at what they call

'socialization in the middle class way of life.' In fact, however, the kinds of learnings they scorn constitute basically acceptable *human* behavior. Kindness and consideration are important in making it possible for people to live in groups and to cooperate. High moral principles, respect for the rights of others, recognition of one's importance as a person—these kinds of standards are essential in any independent society."

2.   Among American Indian students identified as gifted in Oklahoma, only 9% are listed as either full or three-fourths American Indian. By contrast, 68% of American-Indian students identified as gifted have less than one-fourth American-Indian blood (Maker and Schiever 1989, p. 81). This suggests that giftedness is recognized in relation to assimilation to the dominant culture.

3.   Gallagher (1985, pp. 426–427) begins his subchapter on "Culturally Diverse Gifted" with a story titled "Sam's Refrain: Nobody Loves a Smart Boy" that is at once a caricature and veiled condemnation of nonwhite and minority group cultures:

> It is rare that educators have a full appreciation of the diverse pressures that can be placed on talented youngsters who persist in deviating from acceptable cultural norms. Sam had one such experience burned vividly into his memory and which influenced his school behavior from then on.
>
> During one class Sam became enthusiastic about an assignment and the teacher was able to see past the rough exterior and grasp the diamondlike quality of Sam's intellect. For an electric moment their minds touched, and the teacher and Sam had an exhilarating conversation, almost forgetting the rest of the class in their mutual enthusiasm.
>
> That evening as Sam trudged home from school, he turned a corner and suddenly was confronted by five of his male classmates, obviously waiting for him. He was sure that he could handle any one of them physically but equally sure that he was helpless before the group. Cold chills ran up his spine as the largest of the group approaches him. "Hey, Sam, how come you're suckin' up to the teach? We don't like guys actin' too smart, do we?"
>
> A rumble of assent came from the assembled group, and several further highly distinctive suggestions were made as to what might happen to someone who continued such unacceptable behavior. Sam held his ground, but the next day he was very distant to the teacher and resisted all attempts to reinstitute that special relationship. He had made his choice. If he kept his distance from the teacher and continued to excel athletically, his intellectual interests would be accepted, though not without some scorn. It is this type of compromise, in one form or another, that is forced upon talented students coming from a cultural background essentially suspicious of the school or the pursuit of the intellect.
>
> A different problem would face Sam's sister. She might not be threatened so openly in a physical way as Sam, but her aspirations to seek a writing career beyond the home and family, if expressed openly might result in just as thorough an ostracizing as Sam's, in a subculture where women produce babies, not books.

4.   This poem was written by a recent guest editor (Betts 1988, p. 242) of the *Gifted Child Quarterly* and was included within the issue's editorial:

> At last,
> We are beginning to understand you.
> We realize your beauty,

your ability
your potential . . .

A lifetime
of excitement,
joy,
involvement,
creativity and passion
awaits you . . .
but first we must nurture you . . .

We must give you the opportunity
to accept and value
your strengths
and your differences . . .
to accept and value
the strengths
and differences of others . . .

The opportunity
to actively pursue your passions,
your areas of adventure,
and your dreams . . .
to help make our world
a better place in which to live,
where, as you choose,
you may become
the explorers,
the inventors,
the artists,
the poets,
the leaders of tomorrow . . .

But, most importantly,
we must help you become
your true "selves,"
to withstand the pressure
from outside,
and listen closely to
your hearts
so that you may
develop your potential,
and become what
you truly can be,
what you truly are . . .

5.   Karen Flory, a graduate student at the University of Iowa, provided this example of "obliviousness": In a text titled *Exceptional Children* (Hallahan and Kauffman [1990, p. 426]), the authors explicitly attempt to dispel the myth that giftedness is not found as often among the "handicapped" by asserting that at least 2% of handicapped children may be gifted. Implicitly, however, their statistics supported that "myth," as they had earlier estimated that 3% to 5% of the general population is gifted.

6.   The experimental stressor consisted of 100 slides containing "color words" such as *red* or *blue* printed in a color different from that signified by the words themselves. Thus the word *red* might appear in blue colors. These cards were flashed rapidly on screen and the subjects asked to identify the color of the letters, and not to read the "color word." This activity was expected to produce a conflict between the part of the brain responsible for interpreting color and the part responsible for reading.

7.   Hilbert (1987) uses the term "Weberian rationalization" to identify the historical process whereby some entity is abstracted from its many manifestations despite its growing increasingly complex.

8.   *Larry P. v. Riles*, 495 F. Supp. 926 (1979).

9.   Bettleheim's (1958) "Sputnik and Segregation" may be the most prominent exception to this pattern.

Chapter 3

1.   *New York Times*, April 10, 1873, "Inhuman Treatment of a Little Waif—Her Treatment—A Mystery to be Cleared up."

2.   *Education of the Gifted and Talented*, Report to the U.S. Congress by the U.S. Commissioner of Education (Washington, DC: U.S. Government Printing Office, March 1972), pp. 3–4.

3.   In the next chapter I examine the case of William James Sidis, a child prodigy from the first two decades of the century who is now seen as the exemplar of gifted child exploitation.

4.   Ruth Duskin Feldman's (1982, p. 360) *Whatever Happened to the Quiz Kids: Perils and Profits of Growing Up Gifted* was very soft on the "perils" part of her analysis: "Very few of us feel we were unfairly exploited, as Gerard Darrow apparently did. Exploitation can be a two-way street. We were used (kindly) to make the show succeed. But we, in turn, had a rare opportunity we could use to our advantage, and on the whole, most of us did." Although Gerard Darrow, the youngest and perhaps the most popular of the original Quiz Kids, complained that he was ruined by this special attention, Feldman (p. 351) felt that somehow this was Darrow's failure: "It would be easy to say, as with Sidis, that exploitation spoiled Gerard. Branded a prodigy of prodigies, he could not measure up. His family life was hardly ideal, his social and emotional development far from optimum. But neither did he show evidence of the exceptional productive capacity that has been known to transcend troubled youth. . . . Darrow was no child wonder."

Chapter 4

1.   Leta Hollingworth made these comments in a memorandum to the American Council on Education (Harry Hollingworth 1943, p. 119).

2.   H. G. Rickover, *Saturday Evening Post*, March 2, 1957.

3.   M. Hickey, *Ladies Home Journal*, August 1957.

4. *Life*, April 7, 1958.
5. H. S. Galus, *American Mercury*, September 1958.
6. Joel Shurkin's (1992, p. 140) research on Terman's relationship to his gifted subjects shows that, although Terman attributed their successes to giftedness, much could be explained by Terman's behind-the-scene activities on their behalf:

> He would write a letter of recommendation for anyone in the group, if nothing else, stating that the person was in the Terman study of the gifted. He gave them free vocational testing and sent them letters of explanation and advice with the results. He would intervene on their behalf to get them into graduate school or to get them a job. Sometimes they did not even ask; he intervened covertly, leaving the Termites wondering what role he played. Rodney Bear, for instance, thinks his mother may have asked Terman to help get him into Stanford's medical school, but he does not know for sure; Terman did write a letter. He probably helped pay for many of his kids' education by contributing scholarships, always anonymously.

Chapter 5

1. There seems to be the general feeling that all children should be leaders and initiators, that adapting children to these roles is simply good educational practice and, as such, has nothing to do with power.
2. Goddard's (1928, pp. 76–81) text is filled with illustrations of gifted children assuming responsibility for their own education:

> Here is a girl sitting at a table, working away at something. I notice that she is sitting on her foot. How girls love to sit that way—and why should they not? She is looking up something in the encyclopedia, some question that came up in class and she was appointed [to] a committee to look the matter up. Across the room is a boy working all by himself. He seems to be both reading and writing. I go to him and look over his shoulder. He is working in long division, but he has no arithmetic near him. It seems to be a reading book that he is using. Finally I accost him, saying, "What are you doing, my son?" He looks up, pleased at an opportunity to explain, and answers as follows: "I just read in this book that the exports of Alaska last year were valued at $54,938,171. I remember that our history lesson taught us that we paid Russia $72,000,000 for the whole territory. I have just subtracted to see how much more we got in one year than we paid for it." "But you were dividing; what was that?" "Oh, yes, when you spoke, I was dividing $54,938,171 by $7,200,000 to see how many times the cost were the exports for one year. . . ."
> I walk over to the other corner. There are six little first graders. They are standing in front of the reading chart. The smallest boy of the group seems to be acting as teacher. He points to a word on the chart, and the child works it out and pronounces it. If any child does not agree with him, they discuss it; and if they finally do not agree, they put it aside to ask the teacher. Again, *real* education, because they are solving their own problems. They are thinking in their childish way; they are not mechanically doing what somebody else has told them to do.
> There is still a third group over in the other corner. There are the second graders and they are doing spelling. They have elected a little girl to be the teacher, and after a minute or two of observation we know why they elected her. She is a real teacher and they evidently felt it. As we watch from our position in the background,

we note that one boy somewhat larger than the others seems to think it is the proper time to have a little fun on his own account. He accordingly spells and pronounces the word assigned him with an inflection and a manner that attract attention. The little teacher quickly scents mischief and stamps her foot and says emphatically, "William!" That is all. William knows who is the mistress of the situation, and he makes no further attempt at that kind of fun.

3. The Association for Gifted (TAG) proposed to the National Council for Accreditation of Teacher Education that teachers specializing in gifted education should demonstrate:

Knowledge of commonly used tests of cognitive and affective performance that have application to gifted and talented students.

Knowledge of assessment processes and the development of an instructional program built on these processes.

Knowledge of various curriculum adaptations commonly used for gifted and talented students.

Knowledge of various administrative or organizational adaptations and community resources in common use with gifted and talented students.

Knowledge of general characteristics, etiologies, and needs of gifted and talented students from a developmental perspective that require educational adaptations.

Knowledge of special subgroups of gifted and talented students (e.g., underachieving, culturally different, handicapped) that require special identification procedures, planning, and programming.

Knowledge of models of communication and consultation with parents and key professionals.

Ability to plan a sequential differentiated curriculum and execute it with a group of gifted and/or talented students.

Ability to design an educational plan for individual or groups of gifted and/or talented students that takes into account individual strengths and needs.

Mastery of procedures or strategies that can determine the degree of success of a program, curriculum plan, and an individual education plan.

Ability to work with parents and key professionals. (Parke 1991, p. 425)

4. John Feldhusen (1991, p. 115) agrees with Sawyer in a *Gifted Child Quarterly* editorial: "We are in a rut. We continue to operate the same old ubiquitous pull-out programs featuring enrichment, thinking skills training, and project activities and to offer creative problem solving and future problem solving as peripherals to the basic, day-long instructional experiences of gifted and talented youth. . . . We must become part of the total program as it relates to gifted and talented youth." As might be expected, Feldhusen says the chief problem with these seemingly meaningless pullout enrichment programs is not that they are meaningless but that they might be cut because they are meaningless: "By remaining peripheral we have become extremely vulnerable. Programs are being eliminated in schools and all over the United States."

5. Garfinkel (1967, p. 7) gets credit for originating the idea that people never investigate their projects in order "to recognize and describe what they are doing in the first place. Least of all are practical actions investigated in order to explain to practitioners their own talk about what they are doing."

Chapter 6

1.   Delisle (1988, p. 29) illustrates a well-used strategy: "Gifted education has a long way to go before it is perfect, but then, so does every other element of our world."

2.   Gruber (1986, pp. 252–253) provides extraordinarily compelling examples:

William Gilbert, preeminent pioneer of the experimental method, and founding father of the study of electricity and magnetism, worked 18 years to produce *De Magnete* (Gilbert, 1600), at the age of 60.

John Milton conceived of a first provisional plan for his masterwork in 1640. He resumed work on it in 1658 and finished *Paradise Lost* (1665) seven years later, at the age of 66 (Milton, 1655).

Isaac Newton, in his "annus mirabilis" (actually, the two years 1665–1666) began the work in mathematics, optics, and mechanics and gravitation that became the part of his lifework for which he is still almost worshipped. In spite of Newton's faulty recollections in old age, modern studies of the manuscripts show that it really took him the next 20 years to move from these preliminary sketches to *Principia Mathematica* (Newton 1685–1687), which he wrote and published over a two-year period, when he was 45 years old.

Charles Darwin became a professional naturalist during the five-year voyage of the *Beagle*, began the search for a workable theory of evolution soon after returning home, and in about one and one half year's work fashioned the outlines of the theory of evolution. Twenty-one years later he wrote and published *On the Origin of Species* (Darwin 1859), at the age of 50.

Sigmund Freud, from boyhood interested in dreams, made the decisive turn away from somatic medicine when he went to Paris to study with Charcot at the age of 30. Ten years later, in 1891, he began the work that led to his founding masterwork, *The Interpretation of Dreams* (1899) when he was 43 years old (Freud, 1899).

Even the seeming counter-examples of astonishing early achievements display this character of prolonged work. Einstein was only 26 in 1905, and that year he wrote and published six finished articles, each of them fundamental, two of them expounding the theory of special relativity. But he had been thinking about the issues for some 10 years. In 1895 at the age of 16, he had written a paper, "On the Examination of the State of Aether in a Magnetic Field," which he sent to an uncle in Belgium, but which was never published. The same year, he conceived of his now celebrated thought-experiment: What would happen if the observer ran after a light wave with the same velocity as the light itself? In the intervening years leading up to 1905, he continued to think about related questions in an increasingly sophisticated way.

3.   Jarrell and Borland (1990, p. 303) were also struck by Renzulli's ambivalence about standardized tests: "Although an expanded discussion of the creativity-test validity problem can be found in Renzulli et al. (1981, pp. 22–24), a few pages later in the same volume (e.g., pp. 33, 35, 37, 38) one finds suggestions for using creativity tests as part of the identification scheme." In response to these criticisms, Renzulli (1990, p. 326) wrote: "If Jarrell and Borland, or any

other interested critics, want to punch some serious holes in my work, they will need to design some research studies of their own that are based on the formulation of specific hypotheses. This is what my colleagues and I have been doing for the past several years. We have taken the time to test our beliefs by gathering the data, evaluating the findings, and introducing modifications when there was clear evidence that such modifications were warranted. By way of example, one small component of our overall model, the construction and validation of the *Student Product Assessment Form* (Reis 1983), took three years of research and development. Similarly, the *Learning Styles Inventory* (Smith and Renzulli 1984) was four years in the making. That's what research and development are all about."

4. Richert's rhetoric also establishes gifted education's "good intentions." Like Garfinkel's (1967) Agnes, a transsexual who claimed that the penis she was born with was not *intended*, that it was an accident of nature and so could be used neither as a legitimate topic of inquiry nor as evidence that Agnes was not naturally and totally female (e.g., the question of whether Agnes had ever had erections was treated as rude and insulting), so the repeated disavowal of elitist intent makes detailed, in-depth examination of elitist practice awkward and embarrassing.

Chapter 7

1. In the only study I found that compared the effects of a gifted program on both the gifted and nongifted (Roberts, Ingram, and Harris 1992), the findings indicated that gifted students "made significant gains when compared to average ability students receiving special program treatment, as well as gifted and average ability students attending a regular school receiving no special treatment" (p. 33).

Chapter 8

1. The clearest and most dramatic example of how power compels accounts is the confession forced from the prisoner through torture: As Damien the Regicide's flesh was being torn from his body by pincers, and as preparations were being made to draw and quarter him, "several confessors went up to him and spoke to him at length; he willingly kissed the crucifix that was held out to him; he opened his lips and repeated: 'Pardon Lord'" (Foucault 1977a, p. 4).

A less obvious example is Bentham's Panopticon. By creating the illusion and possibility of constant surveillance, the Panopticon impels prisoners to ceaselessly attempt to appear as if they are conforming to the imagined expectations of their keepers. Study of the Panopticon not only reveals that power compels accounts but also that power compels deception. It is the perfect illustration of Foucault's argument that "we are not free to say just anything, that we cannot simply speak of anything, when we like or where we like" (1969, p. 216). Because prisoners are under constant surveillance, not only do they continuously mask the constitutive work whereby their world and their identity appear real, obdurate, and objective, but also they continuously work to mask the role of power. Submission defined and dictated by some external power attempts to cover and deny the existence of that originating power. For this reason, we can imagine that prisoners existing within the Panopticon contrive to make their performances appear "natural," spontaneous, noncontrived. A "doing" and "displaying doing" prisoner (or student, patient, child, female, etc.) that comes about in response to the anticipation of surveillance by some superior power, necessarily includes an effort (either conscious or unconscious) to mask any knowledge or awareness of surveillance. Under observation, the condition that is observed "is constantly required, at the surface of itself, to deny its dissimulation" (Foucault 1965, p. 250).

If the prisoner (student, child, etc.) performance is to come off, the observers must be led to believe that the performance is "natural" (Garfinkel 1967, p. 250) and sincere (Goffman 1959, p. 71). Females who appear to act "feminine" only when observed are seen as nonfeminine. Prisoners who "behave" only because they are being watched are seen as manipulative, fake. Ironically, then, to satisfy the expectations of the keepers engaged in surveillance, prisoners must appear as if their compliance comes about independently of surveillance. Because submission that appears as submission is perceived as spurious, as a mockery of submission, the presence of surveillance motivates prisoners to reiteratively conceal the workings of power in their performances.

The corrective Foucault provides is an awareness of power's ceaseless dissimulation. He (1977a, p. 139) warns of the "small acts of cunning endowed with great power of diffusion, subtle arrangements, apparently innocent, but profoundly suspicious, mechanisms that obeyed economies too shameful to be acknowledged, or pursued petty forms of coercion. . . . They are acts of cunning, not so much of the greater reason that works even in its sleep and gives meaning to the insignificant, as of the attentive 'malevolence' that turns everything to account." Accordingly, the understandings people exhibit should be interpreted with profound skepticism: "The main point is not to accept this knowledge at face value but to understand these sciences as 'truth games'" (Foucault 1988, p. 18).

Perhaps the best known sociological illustration of how power silently organizes accounting practices is Garfinkel's (1974) paper "'Good' Organizational Reasons for 'Bad' Clinic Records." There, Garfinkel (p. 116) notes that record-keepers make their entries "accompanied by their abiding concerns for the strategic consequences of avoiding specifics in the record, given the unpredictable character of the occasions under which the record may be used as part of the ongoing system of supervision and review." However, what Garfinkel identifies as a local feature of record-keeping, the anticipation of supervision and review, Foucault treats as a universal. For Foucault, accounting practices always imply power relations.

2.   This perspective has much in common with the "neofunctionalism" of Jeffry C. Alexander and Paul Colomy (see Alexander 1987; Alexander and Colomy 1990). They also describe a reflexivity between social structures and inter-

pretive activity and emphasize that social structures constrain individual action but are not completely determinative.

3. The "Gifted Children's Center" is a fictional name.

4. The Panopticon design calls for a prison building that encircles an open yard. The cells in the prison ring have two windows traversing the entire thickness of the building. One window faces outside allowing light to illuminate the cell and another window faces the interior yard. At the center of the interior yard stands a tower with wide windows occupied by a keeper who can see into the illuminated cells but who cannot, in turn, be seen by prisoners.

Chapter 9

1. The research of Rebecca Barr and Robert Dreeben (1983) addresses this point. They studied a number of early-grade elementary school classes in which children presumed to have the most reading ability were placed in a fast-learning group and given the most words to learn. Children in a middle or average group were given fewer words to learn. Children in a slow-learning group were given the fewest words. As might be expected, children who were given the most words to learn learned the most words. The critical finding was what happened when, on occasion, children who should have been in the slower group were inadvertently placed in the fast group. These students learned many more words than if they had stayed in the slower groups befitting their presumed ability-level. Dreeben and Gamoran (1986) found the same thing: Racial and class differences in performance are dramatically reduced when children are provided the same instructional materials, expectations, and opportunities. The greater children's exposure to demanding and rigorous instruction, the more they learn.

References

Abraham, Willard. 1958. *Common Sense about Gifted Children*. New York: Harper & Brothers.

Aby, Stephen H. 1990. *The IQ Debate: A Selective Guide to the Literature*. Westport, CT: Greenwood.

Adler, Manfred. 1961. "A study of attitudes toward the gifted child as a causal factor in his socio-personal adjustment." *Gifted Child Quarterly* 5:134–141.

Aguirre, Adalberto. 1979. "Intelligence testing and Chicanos: A quality of life issue." *Social Problems* 27:186–195.

Albert, Robert S. 1969. "Genius: Present-day status of the concept and its implications for the study of creativity and giftedness." *American Psychologist* 24:743–753.

Alexander, Jeffry C. and Paul Colomy. 1990. "Neofunctionalism today: Reconstructing a theoretical tradition." Pp. 33–67 in *Frontiers of Social Theory* edited by George Ritzer. New York: Columbia University Press.

Alexander, Patricia A. and Joseph A. Muia. 1982. *Gifted Education: A Comprehensive Roadmap*. Rockville, MD: Aspen.

American Association for Gifted Children. 1978. *On Being Gifted*. New York: Walker.

Archambault, Francis X., Jr., Karen L. Westberg, Scott W. Brown, Bryan W. Hallmark, Wanli Zhang, and Christine L. Emmons. 1993. "Classroom practices used with gifted third and fourth grade students." *Journal for the Education of the Gifted* 16:103–119.

Austin, J. L. 1962. *Sense and Sensibilia*. London: Oxford University Press.

Ayres, Leonard P. 1909. *Laggards in Our Schools: A Study of Retardation and Elimination in City School Systems*. New York: Charities Publication Committee.

Ayres, Leonard P. 1914. *The Public Schools of Springfield, Illinois*. New York: Russell Sage Foundation.

Barr, Rebecca and Robert Dreeben. 1983. *How Schools Work*. Chicago: University of Chicago Press.

Baum, Susan. 1988. "An enrichment program for gifted learning disabled students." *Gifted Child Quarterly* 32:226–230.

Bayley, N. 1955. "On the growth of intelligence." *American Psychologist* 10:805–818.

Beeghley, Leonard and Edgar W. Butler. 1974. "The consequences of intelligence testing in public schools before and after desegregation." *Social Problems* 21:740–754.

Berger, Peter and Thomas Luckmann. 1967. *The Social Construction of Reality.* Garden City, NY: Anchor Books.

Best, Joel, ed. 1989. *Images of Issues: Typifying Contemporary Social Problems.* Hawthorne, NY: Aldine de Gruyter.

Best, Joel. 1987. "Rhetoric in claims-making: Constructing the missing children problem." *Social Problems* 34:101–121.

Best, Joel. 1990. *Threatened Children: Rhetoric and Concerns about Child-Victims.* Chicago: University of Chicago Press.

Bettleheim, Bruno. 1958. "Sputnik and segregation." *Commentary* 26(Oct.):332–339.

Betts, George T. 1988. "To our gifted children." *Gifted Child Quarterly* 32:242.

Birch, Jack W. 1984. "Is any identification procedure necessary?" *Gifted Child Quarterly* 28:157–161.

Bloom, Benjamin S. 1963. "Report on creativity research by the examiner's office of the University of Chicago. Pp. 251–264 in *Scientific Creativity: Its Recognition and Development* edited by Calvin W. Taylor and Frank Barron. New York: Wiley.

Blumer, Herbert. 1971. "Social problems as collective behavior." *Social Problems* 18:298–306.

Bogdan, Robert and Steven J. Taylor. 1982. *Inside Out: The Social Meaning of Mental Retardation.* Toronto: University of Toronto.

Borkowski, John G. and Virginia A. Peck. 1986. "Causes and consequences of metamemory in gifted children." Pp. 182–200 in *Conceptions of Giftedness* edited by Robert J. Sternberg and Janet E. Davidson. Cambridge: Cambridge University Press.

Borland, James H. 1989. *Planning and Implementing Programs for the Gifted.* NY: Teachers College Press, Columbia University.

Bourdieu, Pierre. 1991. *Language and Symbolic Power.* Cambridge, Eng.: Polity Press.

Bourdieu, Pierre and Jean-Claude Passeron. 1977. *Reproduction in Education, Society and Culture.* London: Sage.

Bowles, Samuel and Herbert Gintis. 1976. *Schooling in Capitalist America: Educational Reform and the Contradictions of Economic Life.* New York: Basic Books.

Bremner, Robert H. 1971. *Children and Youth in America: A Documentary History* (Vol. II). Cambridge, MA: Harvard University Press.

Bridges, Sydney. 1973. *Problems of the Gifted Child—IQ 150.* New York: Crane, Russak.

Burbules, N. 1986. "A theory of power in education." *Educational Theory* 36:95–114.

Burks, Barbara S., Dortha W. Jensen, and Lewis M. Terman. 1930. *The Promise of Youth (Vol. 3: Genetic Studies of Genius).* Stanford, CA: Stanford University Press.

Carroll, Herbert A. 1940. *Genius in the Making.* New York: McGraw-Hill.

Carter, Kyle R. and H. Lee Swanson. 1990. "An analysis of the most frequently cited gifted journal articles since the Marland Report: Implications for researchers." *Gifted Child Quarterly* 34:116–123.

Cathcart, Robert S. 1972. "New approaches to the study of movements: Defining movements rhetorically." *Western Speech* 36:82–88.

Cattell, J. McKeen. 1903. "A statistical study of eminent men." *Popular Science Monthly* 62:359–377.

Chambliss, Daniel F. 1988. "The mundanity of excellence: An ethnographic report on stratification and Olympic swimmers." *Sociological Theory* 7:70–87.

Chapman, Paul Davis. 1988. *Schools as Sorters: Lewis M. Terman, Applied Psychology, and the Intelligence Testing Movement, 1890–1930*. New York: New York University Press.

Cicourel, Aaron V. 1973. *Cognitive Sociology*. London: Macmillan.

Clark, Barbara. 1983. *Growing Up Gifted*. Columbus, OH: Merrill.

Cohen, Ronald D. 1985. "Child-saving and progressivism, 1885–1915." Pp. 273–310 in *American Childhood: A Research Guide and Historical Handbook* edited by Joseph M. Hawes and N. Ray Hiner. Westport, CT: Greenwood.

Cohen, Stanley. 1985. *Visions of Social Control*. Cambridge, Eng.: Polity Press.

Colangelo, Nicholas and Gary A. Davis. eds. 1991. *Handbook of Gifted Children*. Boston: Allyn & Bacon.

Coleman, Laurence J. 1985. *Schooling the Gifted*. Menlo Park, CA: Addison-Wesley.

Conrad, Peter and Joseph W. Schneider. 1980. *Deviance and Medicalization: From Badness to Sickness*. St. Louis: Mosby.

Cooper, Harris M. and Thomas L. Good. 1983. *Pygmalion Grows Up*. New York: Longman.

Cornell, Dewey G. 1983. "Gifted children: The impact of positive labeling on the family system." *American Journal of Orthopsychiatry* 53:322–335.

Cox, Catherine Morris. 1926. *The Early Mental Traits of Three Hundred Geniuses (Vol. 2: Genetic Studies of Genius)*. Palo Alto, CA: Stanford University Press.

Coy, Genevieve L. 1918. "The mentality of a gifted child." *The Journal of Applied Psychology* 2:299–307.

Cravens, Hamilton. 1985. "Child-saving in the age of professionalism, 1915–1930." Pp. 415–488 in *American Childhood: A Research Guide and Historical Handbook* edited by Joseph M. Hawes and N. Ray Hiner. Westport, CT: Greenwood.

Cremin, Lawrence A. 1988. *American Education: The Metropolitan Experience, 1876–1980*. New York: Harper & Row.

Csikszentmihalyi, Mihaly and Rick E. Robinson. 1986. "Culture, time, and the development of talent." Pp. 264–284 in *Conceptions of Giftedness* edited by Robert J. Sternberg and Janet E. Davidson. Cambridge: Cambridge University Press.

Current Literature. 1910. "The boy prodigy of Harvard." 68:291–293.

Curtis, Chad. 1985. "Chad's poem." *G/C/T* 41 (Nov./Dec.):14.

Davis, F. B., E. French., and G. S. Lesser. 1959. "The identification and classroom behavior of elementary school children in five different mental characteristics." Mimeographed research paper, Hunter College, New York.

Davis, Gary A. and Sylvia B. Rimm. 1985. *Education of the Gifted and Talented*. (first edition) Englewood Cliffs, NJ: Prentice-Hall.

Davis, Gary A. and Sylvia B. Rimm. 1989. (second edition) *Education of the Gifted and Talented*. Englewood Cliffs, NJ: Prentice-Hall.

Davis, Helen. 1924. "Personal and social characteristics of gifted children." Pp. 123–144 in *Twenty-Third Yearbook of the National Society for the Study of Education* edited by Guy M. Whipple. Bloomington, IL: Public School Publishing Co.

Davis, Kingsley. 1938. "Mental hygiene and the class structure." *Psychiatry* 1:55–65.

Degler, Carl N. 1991. *In Search of Human Nature: The Decline and Revival of Darwinism in American Social Thought*. New York: Oxford University Press.

DeHaan, Robert F. and Robert J. Havighurst. 1957. *Educating Gifted Children*. Chicago: University of Chicago Press.

Delisle, James R. 1984. *Gifted Children Speak Out*. New York: Walker.

Delisle, James R. 1987. *Gifted Kids Speak Out*. Minneapolis, MN: Free Spirit.

Delisle, James R. 1988. "The role of the gnome in gifted child education: A response to 'In defense of academic rigor'." *Journal for the Education of Gifted Children* 11:20–30.

Delisle, James and Judy Galbraith. 1987. *Gifted Kids Survival Guide II*. Minneapolis, MN: Free Spirit Press.

Delp, J. L. and R. A. Martinson. 1977. *A Handbook for Parents of Gifted and Talented*. Ventura, CA: Ventura County Superintendent of Schools Office.

Descartes, Rene. 1641/1960. *Discourse on Method and Meditations*. (Translated by Laurence J. Lafleur) New York: Bobbs-Merrill.

Dettmann, David F. and Nicholas Colangelo. 1980. "A functional model for counseling parents of gifted children." *Gifted Child Quarterly* 24:158–161.

Dettmer, Peggy. 1991. Gifted program advocacy: Overhauling bandwagons to build support. *Gifted Child Quarterly* 35:165–171.

Dewey, John. 1916. *Democracy and Education*. New York: Macmillan.

Dickinson, Rita Mitton. 1970. *Caring for the Gifted*. North Quincey, MA: Christopher Publishing.

Dizard, Jan E. and Howard Gadlin. 1990. *The Minimal Family*. Amherst, MA: The University of Massachusetts Press.

Dodge, David L. 1985. "The over-negativized conceptualization of deviance: A programmatic exploration." *Deviant Behavior* 6:17–37.

Doe v. Commonwealth Department of Education, 593 F. Supp. 54 (1984).

Douglas, Jack D. 1970. "Deviance and respectability: The social construction of moral meanings." Pp. 3–30 in *Deviance and Respectability* edited by Jack D. Douglas. New York: Basic Books.

Dreeben, Robert and Adam Gamoran. 1986. "Race, instruction, learning." *American Sociological Review* 51:660–669.

Drews, Elizabeth M. 1976. "Leading out and letting be." *Today's Education* 65:26–28.

Eby, Judy W. and Joan F. Smutny. 1990. *A Thoughtful Overview of Gifted Education*. New York: Longman.

Ehrlich, Virginia Z. 1986. "Recognizing superior cognitive abilities in disadvantaged, minority, and other diverse populations." *Journal of Children in Contemporary Society* 18:55–70.

Eliot, Charles W. 1909. *Education for Efficiency and the New Definition of the Cultivated Man*. Boston: Houghton Mifflin.

Evans-Pritchard, E. E. 1937. *Witchcraft, Oracles, and Magic among the Azande*. Oxford: Oxford University Press.

Fabri, Ralph. 1964. "Tribulations of the artistic child (and its parents)." *Gifted Child Quarterly* 8:64–66.

Feinberg, Karen. 1970. "Growing up gifted." *Gifted Child Quarterly* 14:172–173.

Feldhusen, John. ed. 1985. *Toward Excellence in Gifted Education*. Denver: Love.

Feldhusen, John F. 1986. "A conception of giftedness." Pp. 112–127 in *Conceptions of Giftedness* edited by Robert J. Sternberg and Janet E. Davidson. Cambridge: Cambridge University Press.

Feldhusen, John. 1991. "From the editor." *Gifted Child Quarterly* 35:115.

Feldhusen, John, Joyce Van Tassel-Baska, and Ken Seeley. 1989. *Excellence in Educating the Gifted*. Denver: Love.

Feldman, David Henry. 1980. *Beyond Universals in Cognitive Development*. Norwood, NJ: Ablex.

Feldman, David Henry. 1982. *Developmental Approaches to Giftedness and Creativity*. San Francisco: Jossey-Bass.

Feldman, David Henry. 1986a. "Giftedness as a developmentalist sees it." Pp. 285–305 in *Conceptions of Giftedness* edited by Robert J. Sternberg and Janet E. Davidson. Cambridge: Cambridge University Press.

Feldman, David Henry. 1986b. *Nature's Gambit: Child Prodigies and the Development of Human Potential*. New York: Basic Books.

Feldman, Ruth Duskin. 1982. *Whatever Happened to the Quiz Kids: Perils and Profits of Growing Up Gifted*. Chicago: Chicago Review Press.

Ferguson, Phillip M. 1987. "The social construction of mental retardation." *Social Policy* 18:51–56.

Fine, Marvin J. 1977. "Facilitating parent-child relationships for creativity." *Gifted Child Quarterly* 21:487–500.

Fisher, Eleanore. 1981. "The effect of labeling on gifted children and their families." *Roeper Review* 3:49–51.

Foucault, Michel. 1965. *Madness and Civilization*. (Translated by Richard Howard). New York: Random House.

Foucault, Michel. 1972. *The Archaeology of Knowledge*. (Translated by A. M. Sheridan Smith). New York: Pantheon.

Foucault, Michel. 1973. *The Birth of the Clinic*. (Translated by A. M. Sheridan Smith). New York: Pantheon.

Foucault, Michel. 1977a. *Discipline and Punish*. (Translated by Alan Sheridan). New York: Pantheon.

Foucault, Michel. 1977b. "History of systems of thought." Pp. 199–204 in *Language, Counter-Memory, Practice: Selected Essays and Interviews* edited by Donald F. Bouchard. (Translated by Donald F. Bouchard and Sherry Simon). Ithaca, NY: Cornell University Press.

Foucault, Michel. 1977c. "Nietzsche, Genealogy, History." Pp. 137–164 in *Language, Counter-Memory, Practice: Selected Essays and Interviews* edited by Donald F. Bouchard. (Translated by Donald F. Bouchard and Sherry Simon). Ithaca, NY: Cornell University Press.

Foucault, Michel. 1978. *The History of Sexuality* (Vol. 1). (Translated by Robert Hurley). New York: Pantheon.

Foucault, Michel. 1980. *Power/Knowledge*. Translated by Colin Gordon. New York: Pantheon.

Foucault, Michel. 1988. "Technologies of the self." Pp. 16–49 in *Technologies of the Self* edited by Luther H. Martin, Huck Gutman, and Patrick H. Hutton. Amherst, MA: The University of Massachusetts Press.

Freeman, Frank N. 1924. "Miscellaneous experimental and statistical studies of gifted children: Introduction and summary." Pp. 209–219 in *The Twenty-Third Yearbook of the National Society for the Study of Education* edited by Guy M. Whipple. Bloomington, IL: Public School Publishing Company.

Freire, Paulo. 1970. *Pedagogy of the Oppressed*. New York: Seabury Press.

Friedenberg, Edgar Z. 1962. "The gifted child and his enemies." *Commentary* 33(May):410–419.

Froehlich, Carol, Grace McNealy, Ruth Nelson, and Dorothy Norris. 1944. "Gifted children." *Exceptional Children* 10:207–211.

Galbraith, Judy. 1984. *The Gifted Kids' Survival Guide: For Ages 10 & Under*. Minneapolis, MN: Free Spirit Press.

Galbraith, Judy. 1985. "The eight great gripes of gifted kids: Responding to special needs." *Roeper Review* 7:15–18.

Gallagher, James J. 1985. *Teaching the Gifted Child*. Boston: Allyn & Bacon.

Gallagher, James J. 1993. "Comments on McDaniel's education of the gifted and the excellence-equity debate." Pp. 19–21 in *Critical Issues in Gifted Education (Vol. 3: Programs for the Gifted in Regular Classrooms)* edited by C. June Maker. Austin, TX: Pro-ed.

Galton, Francis. 1869. *Hereditary Genius*. London: Macmillan.

Galton, Francis. 1883. *Inquiries into Human Faculty and Its Development*. London: Macmillan.

Galton, Francis. 1889. *Natural Inheritance*. London: Macmillan.

Garfinkel, Harold. 1967. *Studies in Ethnomethodology*. Englewood Cliffs, NJ: Prentice-Hall.

Garfinkel, Harold. 1974. "'Good' Organizational Reasons for 'Bad' Clinic Records." Pp. 109–127 in *Ethnomethodology* edited by Roy Turner. Harmonsworth, Eng.: Penguin.

Garrison, Charlotte G., Agnes Burke, and Leta S. Hollingworth. 1917. "The psychology of a prodigious child." *Journal of Applied Psychology* 1:101–110.

George, R. Karlene. 1989. "Imagining and defining giftedness." Pp. 107–112 in *Critical Issues in Gifted Education: Defensible Programs for Cultural and Ethnic Minorities* edited by C. June Maker and Shirley W. Schiever. Austin, TX: Pro-ed.

George, W. C. 1977. "Parental support—Time and energy." *Gifted Child Quarterly* 21:555–558.

George, W. C., S. J. Cohn, and Julian C. Stanley (Eds.). 1979. *Educating the Gifted: Acceleration and Enrichment*. Baltimore, MD: Johns Hopkins University Press.

Gessell, Arnold. 1921. *Exceptional Children and Public School Policy*. New Haven: Yale University Press.

Ginsberg, G. and C. H. Harrison. 1977. *How to Help Your Gifted Child*. New York: Monarch Press.

Goddard, Henry H. 1912. *The Kallikak Family: A Study in the Heredity of Feeble-mindedness*. New York: Macmillan.

Goddard, Henry H. 1914. *School Training of Defective Children*. Yonkers, NY: World Book Co.

Goddard, Henry H. 1928. *School Training of Gifted Children*. Chicago: World Book Co.

Goddard, Henry H. 1932. "The gifted child." *The Journal of Educational Sociology* 6:354–361.

Goertzel, Mildred, Victor Goertzel, and Ted G. Goertzel. 1979. *Three Hundred Eminent Personalities*. San Francisco: Jossey-Bass.

Goffman, Erving. 1959. *The Presentation of Self in Everyday Life*. Garden City, NY: Doubleday.

Goffman, Erving. 1963. *Stigma: Notes on the Management of Spoiled Identity*. Englewood Cliffs, NJ: Prentice-Hall.

Goldin, Claudia. 1981. "Family strategies and the family economy in the late nineteenth century: The role of secondary workers." Pp. 277–310 in *Philadephia: Work, Space, Family, and Group Experience in the Nineteenth Century* edited by Theodore Hershberg. New York: Oxford University Press.

Goode, Erich. 1969. "Marijuana and the politics of reality." *Journal of Health and Social Behavior* 10:83–94.

Gould, Stephen Jay. 1981. *The Mismeasure of Man*. New York: Norton.

Gowan, J. C. 1955. "The underachieving gifted child: A problem for everyone." *Exceptional Children* 21:247–249.

Greenlaw, Jean M. and Margaret E. McIntosh. 1988. *Educating the Gifted*. Chicago: American Library Association.

Gross, Bertram, M. 1970. "Friendly fascism: A model for America." *Social Policy* (Nov/Dec)1:44–52.

Groth, Norma J. 1971. "Differences in parental environment needed for degree achievement for gifted men and women." *Gifted Child Quarterly* 15:256–259.

Gruber, Howard E. 1986. "The self-construction of the extraordinary." Pp.247–263 in *Conceptions of Giftedness* edited by Robert J. Sternberg and Janet E. Davidson. Cambridge: Cambridge University Press.

Guilford, J. P. 1967. *The Nature of Human Intelligence*. New York: McGraw-Hill.

Guilford, J. P. and R. Hoepfner. 1971. *The Analysis of Intelligence*. New York: McGraw-Hill.

Gusfield, Joseph R. 1981. *The Culture of Public Problems: Drinking-Driving and the Symbolic Order*. Chicago: University of Chicago Press.

Hackney, Harold. 1981. "The gifted child, the family, and the school." *Gifted Child Quarterly* 25:51–54.

Hallahan, Daniel and James Kauffman. 1990. *Exceptional Children*. Englewood Cliffs, NJ: Prentice-Hall.

Harmon, Lindsey R. 1963. "The development of a criterion of scientific competence." Pp. 44–52 in *Scientific Creativity: Its Recognition and Development* edited by Calvin W. Taylor and Frank Barron. New York: Wiley.

Havinghurst, Robert J. 1976. "Conditions productive of superior children." Pp. 251–261 in *The Intellectually Gifted* edited by Wayne Dennis and Margaret Dennis. New York: Grune & Stratton.

Helson, R. and R. S. Crutchfield. 1970. "Mathematicians: The creative researcher and the average Ph.D." *Journal of Consulting and Clinical Psychology* 34:250–257.

Henry, Theodore S. 1920. *The Nineteenth Yearbook of the National Society for the Study of Education (Part II: Classroom Problems in the Education of Gifted Children)*. Bloomington, IL: Public School Publishing Company.

Henry, Theodore S. 1924. "Annotated bibliography on gifted children and their education." Pp. 389–443 in the *Twenty-Third Yearbook of the National Society for the Study of Education* edited by Guy M. Whipple. Bloomington, IL: Public School Publishing Company.

Heritage, John. 1984. *Garfinkel and Ethnomethodology*. Cambridge: Polity Press.

Hilbert, Richard A. 1977. "Approaching reason's edge: Nonsense as the final solution to the problem of meaning." *Sociological Inquiry* 47:25–31.

Hilbert, Richard A. 1987. "Bureaucracy as belief, rationalization as repair: Max Weber in a post-functionalist age." *Sociological Theory* 5:70–86.

Hilbert, Richard A. 1990. "Ethnomethodology and the micro-macro order." *American Sociological Review* 55:794–808.

Hilbert, Richard A. 1992. *The Classical Roots of Ethnomethodology: Durkheim, Weber, and Garfinkel*. Chapel Hill, NC: The University of North Carolina Press.

Hildreth, Gertrude Howell. 1957. *Educating Gifted Children*. New York: Harper.

Hilgard, E. R. and G. H. Bower. 1974. *Theories of Learning*. Englewood Cliffs, NJ: Prentice-Hall.

Hobbs, Nicholas. 1951. "Community Recognition of the Gifted." Pp. 163–184 in *The Gifted Child* edited by Paul Witty. Boston: D. C. Heath.

Hofstadter, Richard. 1959. *Social Darwinism in American Thought*. New York: George Braziller.

Hollingworth, Harry. 1943. *Leta Setter Hollingworth: A Biography*. Bolton, ME: Anker.

Hollingworth, Leta S. 1920. *Psychology of Subnormal Children*. New York: Macmillan.

Hollingworth, Leta, S. 1926. *Gifted Children: Their Nature and Nurture*. New York: Macmillan.

Hollingworth, Leta S. 1927. "Subsequent history of E—; Ten years after the initial report." *Journal of Applied Psychology* 11:385–390.

Hollingworth, Leta S. 1931. "The child of very superior intelligence as a problem in social adjustment." *Mental Hygiene* 15:3–16.

Hollingworth, Leta S. 1935. "The comparative beauty of the faces of highly intelligent adolescents." *Journal of Genetic Psychology* 47:268–281.

Hollingworth, Leta S. 1942/1975. *Children Above 180 IQ*. New York: Arno Press.

Hollingworth, Leta S., Charlotte G. Garrison, and Agnes Burke. 1922. "Subsequent history of E—; Five years after the inital report." *Journal of Applied Psychology* 6:205–210.

Hollingsworth, Patricia. 1990. "Making it through parenting." *Gifted Child Today* 13:2–7.

Holmes, Arthur. 1912. *The Conservation of the Child*. Philadelphia: Lippincott.

Howley, Aimee. 1986. "Gifted education and the spectre of elitism. *Journal of Education* 168:117–125.

Hudson, L. 1960. "Degree class and attainment in scientific research. *British Journal of Psychology* 51:67–73.

Huey, Edmund Burk. 1912. *Backward and Feeble-minded Children*. Baltimore: Warwick and York.

Hughes, Everett C. 1945. "Dilemmas and contradictions of status." *American Journal of Sociology* 50:353–359.

Humphreys, Lloyd G. 1985. "A conceptualization of giftedness." Pp. 331–360 in *The Gifted and Talented: Developmental Perspectives* edited by Frances Degen Horowitz and Marion O'Brien. Washington, DC: American Psychological Association.

Hunt, Joseph M. 1961. *Intelligence and Experience*. New York: Ronald Press.

Isaacs, Ann F. 1965. "Even inanimate objects receive better treatment." *Gifted Child Quarterly* 9:169–170.

Isaacs, Ann F. 1968. "Biblical research III: Modern day problems of the gifted— Are they forecast in the books of Samuel?" *Gifted Child Quarterly* 12:94–105.

Isaacs, Ann F. 1969. "Looking at why giftedness is rejected: Self-identification, self-acceptance, and self-realization." *Gifted Child Quarterly* 13:32–36.

Isaacs, Ann F. 1971. "Biblical research IV: Perspectives on problems of the gifted, and possible solutions as revealed in the Pentateuch." *Gifted Child Quarterly* 15:175–194.

Jarrell, Ranald H. and James H. Borland. 1990. "The research base for Renzulli's three-ring conception of giftedness." *Journal for the Education of the Gifted* 13:288–308.

Kanigher, Herbert. 1977. *Everyday Enrichment for Gifted Children at Home and School*. Los Angeles: National/State Leadership Training Institute on the Gifted and Talented.

Kaplan, Sandra N. 1989a. "Language arts for gifted learners." Pp. 169–178 in *Teaching Gifted and Talented Learners in Regular Classrooms* edited by Roberta M. Milgram. Springfield, IL: Charles C. Thomas.

Kaplan, Sandra N. 1989b (Sept.). "Differentiating curriculum." Alberta Colloquium on Giftedness. Centre for Gifted Education. The University of Calgary.

Karnes, Frances A. and Ronald G. Marquardt. 1991a. *Gifted Children and the Law: Mediation, Due Process, and Court Cases*. Dayton, OH: Ohio Psychology Press.

Karnes, Frances A. and Ronald G. Marquardt. 1991b. *Gifted Children and Legal Issues in Education: Parents' Stories of Hope*. Dayton, OH: Ohio Psychology Press.

Karnes, Frances A. and James E. Whorton. 1991. "Teacher certification and endorsement in gifted education: Past, present, and future." *Gifted Child Quarterly* 35:148–150.

Keating, Daniel P. (Ed.). 1976. *Intellectual Talent: Research and Development*. Baltimore: Johns Hopkins University Press.

Keating, D. P. and Julian S. Stanley. 1972. "Extreme measures for the exceptionally gifted in mathematics and science. *Educational Researcher* 1:3–7.

Keirouz, Kathryn S. 1990. "Concerns of parents of gifted children: A research record." *Gifted Child Quarterly* 34:56–63.

Kevles, Daniel J. 1985. *In the Name of Eugenics*. Berkeley, CA: University of California Press.

Khatena, Joe. 1982. *Educational Psychology of the Gifted*. New York: Wiley.

Kirschenbaum, Robert J. 1989. "Identification of the gifted and talented American Indian student." Pp. 91–101 in *Critical Issues in Gifted Education: Defensible Programs for Cultural and Ethnic Minorities* edited by C. June Maker and Shirley W. Schiever. Austin, TX: Pro-ed.

Kitano, Margie K., and Darrell F. Kirby. 1986. *Gifted Education: A Comprehensive View*. Boston: Little, Brown.

Krueger, Charles. 1981. "To be, or not to be, gifted." *G/C/T*. 17(March/April):16.

Kuhn, Thomas. 1970. *The Structure of Scientific Revolutions*. Chicago: University of Chicago Press.

Lawler, James M. 1978. *IQ, Heritability, and Racism*. New York: International.

Lemert, Edwin M. 1951. *Social Pathology: A Systematic Approach to the Theory of Sociopathic Behavior*. New York: McGraw-Hill.

Liazos, Alexander. 1972. "The poverty of the sociology of deviance: Nuts, sluts, and preverts." *Social Problems* 20:103–120.

Lindsay, Bryan. 1981. "The Prometheus perplex: Leadership giftedness and future studies." *Roeper Review* 3:9–13.

Lisa H. v. State Board of Education, 447 A. 2d 669; aff'd 467 A. 2d 1127 (Pennsylvania 1983).

Ludwig, G and D. Cullinan. 1984. "Behavior problems of gifted and nongifted elementary school girls and boys." *Gifted Child Quarterly* 28:37–43.

Maker, June C. 1993. *Critical Issues in Gifted Education (Vol.3: Programs for the Gifted in Regular Classrooms)*. Austin, TX: Pro-ed.

Maker, June C. and Shirley W. Schiever (Eds.). 1989. *Critical Issues in Gifted Education: Defensible Programs for Cultural and Ethnic Minorities*. Austin, TX: Pro-ed.

Manley, J. R. 1937. "Where are they now?: April fool!" *New Yorker*: 13(Aug. 14):22–26.

Margolin, Leslie. 1993. "Goodness personified: The emergence of gifted children." *Social Problems* 40: 510–532.

Mead, Margaret. 1954. "The gifted child in the American culture of today." *Journal of Teacher Education* 5:211–214.

Mednick, M. T. 1963. "Research creativity in psychology graduate students." *Journal of Consulting Psychology* 27:265–266.

Mehan, Hugh and Houston Woods. 1975. *The Reality of Ethnomethodology*. New York: Wiley.

Mensh, Elaine and Harry Mensh. 1991. *The IQ Mythology: Class, Race, Gender, and Inequality*. Carbondale, IL: Southern Illinois University Press.

Mercer, Jane R. 1965. "Social system perspective and clinical perspective: Frames of reference for understanding career patterns of people labelled as mentally retarded." *Social Problems* 13:18–34.

Mercer, Jane R. 1973. *Labeling the Retarded.* Berkeley: University of California Press.

Merleau-Ponty, Maurice. 1962. *Phenomenology of Perception.* London: Routledge & Kegan Paul.

Merleau-Ponty, Maurice. 1964. *Signs.* Evanston, IL: Northwestern University Press.

Miller, Alice. 1981. *Prisoners of Childhood.* New York: Basic Books.

Miller, Bernard S. 1981. "Gifted children and their families." Pp. 3–23 in *The Gifted Child, the Family, and the Community* edited by Bernard S. Miller and Merle Price. New York: Walker.

Mills, C. Wright. 1940. "Situated actions and vocabularies of motive." *American Sociological Review* 5:904–913.

Mills, C. Wright. 1943. "The professional ideology of social pathologists." *American Journal of Sociology* 49:165–180.

Minner, Sam. 1990. "Teacher evaluations of case descriptions of LD gifted children." *Gifted Child Quarterly* 34:37–39.

Mirman, Norman J. 1970a. "President's message." *Gifted Child Quarterly* 14:144–145.

Mirman, Norman J. 1970b. "President's message." *Gifted Child Quarterly* 14:264–265.

Monahan, Jane E. and Leta S. Hollingworth. 1927. "Neuromuscular capacity of children who test above 135 IQ (Stanford-Binet)." *Journal of Educational Psychology* 18:88–96.

Montour, Kathleen. 1977. "William James Sidis, the broken twig." *American Psychologist* 32:265–279.

Nathan, Carol, N. 1979. "Parental involvement." Pp. 255–271 in *The Gifted and the Talented: Their Education and Development* edited by A. Harry Passow. Chicago: The National Society for the Study of Education.

National Center for Educational Statistics. 1992. *Digest of Educational Statistics.* Washington, DC: Office of Educational Research and Development.

Nelson, Harvey. 1982. "The Identification of black and Hispanic talented and gifted students—Grades kindergarten through six: In search of an educational standard." Pp. 63–80 in *Identifying and Educating the Disadvantaged Gifted/Talented* (Selected Proceedings from the Fifth National Conference on Disadvantaged Gifted/Talented). Ventura, CA: Ventura County Superintendent of Schools Office.

New York Times. 1919. "Young Sidis, 'Harvard prodigy,' sentenced to a year and a half in jail for rioting." May 14, p. 1.

New York Times 1924. "Precocity doesn't wear well." January 11, p. 16.

New York Times. 1988. "Study finds blacks twice as liable to school penalties as whites." December 12, p. A6.

Newland, T. Ernest. 1976. *The Gifted in Socioeducational Perspective.* Englewood Cliffs, NJ: Prentice-Hall.

Nichols, Robert C. 1964. "Parental attitudes of intelligent adolescents and creativity of their children." *Child Development* 35:1041–1049.

Nietzsche, Friedrich. 1901/1909. *The Will to Power.* (Translated by Anthony M. Ludovici). London: George Allen.

Nietzsche, Friedrich. 1887/1910. *The Genealogy of Morals*. (Translated by Horace B. Samuel). London: George Allen.

Nietzsche, Friedrich. 1881/1911. *Dawn of Day*. (Translated by J. M. Kennedy). Edinburgh: Foulis.

Nietzsche, Friedrich. 1880/1964a. *Human, All-Too Human*. (Translated by Paul V. Cohn). New York: Russell & Russell.

Nietzsche, Friedrich. 1886/1964b. *Beyond Good and Evil*. (Translated by Helen Zimmern). New York: Russell & Russell.

North American Review. 1907. "An infant prodigy." April 19 (184:887–888).

Oakes, Jeannie. 1985. *Keeping Track*. New Haven: Yale University Press.

Olstad, Deborah. 1978. "The Pursuit of excellence is not elitism." *Phi Delta Kappan* 60:187–188, 229.

O'Shea, M. V. 1926. "Editor's introduction." *Gifted Children: Their Nature and Nurture* by Leta S. Hollingworth. New York: Macmillan.

Painter, Freda. 1984. *Living with a Gifted Child*. London: Souvenir.

Parker, Jeanette Plauche. 1989. *Instructional Strategies for Teaching the Gifted*. Needham Heights, MA: Allyn & Bacon.

Parke, Beverly N. 1989. *Gifted Students in Regular Classrooms*. Boston: Allyn & Bacon.

Parke, Beverly N. 1991. "Proposed NCATE guidelines for gifted child education." *Journal for the Education of the Gifted* 14:423–426.

Parloff, M. B., L. Datta, M. Kleman, and J. H. Handlon. 1968. "Personality characteristics which differentiate creative male adolescents and adults." *Journal of Personality* 36:528–552.

Passow, A. Harry. 1958. "Enrichment of education for the gifted." Pp. 193–221 in *The Fifty-seventh Yearbook of the National Society for the Study of Education* edited by Nelson B. Henry. Chicago: The National Society for the Study of Education.

Peachman, Marguerite C. 1942. "Attitudes: Their significance in education for the gifted." *Journal of Educational Psychology* 33:183–198.

Pendarvis, Edwina D., Aimee A. Howley, and Craig B. Howley. 1990. *The Abilities of Gifted Children*. Englewood Cliffs, NJ: Prentice-Hall.

Perino, Sheila C. and Joseph Perino. 1981. *Parenting the Gifted: Developing the Promise*. New York: Bowker.

Persell, Caroline Hodges. 1977. *Education and Inequality*. New York: The Free Press.

Pickard, P. L. 1976. *If You Think Your Child Is Gifted*. Hamden, CT: Linnet.

Plowman, Paul D. 1981. "Training extraordinary leaders." *Roeper Review* 3:13–16.

Polakow, Valerie. 1993. *Lives on the Edge: Single Mothers and Their Children in the Other America*. Chicago: University of Chicago Press.

Pollner, Melvin. 1987. *Mundane Reason: Reality in Everyday and Sociological Discourse*. New York: Cambridge University Press.

Pollner, Melvin. 1991. "Radical reflexivity." *American Sociological Review* 56:370–380.

Pressey, Sidney L. 1955. "Concerning the nature and nurture of genius." *Scientific Monthly* (Sept.)81:123–129.

Ransohoff, Daniel J. 1967. "The hippies." *Gifted Child Quarterly* 11:178–181.

Reis, Sally M. 1983. "Avoiding the testing trap: Using alternative assessment instruments to evaluate programs for the gifted." *Journal for the Education of the Gifted* 7:45–59.

Renotsky, Alvin and Jons Green. 1970. *Standard Education Almanac*. Los Angeles: Academic Media.

Renzulli, Joseph S. 1978. "What makes giftedness? Reexamining a definition." *Phi Delta Kappan* 60:180–184, 261.

Renzulli, Joseph S. 1980. "Will the gifted child movement be alive and well in 1990?" *Gifted Child Quarterly* 24:3–9.

Renzulli, Joseph S. 1986. "The three-ring conception of giftedness: A developmental model for creative productivity." Pp. 53–92 in *Conceptions of Giftedness* edited by Robert J. Sternberg and Janet E. Davidson. Cambridge: Cambridge University Press.

Renzulli, Joseph S. 1990. "'Torturing data until they confess': An analysis of the analysis of the three-ring conception of giftedness." *Journal for the Education of the Gifted* 13:309–331.

Renzulli, Joseph S., Sally M. Reis, and L. Smith. 1981. *The revolving door identification model*. Mansfield Center, CT: Creative Learning Press.

Renzulli, Joseph S. and Sally M. Reis. 1991. "Building advocacy through program design, student productivity and public relations." *Gifted Child Quarterly* 35:182–187.

Reynolds, C. R. and M. Bradley. 1983. "Emotional stability of intellectually superior children versus nongifted peers as estimated by chronic anxiety levels." *School Psychology Review* 12:190–194.

Richards, J. M., J. L. Holland, and S. W. Lutz. 1967. "Prediction of student accomplishment in college." *Journal of Educational Psychology* 58:343–355.

Richert, E. Susanne. 1987. "Rampant problems and promising practices in the identification of disadvantaged gifted students." *Gifted Child Quarterly* 31:149–154.

Richert, E. Susanne. 1991. "Rampant problems and promising practices in identification." Pp. 81–96 in *Handbook of Gifted Education* edited by Nicholas Colangelo and Gary A. Davis. Boston: Allyn & Bacon.

Rimm, Sylvia. 1981. "It's dumb to be smart (a not-so-fictitious story)." *G/C/T* 17(March/April):58–60.

Roberts, Christopher, Cregg Ingram, and Carl Harris. 1992. "The effect of special versus regular classroom programming on higher cognitive processes of intermediate elementary aged gifted and average ability students." *Journal for the Education of the Gifted* 15:332–343.

Robinson, N. M. and H. B. Robinson. 1976. *The Mentally Retarded Child*. New York: McGraw-Hill.

Rodger, J. John. 1988. "Social work as social control re-examined: Beyond the dispersal of discipline thesis." *Sociology* 22:563–581.

Roe v. Commonwealth Department of Education. 1987. 638 F. Supp. 929.

Rosenhan, D. L. 1973. "On being sane in insane places." *Science* 179:250–258.

Rosenthal, Robert and Lenore Jacobson. 1968. *Pygmalion in the Classroom*. New York: Holt.

Ross, Alan O. 1964. *The Exceptional Child in the Family: Helping Parents of Exceptional Children.* New York: Grune & Stratton.

Ross, Alan O. 1979. "The gifted child in the family." Pp. 402–407 in *New Voices in Counseling the Gifted* edited by Nicholas Colangelo and Ronald T. Zaffrann. Dubuque, IA: Kendall/Hunt.

Sanderson, Allen R. 1974. "Child labor legislation and the labor force participation of children." *Journal of Economic History* 34:297–299.

Santayana, George. 1924. *Scepticism and Animal Faith.* New York: Scribner.

Saunders, Jacquelyn with Pamela Espeland. 1991. *Bringing Out the Best: A Resource Guide for Parents of Young Gifted Children.* Minneapolis, MN: Free Spirit Publishing.

Sawyer, Robert N. 1988. "In defense of academic rigor." *Journal for the Education of the Gifted* 11:5–19.

Schetky, Diane H. 1981. "The emotional and social development of the gifted child." *G/C/T* 18(May/June):2–4.

Schiever, Shirley W. 1993. "Differentiating the learning environment for gifted students." Pp. 201–214 in *Critical Issues in Gifted Education (Vol.3: Programs for the Gifted in Regular Classrooms)* edited by C. June Maker. Austin, TX: Pro-ed.

Schutz, Alfred. 1944. "The stranger: An essay in social psychology." *American Journal of Sociology* 49:499–507.

Schutz, Alfred. 1945. "The homecomer." *American Journal of Sociology* 50:369–376.

Schutz, Alfred. 1964. "Don Quixote and the problem of reality." Pp. 135–158 in *Collected Papers II: Studies in Social Theory*, edited by Avrid Brodersen. The Hague: Martinus Nijhoff.

Schutz, Alfred and Thomas Luckmann. 1973. *The Structures of the Life-World.* Evanston, IL: Northwestern University Press.

Scott, Robert A. 1970. "The construction of conceptions of stigma by professional experts." Pp. 255–290 in *Deviance and Respectability: The Social Construction of Moral Meanings* edited by Jack D. Douglas. New York: Basic Books.

Shade, Rick. 1991. "Verbal humor in gifted children and students' in the general population: A comparison of spontaneous mirth comprehension." *Journal for the Education of the Gifted* 14:134–150.

Shearer, William J. 1906. "Says New York schools are mental treadmills." *New York Times* March 12, 9:1.

Shorter, Edward. 1977. *The Making of the Modern Family.* New York: Basic Books.

Shumway, David R. 1989. *Michel Foucault.* Boston: Twayne.

Shurkin, Joel N. 1992. *Terman's Kids.* Boston: Little, Brown.

Silverman, Linda Kreger. 1989. "The highly gifted." Pp. 71–83 in *Excellence in Educating the Gifted* edited by John Feldhusen, Joyce Van Tassel-Baska, and Ken Seeley. Denver: Love.

Sisk, Dorothy. 1987. *Creative Teaching of the Gifted.* New York: McGraw-Hill.

Smith, Jacklyn, Barbara Le Rose, and Robert E. Clasen. 1991. "Underrepresentation of minority students in gifted programs: Yes! It matters!" *Gifted Child Quarterly* 35:81–83.

Smith, John David. 1985. *Minds Made Feeble: The Myth and Legacy of the Kallikaks.* Rockville, MD: Aspen.

Smith, L. and Joseph S. Renzulli. 1984. "Learning style preferences: A practical approach for classroom teachers." *Theory Into Practice* 23:44–50.

Smutny, Joan Franklin, Kathleen Veenker, and Stephen Veenker. 1989. *Your Gifted Child: How to Recognize and Develop the Special Talents in Your Child from Birth to Age Seven*. New York: Facts on File.

Spector, Malcolm and John I. Kitsuse. 1977. *Constructing Social Problems*. Menlo Park, CA: Benjamin Cummings.

Spencer, Martin E. 1982. "The ontologies of social science." *Philosophy of Social Sciences* 12:121–141.

Stanley, Julian C. 1976. "Concern for intellectually talented youths: How it originated and flucuated." *Journal of Clinical Child Psychology* 5:38–42.

Stanley, Julian C. 1980. "On educating the gifted." *Educational Researcher* 9:8–12.

Stedman, Lulu. 1924. *Education of Gifted Children*. Yonkers, NY: World Book Company.

Sternberg, Robert J. 1982. "Lies we live by: Misapplication of tests in identifying the gifted." *Gifted Child Quarterly* 26:157–161.

Stewart, Charles J., Craig Allen Smith, and Robert E. Denton, Jr. 1984. *Persuasion and Social Movements*. Prospect Heights, IL: Waveland Press.

Strauss, Anselm. 1959. *Mirrors and Masks*. New York: The Free Press.

Takacs, Carol Addison. 1986. *Enjoy Your Gifted Child*. Syracuse, NY: Syracuse University Press.

Tannenbaum, Abraham J. 1979. "Pre-Sputnik to post-Watergate concern about the gifted." Pp. 5–44 in *The Gifted and the Talented: Their Education and Development* edited by A. Harry Passow. Chicago: National Society for the Study of Education.

Tannenbaum, Abraham J. 1990. "Defensible? Venerable? Vulnerable?" *Gifted Child Quarterly* 34:84–86.

Taylor, Calvin W. 1978. "How many types of giftedness can your program tolerate?" *Journal of Creative Behavior* 12:39–51.

Terman, Lewis M. 1916. *The Measurement of Intelligence*. Boston: Houghton Mifflin.

Terman, Lewis M. 1917. "The Intelligence Quotient of Francis Galton in Childhood." *American Journal of Psychology* 28:209–215.

Terman, Lewis M. 1919. *The Intelligence of School Children: How Children Differ in Ability, the Use of Mental Tests in School Grading and the Proper Education of Exceptional Children*. Boston: Houghton Mifflin.

Terman, Lewis M. 1922. "Were we born that way?" *World's Work* 44(Oct.):660.

Terman, Lewis M. 1925. *Mental and Physical Traits of a Thousand Gifted Children* (*Vol. 1: Genetic Studies of Genius*). Stanford, CA: Stanford University Press.

Terman, Lewis M. 1926. "Editor's preface." Pp. v–ix in *The Early Mental Traits of Three Hundred Geniuses* (*Vol. 2: Genetic Studies of Genius*) by Catherine Morris Cox. Stanford University, CA: Stanford University Press.

Terman, Lewis M. 1954. "The discovery and encouragement of exceptional talent." *American Psychologist* 9:221–230.

Terman, Lewis M. and Melita H. Oden. 1940. "Status of the California gifted group at the end of sixteen years." In *National Society for the Study of Educa-*

tion. Intelligence: Its Nature and Nurture, 39th Yearbook. Bloomington, IL: Public School Publishing Company.

Terman, Lewis M. and Melita H. Oden. 1947. *The Gifted Child Grows Up (Vol. 4: Genetic Studies of Genius).* Stanford, CA: Stanford University Press.

Terman, Lewis M. and Melita H. Oden. 1951. "The Stanford studies of the gifted." Pp. 20–46 in *The Gifted Child* edited by Paul Witty. Boston: D. C. Heath.

Terman, Lewis and Melita H. Oden. 1954. "Major issues in the education of gifted children." *Journal of Teacher Education* 5:230–232.

Terman, Lewis M. and Melita H. Oden. 1959. *The Gifted Group at Mid-Life (Vol. 5: Genetic Studies of Genius).* Stanford, CA: Stanford University Press.

Thom, Douglas A. and Nancy Newell. 1945. "Hazards of the high I.Q." *Mental Hygiene* 29:61–77.

Thorndike, E. L. 1924. "Measurement of intelligence." *Psychological Review* 31:219–252.

Torrance, E. Paul. 1963. "Toward the more humane treatment of gifted children." *Gifted Child Quarterly* 7:135–145.

Townsend, Harvey G. 1924. "The Democratic idea and the education of gifted children." Pp. 145–154 in *The Twenty-Third Yearbook of the Society for the Study of Education (Part 1: Report of the Society's Committee on the Education of Gifted Children)* edited by Guy M. Whipple. Bloomington, IL: Public School Publishing Company.

Tredgold, A. F. 1915. *Mental Deficiency.* New York: William Wood.

Tuttle, Frederick B., Jr., and Laurence A. Becker. 1983. *Characteristics and Identification of Gifted and Talented Students.* Washington, DC: National Education Association.

Vail, P. L. 1979. *The World of the Gifted Child.* New York: Walker.

Van Sickle, J. H. 1910. "Provision for gifted children in public schools." *Elementary School Teacher* 10:357–366.

Van Tassel-Baska, Joyce. 1989a. "The disadvantaged gifted." Pp. 53–70 in *Excellence in Educating the Gifted* edited by John Feldhusen, Joyce Van Tassel-Baska, and Ken Seeley. Denver: Love.

Van Tassel-Baska, Joyce. 1989b. "The role of the family in the success of disadvantaged gifted learners." *Journal for the Education of the Gifted* 13:22–36.

Walker, Sally Yahnke. 1991. *The Survival Guide for Parents of Gifted Kids: How to Understand, Live With, and Stick Up for Your Gifted Child.* Minneapolis, MN: Free Spirit Press.

Wallace, A. 1986. *The Prodigy: A Biography of William James Sidis, the world's greatest child prodigy.* London: Macmillan.

Wallach, M. A. 1976. "Tests tell us little about talent." *American Scientist* 64:57–63.

Wallach, M. A. and C. W. Wing, Jr. 1969. *The Talented Students: A Validation of the Creativity-Intelligence Distinction.* New York: Holt, Rinehart and Winston.

Weber, Max. 1930. *The Protestant Ethic and the Spirit of Capitalism.* (Translated by Talcott Parsons). London: George Allen.

Weiler, Dorothy. 1978. "The alpha children: California's brave new world for the gifted." *Phi Delta Kappan* 60:185–187.

Whalen, Jack, Don H. Zimmerman, and Marilyn R. Whalen. 1988. "When words fail: A single case analysis." *Social Problems* 35:335–362.
Whipple, Guy Montrose. 1919. *Classes for Gifted Children.* Bloomington, IL: Public School Publishing Company.
White, Patricia. 1983. *Beyond Domination.* London: Routledge & Kegan Paul.
Whitlock, Sue M. and Joseph P. DuCette. 1989. "Outstanding and average teachers of the gifted: A comparative study." *Gifted Child Quarterly* 33:15–21.
Whitmore, Joanne. 1980. *Giftedness, Conflict, and Underachievement.* Boston: Allyn & Bacon.
Whitmore, Joanne. 1987. "Conceptualizing the issue of underserved populations of gifted students". *Journal for the Education of the Gifted* 10:141–154.
Wilson, Thomas P. 1991. "Social structure and the sequential organization of interaction." Pp. 22–43 in *Talk and Social Structure* edited by Deirdre Boden and Don H. Zimmerman. Cambridge: Polity.
Wittgenstein, Ludwig. 1953. *Philosophical Investigations.* New York: Macmillan.
Witty, Paul A. 1936. "Exploitation of the child of high intelligence quotient." *Educational Method* 15:298–304.
Wolfle, Dael. 1951. "Intellectual resources." *Scientific American* (Sept.)185:42–46.
Woodbridge, Frederick J. E. 1940. *An Essay on Nature.* New York: Columbia University Press.
Wooding, G. Scott and Bingham Ronald D. 1988. "Gifted children's responses to a cognitive stressor." *Gifted Child Quarterly* 32:330–332.
Yoder, G. F. 1894. "A study of the boyhood of great men." *Journal of Genetic Psychology* 3:134–156.
Zappia, Irene Antonia. 1989. "Identification of gifted Hispanic students: A multidimensional view." Pp. 19–26 in *Critical Issues in Gifted Education: Defensible Programs for Cultural and Ethnic Minorities* edited by C. June Maker and Shirley W. Schiever. Austin, TX: Pro-ed.
Zelizer, Vivian A. 1981. "The price and value of children: The case of children's insurance." *American Journal of Sociology* 86:1036–1056.
Zelizer, Vivian A. 1986. *Pricing the Priceless Child: The Changing Value of Children.* New York: Basic Books.
Zimmerman, Don H. and Melvin Pollner. 1970. "The everyday world as phenomenon." Pp. 80–103 in *Understanding Everyday Life* edited by Jack D. Douglas. Chicago: Aldine.
Zimmerman, Don H. and Wieder, Lawrence D. 1970. "Ethnomethodology and the problem of order: A comment on Denzin." Pp. 221–238 in *Understanding Everyday Life* edited by Jack D. Douglas. Chicago: Aldine.
Ziv, Avner. 1977. *Counselling the Intellectually Gifted Child.* Toronto: University of Toronto.

Name Index

Subject Index

Ability tracking, 11–12, 19–20

Academic skill assessments, 94–96 (*See also* IQ testing)

Adult success and giftedness
constancy of giftedness and, 59–65
Cox's study of geniuses and, 68–71
"early ripe, early rot" argument and, 58–59
historic record and, 65–68, 72
mental illness and, 64
social class and, 71–75
women's careers and, 64

Alcoholism, 61

Ancestors of gifted children, 6

Anti-gifted
contemporary images of, 44–46
emergence of, 38–44
parents and, 39–40
"survival" guides for gifted children and, 45
teachers and, 41–44
victimization of gifted children and, 38–46

Aristocracy, gifted children and, 5–6

Behavior of gifted children
discipline and, 7, 107–108
model classroom, 7–8
negative, 127–133

Blacks, 22–24, 27–28

Career aspirations of gifted children, 2, 28–29, 64

Carroll, Herbert A., 39–40, 41–42

Children's Mirth Response Test, 116–117

"Child-saving" movements, 36 (*See also* Gifted child movement)

Christian virtue, 7, 135–137

Class status (*See* Social class)

Creativity, 133–134

Cultural pluralism, 20–21

Descriptors of gifted children, 23–25

"Disadvantaged gifted," 22–23

Discipline
behavior of gifted children and, 7, 107–108
Foucalt's definition of, 121, 122, 124
Gifted Children's Center and, 123–127
giftedness and, 121–123
Goddard's definition of, 7
negative behavior and, 127–133

Documentation of giftedness (*See also* specific names of scholars)
by Cox, 68–71
by Goddard, 10–12, 15–17
by Hollingworth, 9–10, 12–14, 17–18, 60
by Terman, 9–10, 14, 17, 60–65